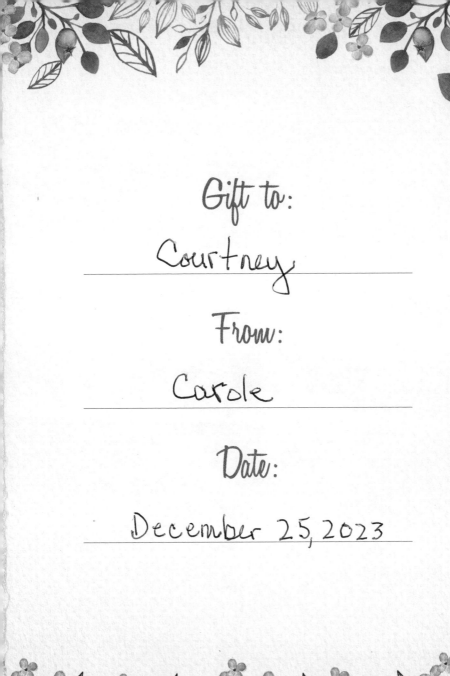

Gift to:

Courtney

From:

Carole

Date:

December 25, 2023

Walking in Grace

DALENE REYBURN

CHRISTIAN ART
PUBLISHERS

Published by Christian Art Publishers
PO Box 1599, Vereeniging, 1930, RSA

© 2017
Second edition 2020

Cover designed by Christian Art Publishers

Images used under license from Shutterstock.com

Haikus on March and August section pages taken from *Dragons and Dirt*

Scripture quotations marked NLT are taken from the *Holy Bible*, New Living Translation. Copyright © 1996, 2004, 2015 by Tyndale House Foundation. Used by permission of Tyndale House Publishers, Carol Stream, Illinois 60188. All rights reserved.
Scripture quotations marked NIV are taken from the Holy Bible, New International Version® NIV®. Copyright © 1973, 1978, 1984, 2011 by International Bible Society. Used by permission of Biblica, Inc.® All rights reserved worldwide.
Scripture quotations marked MSG are taken from taken from *The Message*. Copyright © by Eugene H. Peterson, 1993, 1994, 1995, 1996, 2000, 2001, 2002. Used by permission of NavPress Publishing Group.
Scripture quotations marked AMPC are taken from the *Holy Bible,* Amplified® Bible, Classic Edition. Copyright © 1954, 1958, 1962, 1964, 1965, 1987 by The Lockman Foundation. Used by permission. All rights reserved.
Scripture quotations marked ESV are taken from the *Holy Bible*, English Standard Version. Copyright © 2001 by Crossway Bibles, a division of Good News Publishers. Used by permission. All rights reserved.
Scripture quotations marked NASB are taken from the *Holy Bible*, New American Standard Bible. Copyright © 1960, 1962, 1963, 1968, 1971, 1972, 1973, 1975, 1977, 1995 by The Lockman Foundation. Used by permission. All rights reserved.
Scripture quotations are taken from the *Holy Bible*, GOD'S WORD Translation. Copyright © 1995 by God's Word to the Nations. Used by permission of Baker Publishing Group. All rights reserved.

Set in 11 on 12 pt Avenir LT Std
by Christian Art Publishers

Printed in China

ISBN 978-1-4321-3167-8

22 23 24 25 26 27 28 29 30 31 – 18 17 16 15 14 13 12 11 10 9

To Murray –
for all the ways your love keeps me keeping on.

And to Nicole, Meagan, Annabelle, Caroline and Isla –
may you grow up to be brave women who love the truth,
and walk in grace.

CONTENTS

JANUARY: Rhythm, radiance and changing the world

FEBRUARY: Broken, brave and beautiful

MARCH: Slay dragons, scrub dirt

APRIL: Character, calling and simple success

MAY: Billboards, bank accounts and deep peace

JUNE: Lay low, sing loud

JULY: Strong spirit, soft heart

AUGUST: Four-part harmony

SEPTEMBER: Break bread, build bridges

OCTOBER: Night-lights and lullabies

NOVEMBER: Feet first

DECEMBER: Rock hard

JANUARY

Rhythm, radiance and changing the world

"Do all you can with what you have in the time you have in the place you are."

– Nkosi Johnson, AIDS activist, b. 1989 d. 2001

A no-fear new year

Do not be afraid or discouraged, for the LORD will
personally go ahead of you. He will be with you;
He will neither fail you nor abandon you.

Deuteronomy 31:8 NLT

Moses said it brave before all Israel – that Joshua should be strong and courageous – because he knew what it was to stand on the brink of the future. He also knew the God who already wholly knew the unknown days that lay ahead.

And today you're stepping onto the blank pages of a new year. You've never come this far, and it can be kind of terrifying to think about inking the future. Like Joshua and like Moses before him, you don't know what might be waiting when you turn the pages.

But this brand-new year can be your fearless worship. Your gift to God of 365 small steps of obedience. Your living declaration that faith and fear can't coexist in your heart. And, like worship often is, living this year may be difficult and devastating and exhilarating and deeply satisfying. But when you wake up each new day to weave your moments and movements, your thoughts, words and whereabouts, into the rhythm of spirit-and-truth real-life worship, thank God for the potential preloaded in the months ahead. And remember that He is 365 steps ahead of you. And then some.

What big or small fear for the year can you surrender to God today?

Jesus, I give You this year and my fear.
Please make something beautiful. Amen.

Look forward to looking back

… just as you accepted Christ Jesus as your Lord, you must continue to follow Him. Let your roots grow down into Him, and let your lives be built on Him. Then your faith will grow strong in the truth you were taught, and you will overflow with thankfulness.

Colossians 2:6-7 NLT

As you set goals for this year, consider what you want to be most grateful for twelve months from now. Pick a theme for the year – like gentleness, wisdom or consistency – that will help keep you on track. Getting into the habit of living out of a particular idea informs your priorities and decisions. Like, I'd love to get to the end of this year and say, "I'm so grateful that I was patient with my kids!" So I'm picking patience as a theme.

The themes of this devotional are *truth*, *courage*, *excellence* and *beauty*. Maybe start there. What could these themes look like for you? In which areas of your current context could you be brave enough to face up to the truth, seek to live excellently, and create beauty – for God's glory? What is God putting on your heart about this year, and about where you should spend your time, money, energy and emotional capacity? Listen. Obey. You'll be glad you did.

What do you want to be thanking God for a year from now?

Jesus, help me to make character decisions today in line with what I want to be praising You for in the future. Amen.

Stop and ask

Trust in the LORD with all your heart; do not depend
on your own understanding. Seek His will in all you do,
and He will show you which path to take.

Proverbs 3:5-6 NLT

This is an extreme command: surrender to God completely in absolutely every facet of your life. Yet it comes with a radical, life-altering promise: He will give you clear directions.

We can't afford to miss this. Don't head out any further into another year's spaghetti maze of bright light highways, overhead flyways and oncoming traffic unless you've surrendered to God.

Decide today to risk everything on Jesus – your inside and your outside life. And don't convince yourself that you know exactly where you're going – that you don't need to stop and ask for directions. No one has a totally reliable moral compass.

Rather – at every meeting of great minds or mundane trundling through frozen food aisles – keep asking God to show you His will, His way, in His strength, and for His glory. And then breathe deep peace and know: He will give you the coordinates you need, at least for the next step.

If you know you're scared and stalling, or if it feels like you're falling into this new year – flailing and failing – would you take a moment today for quiet surrender?

*God, I'm struggling to trust You. I want to go
my own way. But I know You see things that I don't.
Please pick out the right path for me.* Amen.

Simplify

I don't mean to say that I have already achieved these things …
But I press on to possess that perfection for which Christ Jesus
first possessed me. No, dear brothers and sisters, I have
not achieved it, but I focus on this one thing: Forgetting the past
and looking forward to what lies ahead, I press on to reach
the end of the race and receive the heavenly prize for
which God, through Christ Jesus, is calling us.

Philippians 3:12-14 NLT

Paul had a way of distilling pure truth from the muck of life. He understood that he couldn't change his past but he had the courage to face it down and put it in its place – which was, behind him. He understood that, facing forward, his highest, simplest priority was to become more and more like Jesus.

Remembering what will really matter in the end helps to simplify – beautify – your life today. It quiets the noise of the present and the voices of the past. It gives clarity and perspective and scatters distractions that yank you in dead-end directions. And a new year is a gift – a chance to clear the trappings and to weight things wisely: your relationships, work, ministry and other time and energy expenses. Channel every decision, every interaction, in the direction of setting your hope simply on Jesus.

Could you do one thing today to simplify your life?

Jesus, let the truest, most beautiful thing
about me be that I simply follow You. Amen.

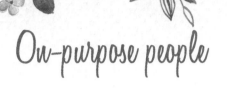

On-purpose people

Don't just pretend to love others. Really love them.

Romans 12:9 NLT

Love isn't fake or feeble. Jesus said that it's our real, hard-core love that sets us radically apart from the world (John 13:35), which rests unsteady on appearances and selfishness. Christ's love is heavy and sure. Solid and stable. And His love compels us to see the people who cross our paths and parking lots or who arrive in our inboxes and at our front doors as *on-purpose* people. As in, they fill our days, on purpose.

Your heavenly Father already knows the people who will be written into your story this year. Pray for discernment, wisdom and insight to read them right. Get a sense of where they're coming from, where they're going and how they're getting there – practically, emotionally and spiritually. Pray that God will give you His heart for them, so that you will really see them, and really love them.

Whether you're shaking the hand of a statesman or greeting the cleaner in the ladies' room, learn to take those moments – contrived and intentional or random and seemingly insignificant – equally seriously. Set the gentle, striking example to others of spending less energy trying to be interesting and more energy being interested in others.

Are there people in your life that you tend to overlook? How could you start seeing them and loving them on purpose?

Lord, let me not waste a single interaction by offering anything other than warm words of life. Amen.

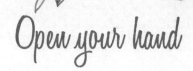

Open your hand

Then the LORD asked him, "What is that in your hand?"

Exodus 4:2 NLT

Moses doesn't think he has much to contribute to God's master plan for His people. He's just a shepherd with a staff. And yet that's exactly how God uses him. He dares Moses to take *just what he has* and trust God to use it in ways Moses can't imagine. God turns the staff in Moses' hand into a snake, and it's the sign that gets Pharaoh's attention. Eventually, Pharaoh lets God's people go. And the rest is history.

You have something in your hand too. Something to offer. It may not be much, but that's the wonder of it. Because God can transform what is simply surrendered to Him into something dazzling – something astoundingly beautiful and effective.

Make it your simple act of obedience this year to open your hand and sow whatever seeds you're clutching there. Sow truth. Sow excellence. And when your hand is empty? When you think you have nothing left to sow, you may be surprised to find another bag of seed at your feet. Dip your hands back into that bag. Dig for more seeds. Drop them into the soil you're standing on. Trust God for the harvest. Then do it again.

What are you holding? Will you give it to God – let Him use it?

Jesus, this is all I have in my hand. I'm giving it to You, and trusting that You can turn it into Your glory. Amen.

It starts with you

The way of the righteous is like the first gleam of dawn,
which shines ever brighter until the full light of day.

Proverbs 4:18 NLT

It's a breathtaking paradox that we grow more effective and more beautiful the older we get, because we grow into the fullness of Christ. We *never* no longer have what it takes to change the world.

And you do want to change the world, right? You want honest politicians. Superb schooling. Nature conservation. Accessible medical care. An end to domestic violence and child abuse. Yet each society's evils devolve into more and more sinister shapes and forms unless the people in that society change. So before it's possible to start righting the wrongs, we need Christ's light to dawn in people's hearts. Because changed hearts change behavior – which changes society.

It starts with you. In the Hebraic tradition of reaching others for change and influence they say, "One is obligatory. Two is a privilege." You are the obligatory one. And the lives you touch are the privilege. Because if *just you* can change the world will be different. And if *just one other person* whose life rubs up against yours can change, the difference doubles and suddenly you're not just a dreamer, you're a revolutionary leaving the planet better than you found it.

Are you intentional about glowing brighter by the day – inspiring others to look to Jesus as the source of positive change?

Jesus, You are the hope of the world. Use me. *Amen.*

What stops you being you?

For we are God's masterpiece. He has created us anew in Christ Jesus, so we can do the good things He planned for us long ago.

Ephesians 2:10 NLT

You're God's masterpiece. So what holds you back from being and doing what God planned long ago for you to be and do, today and all your numbered days to come?

If what's true for me is true for you, then you've lived things that make you long for the world to be different. You carry things in your heart that you wish you didn't have to. You get discouraged, and not taken seriously. Some days you dream dreams and close deals and some days you scrape last night's projectile vomit off the bunk beds. You look back with regret. You look forward with fear. And you live a mediocre present. You allow the fear of not mattering much to keep you from what matters most.

You could decide today to be done with wasting your time and potential. You could start to decode the God-dreams woven into your DNA because He has grown in you a passion for His glory and because He calls you a masterpiece – made new for Kingdom assignments preplanned by the Creator. That is some kind of wonderful.

Are you living the truth that, despite the external and internal challenges of life, you've been made new and God has planned your purpose?

Lord, let me be and do what You shaped me for. Amen.

Living the wonder

He died for everyone so that those who receive His new life
will no longer live for themselves. Instead, they will live
for Christ, who died and was raised for them …
This means that anyone who belongs to Christ has become
a new person. The old life is gone; a new life has begun!

2 Corinthians 5:15, 17 NLT

Take a moment. Let that sink … and settle: *A new life has begun.*

Jesus took on Himself the punishment that you had coming so that you could walk free and clean into the destiny He designed for you. The pressure's off to earn your future.

And you – beautiful new you – have been uniquely crafted and gifted. There are things in you uncommon to any of the seven billion other people crowding these continents. You have unique opportunities and a unique calling. You get to live this new life for Jesus in a unique area of influence. Of course, the wonder that surrounds your life like so much stardust is there because God broke into darkness with blazing hope to call you Redeemed. Beloved. And all your wonder shines wondrous only when you know that you are not the main character of the story. When you live the wonder for His glory, not yours.

Looking back, can you trace the truth that the old life is gone and a new life has begun?

Jesus, thank You that Your sacrifice made wide-open wonder-spaces for me to live for You. Amen.

Shoot for perfect, walk in grace

Then Jesus stood up again and said to the woman, "Where are your accusers? Didn't even one of them condemn you?" "No, Lord," she said. And Jesus said, "Neither do I. Go and sin no more."

John 8:10-11 NLT

Jesus always pointed to the ideal – how people should live. Yet He never condemned those who fell short of it. He never lowered the bar or made excuses for sin. Rather, He called people to holiness. He pressed them to repent with the urgency of a compassionate God, so that they would know the freedom of redemptive grace. His forgiveness of the woman caught in adultery is absolute, yet His charge is insistent: "Go and sin no more."

Your life may look totally different from hers, but living out your gratitude for God's lavish grace by loving and honoring Him – it's what will change you too, and change the world. Because changing the world depends on a commitment to obedience that demands truth and courage. What needs to be done (truth) needs to be done (courage) and the doing is beautiful obedience. You need to be brave to lean hard into truth, but it will set you free to live fully – in the kitchen or the car or the boardroom or the bedroom. And you – living fully, free, forgiven – that's where change begins.

Have you accepted God's gift of total forgiveness?

Jesus, thank You for setting me free. Strengthen me to use my freedom to glorify You before a watching world. Amen.

You can once you realize you can't

"And I will give you a new heart, and I will put a new spirit in you. I will take out your stony, stubborn heart and give you a tender, responsive heart."

Ezekiel 36:26 NLT

Trying to change your own heart is like trying to steer a motorboat that's been put on autopilot. You can override the set of the steering wheel for a while – force the boat to go in the direction you choose – but eventually your arms will get too tired. You'll have to let go. And the boat will go right back to heading in the direction it's been programmed for.

Maybe you've tried heart change on your own – tried to override your heart's autopilot – grown weary – and let go? Because the truth is you can never change yourself. You can never create your own "tender, responsive heart." But the sure hope you have is that you can build canals to channel the staggering floods of changing grace.

True and lasting heart change will happen when you surrender to the Savior your beauty and your brokenness, trusting Him to bring about the change so that the space and potential you have for Kingdom influence can become a stunning and significant reality.

Have you been trying too hard to change bits of you – to be "good enough" – instead of trusting God to do the changing?

Father, I can't change me. Change me! I need You to give me a new heart, and a new spirit. Amen.

The irresistible rhythm of beautiful routine

Walk with me and work with me – watch how I do it.
Learn the unforced rhythms of grace. I won't
lay anything heavy or ill-fitting on you.

Matthew 11:29 MSG

Routine has a bad rap. It's lumped with the boring and ordinary. Like it's dull. Unexciting. Life over-rehearsed. But if you dare to dig deeper than the daily mundane you'll discover the glittering truth that routine is essential for creating rhythm, and there's nothing tedious about rhythm.

It's regular rhythm that draws people in and onto the dance floor. It's what makes us laugh easy. It's what gets into the soul, lifts the mood, lightens the spirit. You can't dance spontaneously unless you can hear a steady beat.

And Jesus said that if we walk with Him – the daily one-foot-in-front-of-the-other routine of following Him – it wouldn't be heavy, or boring, or ordinary. He said He would lend rhythm to our steps, and it would be something beautiful. Because the excellence and beauty of our routine determines the excellence and beauty of our freedom.

What's your routine like? (If you have one?). Do you see it as something that ties you into the ordinary, or sets you free to enjoy the extraordinary?

Jesus, I want to walk with You, work with You, watch You. Choose my rhythm and routine. Turn my life into a beautiful beat that people can't ignore, and that draws them to You. Amen.

Momentum

So let's not get tired of doing what is good. At just the
right time we will reap a harvest of blessing if we don't give up.

Galatians 6:9 NLT

Routine creates momentum. If you are in the habit of doing something every day, it's easy to keep doing it every day after that, because the habit – the routine – has you riding a wave of your own
making, simply because you kept on choosing to ride it.

Momentum also saves you from making a bunch of decisions
that can take care of themselves. Like, you don't really decide each
morning to make coffee or brush your teeth. These doings are just
part of your routine, so you don't waste time or energy pondering
them. And the time and energy saved through good habits and
healthy routines free you up to get busy changing the world.

Never underestimate the power and significance of your routine,
even as you wonder if this year's routine is going to look much
the same – and equally dismal – as last year's. Appreciate how the
stability, predictability and momentum that routine brings can set
you free to take on the challenges and adventures of life, and un-
lock your potential in more stimulating ways.

Are you brave enough to create excellence this year, by committing
to a routine?

God, help me not to grow weary of day in,
day out doing good. I trust that in due course
I will reap the freedom fruits of momentum. Amen.

Keeping time with time

"Don't be afraid, for I am with you. Don't be discouraged,
for I am your God. I will strengthen you and help you.
I will hold you up with My victorious right hand."

Isaiah 41:10 NLT

We read Scriptures like this all the time, yet we don't seem to believe them. We don't *really live* as if we believe that there's nothing to be afraid of. You may be in a season of looking eagerly to the future, whiling away the present with breathless expectation. But a time will almost certainly come when the future will loom ominous and reach into the present to steal your joy. When that happens, hold tight to the truth that God holds you tight where you are, strengthening you and helping you.

Keep your thoughts in today. The future will arrive in good time. It cannot and will not get to you a moment sooner than it's due. You are and only ever can be present *now* – alive in this moment *now*. Walk at time's pace. Don't lag in the past, and don't rush ahead.

Are you prone to the crippling fear of the future? How can you remind yourself today that today is all you know for sure, and that God is with you?

God, I'm so glad You're in my present circumstances.
Give me the courage to make an excellent, beautiful now.
Thank You that You're already in my future, and
we can talk about it when I get there. Amen.

Beat your own drum

Make it your goal to live a quiet life, minding your own business and working with your hands, just as we instructed you before.

1 Thessalonians 4:11 NLT

Being told to mind your own business usually comes with a bit of aggression. It's a warning to back off. But Paul's instruction here to the Thessalonian believers is beautifully liberating. He's urging them to get down to their gifting, live it out and enjoy it, without looking around to see who else is doing what, and what else is going down.

Your capacity and your priorities will vary depending on your stage of life. Whether you're single, an empty-nester, or the mom of three toddlers – this may affect, say, how you host a dinner party. (Or if you host a dinner party.)

Don't beat yourself up because your friend or your mom-in-law or your boss has all her ducks in a row, and you're not even sure you have ducks anymore. Stop trying to tap your foot to a rhythm that's not right for your life. Be brave, and find the pace – and the peace of mind – that works for you in your current season. You're not your most excellent, or your most beautiful, when you're dancing to someone else's tune. Dance to your own.

Are you trying to beat out the rhythms of your life according to someone else's schedule, gifting, life circumstances or apparent capacity?

Creator God, help me do what You would have me do, excellently and beautifully. Amen.

Forecast: Change, with a chance of curveballs

For everything there is a season,
a time for every activity under heaven.

Ecclesiastes 3:1 NLT

Change shouldn't surprise us as much as it does, because it's synonymous with time. Or rather, change is how we know that time has *happened*. Like, the microwave pings something warm. Suddenly, the world is slightly different from what it was a few seconds ago, because what was frozen is now defrosted. Change has taken place, which shows that time has passed.

The reason change sideswipes us is because we hang our hopes on our circumstances, which we naively convince ourselves will *not* change with time. Then, when they inevitably do change, we're horrified.

While we can and should appreciate our circumstances, we need a healthy awareness that they are not forever, and subject to the changing influences of time. A safer bet is to stack all our hope on Jesus, then watch expectantly, and without fear, for the weather to change.

What changes are blowing in with the weather in your world? What courage do they demand of you?

God of time, help me remember that change isn't just likely, it's inescapable. Give me the grace to dress accordingly when it happens. Amen.

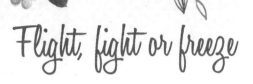

Flight, fight or freeze

Jesus Christ is the same yesterday, today, and forever.

Hebrews 13:8 NLT

The truth is that as much as we all want to do what we can to see the world become a better place, negative change – adverse change beyond our control that alters our reality – can paralyze us and stop us making the positive change we long for. Negative change makes for a shape-shifting, unpredictable reality. Things we thought we could count on can disappear or morph into unrecognizable horror.

Negative change – like retrenchment, or an autoimmune disease that has reshaped your life irrevocably – can have you backing into a cave, wasting your energy on fury. Or running to anywhere but here and now. Or stagnating into same-old-same-old. You fight, take flight or freeze.

If you *choose* change – like swapping your aisle seat for a window – then great. But change that you *don't choose* is threatening. It's a force outside of you that snuffs your resolve to give your best self to the world because suddenly the world isn't what it was. Suddenly the calm assurance and confidence you'd fostered around a set of circumstances falls away. You spend emotional, intellectual and spiritual resources recalibrating. It costs you time to adjust.

When the swirling world around you changes, cling brave to the truth you are anchored in the One who *never* changes.

Are you facing difficult changes that have you fighting, fleeing or freezing up?

O God, thank You that You are my constant. Amen.

A change is (not always) as good as a holiday

Joshua then commanded the officers of Israel, "Go through the camp and tell the people to get their provisions ready. In three days you will cross the Jordan River and take possession of the land the LORD your God is giving you."

Joshua 1:10-11 NLT

The Israelites, under Joshua's command, weren't crossing the Jordan to picnic in a new spot. They could scarcely guess the magnitude of the culture-altering changes ahead of them. They were heading into battle after battle in unfamiliar enemy territory. And yet God had plans to use this season of hostile change to change and restore the hearts of His people.

The changes you face in your life won't always be pleasant or convenient. They will likely leave you hurt, confused, angry or dazed. But you can trust that God will use the changes to give your faith a strength and elasticity that it could never otherwise attain. You can also trust that although you experience your life as a surprising, spontaneous, strenuous adventure – it's none of those things to the God who is never taken by surprise, and whose plans are from eternity past.

If you aren't facing hectic, disorientating change right now – do you know someone who is? How can you cheer for her, today, so that she's encouraged to be brave through this season?

Jesus, I pray for peace amidst the confusion of change, and I trust that You are using all this change, to change me. Amen.

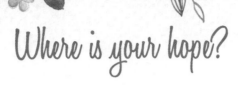

Where is your hope?

"Then you will know that I am the LORD;
those who hope in Me will not be disappointed."

Isaiah 49:23 NIV

When you've been hit by the shock waves of change, you've probably asked angry questions and shaken angry fists. Maybe you've thought about running away from the changes. Maybe you've even tried to subsist in a kind of cold indifference. If you've mentally mined the shafts of fight, flight and freeze, you'll have realized that they're all dark dead-ends. None of them change you, or the world, for good. If you've tapped at their source where fear froths hot and irrational and tunneled deeper still to the soul-pit where things hurt and heal, you will have heard that the God-whisper is always the same: *Where is your hope?*

Hoping that the things of this world will stay the same, or change to suit your comfort or convenience, will only ever lead to disappointment. The fear might shrink back a bit. But probably it will swell and return vicious. Because if you put your hope in anything or anyone other than the Creator of serenity and stability, you'll be let down. How incredible to *know* that Creator, and know that you need never live a life devoid of purpose or hope.

Are you brave enough today to ask God to shine a light on your heart and show you if you're putting your hope in something other than Him?

God of power and peace, I put all my hope in You. Amen.

How the unchanging God changes everything

With Your unfailing love You lead the people You have redeemed. In Your might, You guide them to Your sacred home.

Exodus 15:13 NLT

On the other side of the Red Sea – bondage behind them – Moses praised God for rescuing His people. There's beautiful irony in the fact that the massive change He had brought about for them was in accordance with His changeless love and faithfulness – His immutable character of holy integrity. Because only the changeless God can bring about lasting change.

So when you have your own sea to cross, trust the sovereign God who *never changes*. If your peace and your pace come from Him, if you believe He is who He says He is, and if you trust Him to shepherd and shape your calling and the conditions of your life – then you needn't be afraid. God speaks light, flings stars, multiplies cells and sets the fetal heart beating. He's way ahead of online cultures that morph and mushroom overnight. He's bigger than politics, bigger than physical safety or danger, bigger than what's trending today and forgotten tomorrow, bigger than the landscape and the velocity of change. He's far, far bigger than fear. And He can part the waters.

How has the unchanging love of God changed your own heart? Does it make you brave to accept – even embrace – change in the world around you?

Jesus, I want Your changeless character to change me – so that I can bring about God-honoring changes in this world. Amen.

Catalyst

It was by faith that Abraham obeyed when God called him
to leave home and go to another land that God would give him
as his inheritance. He went without knowing where he was going.

Hebrews 11:8 NLT

If change leaves you dazed – insecure – ineffective – think about the people throughout history who were confronted by change and became revolutionaries.

Like, Abraham and his wife who left their homeland *not knowing where God was taking them*. They built a nation. Moses got that nation to follow him into a desert. God gave him a timeless covenant that has shaped cultures for millennia. Ruth lost her husband and her home and followed her mom-in-law to strange territory. God gave her new love and a place in the lineage of Christ. Some friends watched their only Hope bleed on a cross. God raised that Hope. He filled those friends. He sent them. And they changed the world.

So maybe change is the catalyst. Maybe unsolicited change at its scariest is handing you unprecedented opportunities to effect the change you hope for. Strangely, the chaos of change can suck you into the eye of the storm where things are quiet. Perspective is distilled. Truth becomes clear. You can resolve again to maximize your time. Search for what God has put inside you. Because changed circumstances demand that you find the courage and conviction to act.

How has catastrophic change mobilized you or others for good?

*Lord, make something beautiful from
the changes all around me.* Amen.

No surprises

"For I know the plans I have for you," says the LORD.

Jeremiah 29:11 NLT

There's incredible peace and relief in the truth that nothing – not even the disastrous or the devastating upending of your life plan and picture – takes God by surprise. We label certain circumstances as 'change' because they have turned out differently to how we thought or hoped or planned or expected them to turn out. We forget so quickly that, with God on the throne, they've turned out exactly the way He knew they would.

You can be sure that, so long as you're still part of life on this planet, you'll be part of more changes too. Negative, blindsiding changes that will steal your keenness to make some positive, beautiful changes. In some parts of the world infrastructure will crumble and in other parts of the world castles will be built on complacency. But rest in the big picture reality that in every part of the world there is Jesus. Where lands and lives are decimated, He plants hope. Where change razes, He raises. And He knows the plans He has for you.

Are you wondering if God really has your best interests at heart? Are you wrestling with the truth that He saw your present circumstances coming, and He did nothing to avert them? Maybe, rather ask: would it be worth trusting in a God who didn't completely know and hold the future?

God, I'm so very glad that You never say, "Oops." Amen.

You'll never walk alone

"I will not in any way fail you nor give you up nor leave you without support. [I will] not, [I will] not, [I will] not in any degree leave you helpless nor forsake nor let [you] down (relax My hold on you)! [Assuredly not!]"

Hebrews 13:5 AMPC

If you're freaked out by change, stop trying to fight the fear on your own. Stop running. Stop hiding. Remind yourself that God is inside time – outside time – all the time. He summons each new generation from the beginning of time (Isaiah 41:4). He prepared beforehand the Kingdom ground He wanted you to plough (Ephesians 2:10). He knew the physical and spiritual contours of the continent on which He placed you long before He did the placing. He knows how the journey's terrain will change as you walk it. And He promises never to loosen His grace-grip on your life.

When Israel's troops faced their enemies, the priest would address them before battle, saying: "Listen to me, all you men of Israel! Do not be afraid as you go out to fight your enemies today! Do not lose heart or panic or tremble before them. For the Lord your God is going with you! He will fight for you against your enemies, and He will give you victory!" (Deuteronomy 20:3-4).

How would dwelling on God's abiding presence change your stress levels?

Jesus, help me remember that, whether I "feel" it or not, You are always with me. Amen.

Hero

Then, since Rahab's house was built into the town wall, she let them down by a rope through the window. "Escape to the hill country," she told them. "Hide there for three days from the men searching for you. Then, when they have returned, you can go on your way."

Joshua 2:15-16 NLT

Like you and me, Rahab wasn't perfect. But she was a hero. In a desperate situation fraught with unforeseen change and likely disaster, she saw things clearly. And she found the courage to do the right thing in the right way at the right time.

You'll know from your own experiences that mediocrity isn't transformed into significance when the road is smooth. It's in calamity brought on by the mudslides of change that the hero in you – the world changer who isn't living for the applause of people – is brave enough to cling to weapons of truth, knowing that there is One who fights with you, and for you. Time and energy you once spent floundering in the dark of anxiety is channeled into excellence, into making a difference in the world, and a world of difference.

Where is God calling you to step out heroically, rather than shrink back fearfully?

God, make me brave. I want to be a hero:
a difference-maker that points all the glory to You. Amen.

Change: bring it on

Dear friends, you always followed my instructions when I was with you. And now that I am away, it is even more important. Work hard to show the results of your salvation, obeying God with deep reverence and fear. For God is working in you, giving you the desire and the power to do what pleases Him.

Philippians 2:12-13 NLT

As difficult as adverse change can be, it's so important to remember that change is God's will for you. He redeemed you to change you. He longs to change you into the best, most beautiful version of you: the you that looks like Jesus. It's one of the most staggering mysteries of faith – that God is at work inside of you, changing your inclinations and your wants, so that you *want* to want to be like Jesus.

And He doesn't just give you the *want*. He gives you the *how*. He equips you with Holy Spirit power and Word wisdom and people in your community who care for you and cheer you on. You have every reason to be excited and expectant.

How could you show the results of your salvation today, knowing that your willingness and ability to do so are gifts from God?

Almighty God – bring on the change. Make me beautifully different – unusually excellent – for Your glory. Amen.

Moving on

Jesus came and told His disciples, "I have been given all authority in heaven and on earth. Therefore, go and make disciples of all the nations, baptizing them in the name of the Father and the Son and the Holy Spirit. Teach these new disciples to obey all the commands I have given you. And be sure of this: I am with you always, even to the end of the age."

Matthew 28:18-20 NLT

Jesus' disciples were faced with overwhelming change. Jesus had died, been buried and resurrected. Now He was leaving them with a new set of instructions that must have landed heavy and sobering on His friends: *Go out and change the world with the truth about Me.* And yet Jesus clearly called them into this season of change. He called them to move forward in obedience when it would have been easier to wallow in their grief or confusion – stagnant and passive. And again, He assured them of His presence.

Jesus is calling you to change too. He has Kingdom plans for you and obeying His call will mean moving – following – changing as you listen for His voice.

What does obedience look like in your life today? How are you moving forward in faith?

Jesus, thank You that I needn't fear the unknowns involved in moving on, up or forward, because I know You are with me. Amen.

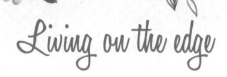

Living on the edge

For we live by believing and not by seeing.

2 Corinthians 5:7 NLT

It's a common cultural quip – *Live on the edge.* When people say it, what they usually mean is, *Take a risk, Live a little, Have some fun.*

The horizon of change shifts constantly. You're on the rim of the future all the time. You're living on the edge, whether you like it or not. But as a believer, it means something so much more exciting than just living crazy or being a little daring. Living on the edge of your earthly future and eternity means conceding all your dreams to the great *I Am* – leaving your case in His hands the way Jesus did (1 Peter 2:23). It means living the spilling-over life that Jesus promised (John 10:10). It's the joyride and the faith adventure of stepping into God's best for you.

So when cliffs drop below you, paths fall away and changes erupt all around? Rejoice. You're living on the edge. Just keep your feet on the Rock that is impervious to tremors. Because *I Am* still is.

Do you feel as if God has you at the very edge of your capacity in some – or all – areas of your life? Are you thrilled? Terrified? Exhausted? All three?

God, if You don't come through for me, I've got nowhere to turn. Thank You for bringing me to this place of total dependence on You – my hope and rescue. Amen.

Contagious radiance

Let us hold tightly without wavering to the hope we affirm,
for God can be trusted to keep His promise. Let us think of
ways to motivate one another to acts of love and good works.

Hebrews 10:23-24 NLT

One way to find your own rhythm and radiance is to create it for others. Helping your kids, your spouse, a friend or a colleague to find their particular cadence can calm them, energize them, and give them perspective. All it takes is being intentional – reading them right – so that you can do what you can to love them.

Someone close to you may need the upbeat rhythm of encouragement. Someone else may need to be slowed down before they burn out. And offering encouragement – putting the wind in someone else's sails – is win-win.

The spin-off for you is that you're your most beautiful – your most radiant – when you've forgotten about you, because you're pouring yourself into someone else.

How can you add rhythm or radiance to someone else's life, just today, in just one small way?

Lord, help me to see and meet the needs of those around me, so that they find the rhythm again that lends them momentum to keep on keeping on living a brave, beautiful, excellent life. Amen.

Do well what only you can do

But as for me and my family, we will serve the LORD.

Joshua 24:15 NLT

If you have a career, or if you volunteer at church or at your kid's school, then you have responsibilities to fulfill to avoid reproach. There are things you need to do to avoid being fired or asked to stop serving at the cake sale.

Our excellence in the workforce honors God. But sometimes, we try so hard to please third party people that we make decisions to the detriment of those who really matter – our family or friends. Maybe you're desperate for no one to think badly of you so you bend every which way to placate when you're in the public eye – and neglect the people in your life who really matter. It's a weird thought, but who are the people you're exhausting yourself to impress? They probably won't be at your funeral. The ones getting your leftovers? They will be.

There are jobs anyone can do – like being a tax attorney or selling hotdogs to ten-year-olds. And then there are jobs only you can do – like being the wife to your husband, mother to your children, daughter to your parents, or BFF to your BFF. Do well the jobs that only you can do.

Could you manage your time differently today, to bless and encourage those God has placed uniquely in your life to love?

Jesus, help me to wow the near and dear before I try to wow the far and wide. Amen.

The face that launched a thousand ships

The LORD, the Mighty One, is God, and He has spoken;
He has summoned all humanity from where the sun rises
to where it sets. From Mount Zion, the perfection
of beauty, God shines in glorious radiance.

Psalm 50:1-2 NLT

According to the myth, Helen of Troy's beauty changed the course of history. Her capture led to the mobilization of a nation, and war. It's an extreme (and fictitious) example, but it does illustrate that beauty has power.

And you – believing woman – daughter of the King – you're beautiful. You've been clothed in righteousness (Isaiah 61:10). God's radiance has taken up residence in you, and you're making history. He has you and only you on your particular earthly mission. Enjoy that. Enjoy your potential. Enjoy your beauty. Use it wisely, because true beauty – the kind that can't help spilling out if it's in you – is powerful enough to bring about lasting change.

If you're not sure what to do with your unique beauty – where and how to live it out – ask yourself: In light of where I've come from, where I am now, and where I want to go – what is the wise, excellent, beautiful thing for me to do, today?

Can you think of someone whose unmistakable inner beauty has influenced those around her, and brought about positive, lasting change?

God, I want to be really, royally beautiful, from the inside out. Change me, so that I can change the world around me, for Your glory. Amen.

Compelled to be content

The LORD directs the steps of the godly.
He delights in every detail of their lives.

Psalm 37:23 NLT

Whatever life is throwing at you, hiding this Scripture in your heart is the secret weapon you need to quell the restless discontent and find peace. Because owning the fact that God is in *every detail* of your life compels you to relax. Nothing escapes His notice. But even more than that – *He delights* in the detail.

Don't buy the lie that God is too busy running the universe to notice, never mind care about, your kid's test result, your broken washing machine or your broken marriage. He sees and cares about how that date stood you up or how someone has moved the goal posts in your career, your community or your comfort zone. Again.

We're one month down; eleven to go. Carry this priceless truth with you as the year picks up speed and noise levels rise and re-sponsibilities and uncertainties, changes and challenges, crowd your heart and your headspace. God is in the details. Be content.

What is stealing your contentment? (Make a list.) Would you commit even the small, seemingly insignificant nagging minutia to the God who delights in your every step?

Jesus, thank You for being in the details of today, and all my tomorrows. Amen.

FEBRUARY

Broken, brave and beautiful

"We can ignore even pleasure. But pain insists upon being attended to. God whispers to us in our pleasures, speaks in our conscience, but shouts in our pains: it is His megaphone to rouse a deaf world."

– *C. S. Lewis*

What you didn't sign up for

"Here on earth you will have many trials and sorrows.
But take heart, because I have overcome the world."

John 16:33 NLT

Pain and tragedy – whatever shape they take – can stop you from using your time and potential to be all that God created you to be. But to begin grappling with, and combating, suffering, you need to acknowledge its presence – or potential presence – in your life. Jesus helped us with that. He never downplayed glorious, joyous truth, and He never sugar-coated difficult, sobering truth. He told us clearly that we shouldn't be surprised by suffering – that it would certainly be part of our journey. And so if life hasn't happened to you yet? At some point, it will.

This may sound macabre, but really it's not. Having a real, it-is-what-it-is perspective on suffering will lend you calm acceptance. Sure, you didn't wish for suffering, plan it or necessarily expect it, and in the midst of it you probably don't feel like being a proverbial sunbeam for Jesus. But you needn't be shocked or paralyzed by the storm raging. Rather, you can be brave, because your Savior has calmed it. You may even begin to see the shafts of light and joy, beauty and hope.

Could you journal about a time you felt indignant, debilitated or stunned by grief or trauma in your life?

Jesus, You told us what to expect in this life.
Help me trust in Your promise: that You
have overcome the world, and my suffering. Amen.

Weapons of truth

Put on salvation as your helmet, and take
the sword of the Spirit, which is the word of God.

Ephesians 6:17 NLT

We've all seen the dragons of suffering from a distance. We smell the smoke when they spit fire on other people's lives. But when they stalk you silent – swiftly ambush you and breathe ugly in your face – and you realize you're in the fray, you can feel shocked and unprepared.

But here's the wonder: if you look down, you may see that you're holding weapons. You may not have noticed them before because up to now you haven't really needed them. Yet out of habit or instinct, you've kept them more or less polished and sharp. God hasn't thrust you clumsy into combat with brand new equipment. Quietly and consistently – for years maybe – He's been supplying the weapons you need to survive this battle.

And your weapons? They're made of Word truth. Cling to them. They are powerful against the scales and flailing tales of the enemy. They are your hope of victory.

What habits could you put in place to make God's Word part of your battle strategy and your everyday thinking? Whatever dragon is breathing fire on you today, what could you do to face it with weapons of truth?

*God, make me brave. Tighten my grip
on the sword of the Spirit –Your Word.* Amen.

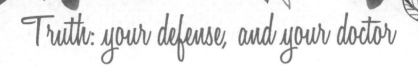

Truth: your defense, and your doctor

He sent out His word and healed them,
snatching them from the door of death.

Psalm 107:20 NLT

You need the truth of God's Word to help you stand firm against waves of tragedy, and waves of lies from enemy lips. And yet truth is more than your defense. It's also your doctor.

Because when suffering hits and the dragon's claws rip open your heart, you have to find the courage to get truth salve into the bleeding mess of raw flesh no matter how much it hurts. Without truth, infection will fester.

The Bible is not just a feel-good book of decent advice and inspiring stories. It has supernatural power to change hearts and minds, lives and circumstances (Romans 1:16, Hebrews 4:12). It finds you in the midst of the war you're waging and brings hope, healing and perspective when the world can offer you none of those things.

What part of your life needs the truth of God's Word to stop the bleeding of your heart? How much time have you spent in God's Word since the battle started raging?

Heavenly Father, thank You that You haven't left me to tend my own battle wounds. Thank You for beautiful truth, which heals and gives me the courage I need to go on. Amen.

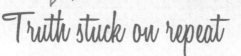

Truth stuck on repeat

He is the Rock; His deeds are perfect. Everything
He does is just and fair. He is a faithful God
who does no wrong; how just and upright He is!

Deuteronomy 32:4 NLT

When you're in the throes of trauma, tragedy or just a bad day, it's hard to *feel* as if you *really* believe that God is perfect in power, perfect in wisdom, and perfect in love.

But the longer you live by this truth, the more likely it is to become your default. When you build your life around the certainty of God's character, then even when it seems as if life is imploding, you'll *know* somehow, still, that your God is almighty, all knowing, all loving. He's not cruel, capricious or too busy attending to the universe – back turned on you while your agony unfolds. You'll know it *can't* be so – no matter how your ears ring with the roar that God doesn't love you, that He's punishing you, that these circumstances beyond your control are somehow your fault, or that this is just a random act of the cosmos.

Friend, get this stuck on repeat: He is perfect in power, perfect in wisdom, perfect in love.

Do you secretly – or maybe not so secretly – struggle to believe that God is perfect in power, wisdom and love?

God: despite what's going on in my life, I trust that
Your plans are wise and good, You love me completely,
and You hold my life in perfect power. Amen.

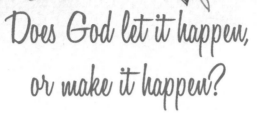

Does God let it happen, or make it happen?

Though He brings grief, He also shows compassion because of the greatness of His unfailing love. For He does not enjoy hurting people or causing them sorrow … Who can command things to happen without the Lord's permission? Does not the Most High send both calamity and good?

Lamentations 3:32-33, 37-38 NLT

When hard times steamroll your life, debates will rage around you in whispers – did a loving God *allow* this, or did a sovereign God *ordain* it?

And the answer is, *yes.*

Because really, it's two sides of the same coin. And God doesn't gamble. He hasn't flipped that coin flippant over all that hangs in the balance of your life, to see how it will land. You may never breathe the fresh air of deep peace this side of eternity until you settle the fact that you can't fully grasp the perfect paradox of God's multifaceted character, or how His attributes coexist in compassion, goodness, perfection, power and holiness. But they do. And your name is written on the palms of His hands.

In the face of tragedy, is it easier for you to make peace with God's sovereignty or God's love? Would you be content to serve a God who was only compassionate, or only powerful?

Sovereign God of love, I know that You hold together all the atoms of existence, for Your glory. Some days, all I see is pain and mess that make no sense. Help me to trust that You're loving me through this. Amen.

Ask the right question

Not a single person on earth is always good and never sins.

Ecclesiastes 7:20 NLT

Why do bad things happen to good people? I've asked it. You probably have too.

Yet it's possible that that's the wrong question. Because you, me and everyone, we're not good people. We have a debilitating congenital sin defect. We're living on pure grace and borrowed time. When Adam fell, he took creation with him (Genesis 3). In this life we can't shake off all the consequences of that cataclysm. The world is broken. Terrible, inconvenient things happen. It's not fair. But it's true.

So the question to ask – resting and wrestling with the sure hope that God sees things we don't and will judge the world with fairness and righteousness when He rolls up all of history in His glory – is not, "Why?" The question is, "What now?"

The truth is, no one ever got over suffering by having it explained. Suffering is generally irrational. It manifests in our lives as something that lashes out random and indiscriminate and mysterious. But mysteriously – wondrously – it holds the power to change our hearts.

So, what now?

Jesus, I don't feel as if what I'm facing is fair. But help me ask the right questions. Help me to be brave, to live excellently and to let pain do its mysterious, beautiful work, making much of You through my life. Amen.

There's help

Those who look to Him for help will be radiant
with joy; no shadow of shame will darken their faces.

Psalm 34:5 NLT

When you're going through hard times – mild or severe – there's help available. Psychologists and psychiatrists. Pastors, preachers, teachers and dieticians. Support groups and self-help seminars. You can call your mom or your best friend. Appeal to your boss or your bank manager. Buy something on eBay. And where God has opened up a channel of help or support, pray for wisdom and take advantage of the resources that He has provided.

Yet ultimately, unless a shift of perspective has taken place in your heart – unless you've recognized that God is on His throne – all the help you seek might bring temporary relief, but it won't alleviate the grief, fear, pain or disappointment lodged in your soul. Only God can do that. He wrote to you – over thousands of years – and He saw to it that His words were preserved and protected so that even where you find yourself today in your twenty-first century reality, His words bring peace, and the radiance of joy.

Do you see God's Word as your mainstay – your help and healing?

God, You invented communication, and You are never
silent in my life because I have Your living Word. Thank You!
Help me to turn to Your promises, Your commands
and Your wisdom – to listen and live well. Amen.

Brand-new ancient words

Open my eyes to see the wonderful truths in Your instructions.

Psalm 119:18 NLT

My four-year-old said to me the other day, "Mom, I know all the episodes in the Bible!" I'm chuffed that he feels he has a good grasp on the Scriptures, but I want to teach him that not one of us dare ever think that we've got God's Word waxed. That it can't teach us anything new. That we understand each textured layer of the shimmering depths of the God-breathed Scriptures.

And there's nothing quite like distress to drive you back to God's Word and have you scrabbling desperate from Genesis to Revelation. Because it's in God's Word that you'll find warm familiar hollows to stop and rest. Breathe the air and remember the view from truths you have long loved. And gasp awestruck at old words made new because of the view from the precipice you're on.

For each different set of circumstances that presents itself, old, unchanging Word truth will light up in new and glorious ways, empowering you to live brave and beautiful, right where you are.

Have there been days – maybe even whole seasons – when you've felt that God's Word is redundant, or irrelevant to what you face?

Father, I don't want to ignore or avoid Your Word for so long that bright truth gathers dust in my heart and mind. Keep drawing me into the freshness of Your inspired narratives, poetry and instructions. Amen.

But God

> You intended to harm me, but God intended
> it all for good. He brought me to this position
> so I could save the lives of many people.
>
> *Genesis 50:20* NLT

Joseph's life – and the way he lived it – is an incredible example of trusting God through intense hardship for the long haul. It's easy for us to read a few chapters of Genesis and see the golden thread of God's ingenious plan being strung out in Joseph's generation and for all eternity.

But Joseph lived all that. Day by slow difficult day. And when he was in the thick of it, he couldn't see how rejection, slavery, prison or politics could possibly bring light and life. He just kept trusting. Kept obeying. And decades into a grim life he was able to say with perfect peace to his brothers – his betrayers – that God can bring good where it's impossible to see any.

You may never know or understand the reason for your heartbreak, or your flat tire on the way to work. And even knowing and understanding the reason may not make living through the hassle or the heartbreak any easier. *But God.* But God is threading something golden through the seamless plan He has for you.

Can you look back on your life and acknowledge that God transformed what you saw only as disaster, into favor or freedom?

*Kind and mighty King, I don't see the good
You will bring. But I trust You. Amen.*

No good thing

For the LORD God is our sun and our shield.
He gives us grace and glory. The LORD will withhold
no good thing from those who do what is right.

Psalm 84:11 NLT

You might want to stick that on the fridge. Or wear it as a harness – your ultimate safety and stay on the cliffs of difficulty.

Because the Lord is your sun: bringing light when your world goes dark. He's your shield: protecting you from the enemy's flaming arrows. He gives you grace: daily, sufficient, undeserved favor and new mercies every morning (2 Corinthians 12:9, Lamentations 3:23). He gives you glory: *His* glory reflected in your life and lived to honor Him.

If you've trusted in His righteousness, not yours, He will withhold no good thing from you. Which means that if freedom from your circumstances is *good* for you – good in the Kingdom sense, the more-like-Christ sense – then God will not withhold it. Hard as it is to swallow, whether or not something *feels* good to you as it slips or sticks or stabs jagged in your hands – this *feeling* is not the flawless texture of eternity. If God is withholding freedom or healing or relief from struggle or inconvenience – there's an excellent, beautiful reason.

Will you be brave and trust that God is accomplishing good in your life?

Jesus, it's hard to believe there's a reason You're
withholding what I think would be so good.
But You are God, and I am not. Strengthen my faith! Amen.

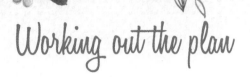

Working out the plan

The LORD will work out His plans for my life – for Your faithful love, O LORD, endures forever. Don't abandon me, for You made me.

Psalm 138:8 NLT

If life is going swimmingly for you, this is the best time to establish your personal policy on tough times. Because disappointment or tragedy can leave you feeling the very worst kind of alone and unloved, and that's not conducive to preaching truth to yourself. When you feel – or really have been – abandoned, you need to have a thick, soft layer of solid truth to collapse on.

So would you believe with the psalmist that, no matter how things look from an earthly perspective and no matter how you feel, God has not abandoned you – and will never abandon you? He created you and He created plans for your life and because His faithful love is everlasting, He will bring the plan and purpose for your life to fulfillment.

You'll also need to know up front that God's plans are almost certainly going to look way different from yours. And since He can see the past and the future, and since He is inside time and outside at the same time, you can count on Him to know what He's doing.

Would it make your day more beautiful to know that God hasn't abandoned you but is crafting meticulous life plans for you?

Creator God, I'm so glad that it's not totally up to me to plot my life's course. Have Your way. Amen.

Blinded by the burden

I will lead the blind by ways they have not known,
along unfamiliar paths I will guide them; I will turn the darkness
into light before them and make the rough places smooth.
These are the things I will do; I will not forsake them.

Isaiah 42:16 NIV

Our eldest son is visually impaired, so I can totally live into this verse about the blind. I sense the fear of what it's like – practically and physically – to go down a rough road you've never walked. But then I imagine how it must feel for that fear to dissipate because someone takes your hand. The perpetual darkness is miraculously turned to light. You're not tripping over your own humiliation before the crowds. You're not even stubbing your toe because the uneven places are ironed out smooth.

If you're carrying something uncomfortable, confusing, heavy or heartrending today, and you're stepping out in the dark on a narrow mountain path, know that, even as the ragged rocks are cutting your feet, the sun will rise and the way forward will be made clear. It's God's promise to you.

Could you set yourself some sort of reminder today – leave your running shoes at the front door? – so you won't forget that God is leading you to the next smooth step, even though you can't see it?

God of light and guidance, thank You that You haven't left me on a treacherous, shadowed road alone. Amen.

Look up

"What sorrow awaits those who argue with their Creator. Does a clay pot argue with its maker? Does the clay dispute with the one who shapes it, saying, 'Stop, you're doing it wrong!' How terrible it would be if a newborn baby said to its father, 'Why was I born?' or if it said to its mother, 'Why did you make me this way?'" This is what the LORD says: "Do you question what I do for My children? Do you give Me orders about the work of My hands? I am the One who made the earth and created people to live on it. With My hands I stretched out the heavens. All the stars are at My command."

Isaiah 45:9–12 NLT

In the midst of what's dreary or difficult, there's always the sky. Maybe tonight – after kids' bedtimes or late night emails – you could take thirty seconds to stare out at the night and think about this Scripture.

The One who stretched out the heavens may be stretching you in aching ways, but the truth is that the light from some of the stars you see has been traveling towards you for centuries and God is way ahead of you – He *got* this. As the heavens are higher than the earth, so His ways are higher than your ways (Isaiah 55:9).

It's ok to argue with God. Have you ever had the last word?

God, it's a glorious mystery.
You are the Potter. I am the clay. Amen.

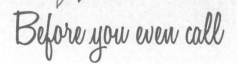

Before you even call

"I will answer them before they even call to Me. While they are still talking about their needs, I will go ahead and answer their prayers!"

Isaiah 65:24 NLT

We scarcely recognize most of the time that these words have been, are and will be true in our lives. We're so self-absorbed that we hardly take note of the daily interventions of a good God who doesn't just watch over us ambivalently but who is actively, intentionally involved in supernaturally planning and providing for us. He meets our needs before we even know that they're needs.

But when you know your need because it tastes bitter and smells like defeat and feels like fear – then you need to cling brave to the knowing that before you even called out to Him above the noise of your need, He had answered.

Can you remember a time when God's grace began to surface in your life to provide for a need you had no idea you would ever have?

Thank You, Almighty God, that You are already at work in my future, willing and working things out for Your glory and my good. Thank You that You know my current and coming needs, and You will answer. Before I even call to You, You will answer. Amen.

When everyone wants to help

We have studied life and found all this to be true.
Listen to my counsel, and apply it to yourself.

Job 5:27 NLT

Job's friends probably really wanted to help him. But their criticism and insensitivity made things worse for Job, who was facing seismic personal disaster.

If you're part of an amazing community of people who are eager to share your life – happiness, humdrum or heartbreak – it may be hard to handle when those people step close to shoulder a burden for you. Or, unintentionally, kill you with kindness.

People's understanding of your struggle is almost always one-dimensional. It's your struggle, not theirs. Similarly, even if you've gone through an identical trauma to someone else, you won't fully understand what they're going through because the way each of us translates distress or disillusionment into our circumstances, differs.

Still, you need to find space for the way people love you, and want to help. They see just a small corner of your hardship, but they're eager to give hope where they can. Let them. You don't have to take all their advice. But try to extend grace, as you would hope it would be extended to you when you say the wrong thing at the wrong time to a person in pain.

Have you ever been mad at someone who told you to cheer up in the midst of intense anguish?

God, thank You for people who genuinely care.
Help me to judge them on their intentions, not their actions. Amen.

Fragrance

Then Mary took a twelve-ounce jar of expensive perfume …
and she anointed Jesus' feet with it, wiping His feet
with her hair. The house was filled with the fragrance.

John 12:3 NLT

Judas is indignant about Mary's extravagant – wasteful? – act. "We could have sold that perfume and given it to the poor," he says.

But Jesus makes it extremely clear that He is deeply moved by her sacrificial, humble worship. He immediately protects her. "Leave her alone," He says. "Why criticize her for doing such a good thing to Me?" (Mark 14:6).

Mary must have known that she would be met with opposition. Breaking that jar and pouring out the perfume was a desperate act. And her own brokenness was mirrored in the breaking of the jar because what makes us desperate is brokenness – the world's, other people's, and our own.

But Mary needed a Savior – more than she needed not to be thought of as weird. She knew she was broken and she knew what to do with her brokenness. She took it straight to the feet of her King and left it there – a brave act, in front of a room full of critical onlookers. What Jesus saw was a woman who lavished on Him an extraordinarily expensive gift, and all of herself.

Will you offer the fragrance of your brokenness to the King?

Jesus, even in my brokenness, I want to be brave
enough to worship You extravagantly. Amen.

Raw deal?

"You parents – if your children ask for a loaf of bread, do you give them a stone instead? Or if they ask for a fish, do you give them a snake? Of course not! So if you sinful people know how to give good gifts to your children, how much more will your heavenly Father give good gifts to those who ask Him."

Matthew 7:9–11 NLT

I love cooking cheesy-bacon-pasta for my boys because it's their *best*, as they say. I delight in delighting them. I also love cooking broccoli for my boys. It's their *worst*. I cook it anyway. Not to spite them or ruin their fun or exert my authority. I give it to them because I know better. I know that it's good for them.

Getting over the distaste of adversity has to do with your view of God the Father, who delights in delighting you. He's the Father who knows which nutrients will feed your soul.

It might feel as if God is only dishing out broccoli. Like, you'll throw up if you even *smell* it. But Jesus made it clear that God hasn't ripped you off. He promised you abundant life (John 10:10). And He proved that promise of life by laying down His own.

Could you trust God today that the stone or the snake in your hand is really a loaf or a fish?

Jesus, thank You for reassuring me that my heavenly Father has my very best interests at heart. Amen.

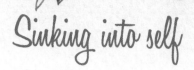

Sinking into self

*Then I realized that my heart was bitter, and I was
all torn up inside. I was so foolish and ignorant.
Yet I still belong to You; You hold my right hand. You guide
me with Your counsel, leading me to a glorious destiny.*

Psalm 73:21-24 NLT

If you want the perfect picture of self-pity – and how to get out of it – go and read all of Psalm 73, by Asaph. The first sixteen verses are really just him throwing a fabulous pity party – streamers, balloons, everything. It's a blast. He's complaining about how unfair everything is, and wondering why he even bothered ever to follow God because it really hasn't been working out for him. The turning point comes in verse 17, where he says, "Then I went into Your sanctuary, O God …" He seeks God. He gets perspective. He forgets himself. He's happy.

A bad day can send you spiraling into self-pity – to the point that how desperately sorry you're feeling for yourself actually becomes more destructive than the bad day. Your self-pity might be legitimate. But it still saps your strength. Even if it's the last thing in the world you feel like doing, because of how low you are, seek God. And seek others who are seeking God.

Is self-pity suffocating your desire to seek God?

O God, get me out of this spiral. Help. Amen.

Why I know you won't give up

That is why we never give up. Though our bodies are dying, our spirits are being renewed every day. For our present troubles are small and won't last very long. Yet they produce for us a glory that vastly outweighs them and will last forever! So we don't look at the troubles we can see now; rather, we fix our gaze on things that cannot be seen. For the things we see now will soon be gone, but the things we cannot see will last forever.

2 Corinthians 4:16-18 NLT

Despite the stop-start confusion of this ups-and-downs life, there's soul-soothing rhythm in Paul's holy arguments for a God of grace who causes all things to work together for good and won't let anything get between you and His love (Romans 8). That's reason enough not to give up.

But maybe words like that have been Band-Aided glibly over your life for as long as you can remember and you can't *feel* them anymore. I'm praying you'd remember the truth: you're a child of God. Giving up isn't your thing. You know God. You know He knows you. You know this life isn't the main event. There's a point to it all. He'll come through for you. And it will be glorious.

Can you imagine the weight of eternal glory offsetting the stress or suffering you hold today?

Jesus, thank You that no matter what's happening on the outside of me, You continually renew, refresh and rejuvenate the inside of me. Amen.

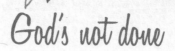

God's not done

And I am certain that God, who began the good work within you, will continue His work until it is finally finished on the day when Christ Jesus returns.

Philippians 1:6 NLT

When Paul wrote his letter to the Philippians from inside a Roman prison, he had no idea how it would find its way to your heart. But millennia later, God is speaking those words to you, to reassure you that He won't leave you in a prison of depression. He won't leave you chained to disillusionment.

Friend, you can cling to the promise: God isn't done with you. Until He lends you that last breath and calls you home forever, He's continually crafting – chiseling – shaping – molding you – more and more into the image of His Son.

It may feel now as if you'll never get out of or through or over the barrier or the addiction or the sin-struggle you're fighting. It may feel as if you'll always just look like the ugliest version of you, and never like Jesus. But He has declared that He will accomplish His perfect plans for you. Keep dreaming. Keep taking every next small step of obedience. God's not done.

Would it change how you feel about the disappointment, desperation or distress you're carrying, to know that God hasn't dumped you with it and walked away?

Father, never stop chipping away at me. Make me a masterpiece. Amen.

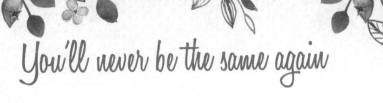

You'll never be the same again

Why am I discouraged? Why is my heart so sad? I will put my hope in God! I will praise Him again – my Savior and my God!

Psalm 42:5-6 NLT

The darkest time you've ever lived through – it changed you, didn't it? Irrevocably. It's as if your heart got ripped right down the middle and the insides lay exposed. The rip was painful but it tore open areas that had always been covered up. Like whole chambers of compassion that had been lying dormant.

A new kind of love started bleeding from the rip. People could walk into your heart far more easily. There was an easy-access gash and no effective queuing system. It's made your heart crowded, much heavier, and harder to carry around some days, but it's also pumping in a brave, totally alive kind of way. And maybe it startled you to realize it wasn't so much just you anymore. There was more of Jesus *in* you.

But suffering is a double-edged sword. It could just as easily ensnare you with cynicism, convincing you to string up barrier tape and no entry signs across your heart-rip. Some people are made meaner, harder and more cantankerous by suffering. They're positively unbearable. Suffering doesn't automatically turn everyone angelic. But in the life yielded happy to Christ, it brings extraordinary, beautiful change.

Has your own suffering grown your empathy for others?

God, take my heart-rip. Make it beautiful, so people would see, and know You. Amen.

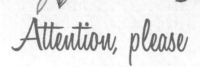

Attention, please

But by means of their suffering, He rescues those who suffer. For He gets their attention through adversity.

Job 36:15 NLT

Pain will get your attention. When tragedy explodes in your life, it will blow open your perspectives and priorities. You'll see the things that have always preoccupied you for what they really are: preoccupations.

Like change, suffering can be a catalyst that awakens something in you – a deeper urge and urgency to live fully. To invest your time and your potential in things that matter more. And that is such an excellent thing.

You'll have hard days when you'll need to readjust your dreams or squash the sadness, but know that as Elisabeth Kübler-Ross says: "The most beautiful people we have known are those who have known defeat, known suffering, known struggle, known loss, and have found their way out of the depths. These persons have an appreciation, a sensitivity, and an understanding of life that fills them with compassion, gentleness, and a deep loving concern. Beautiful people do not just happen."

Of course, suffering doesn't necessarily happen to you only because you weren't listening to God! But would you think about how He may be using it to get your attention?

Gracious, loving God, thank You for doing whatever it takes –using whatever comes – to bring me back to You. Amen.

Next right thing

Show me the right path, O LORD; point out the road for me to follow.

Psalm 25:4 NLT

When you don't know which way to turn – in your career, your finances, a friendship or a family connection – the courageous resolution to stick to in tough times is the decision to keep on doing the Next Right Thing.

You could start today. Because it doesn't take long to see how a whole lot of next right decisions – a whole lot of five minute slots – stack up into days, weeks and years, and the momentum that builds as you live intentionally will free you, eventually, to find headspace for perspective, bigger decisions and long-term planning.

Before you know it, another day will be done. And then a few more days. And then years. And then you'll be through what you face now and you'll have developed a habit that boils life right down to the instant. Reduces it to something rich and thick. Allows you to taste the given moment. Because the given moment is all you ever really have.

You may feel as if you don't have strength to make it through today. But could you just do one thing – the Next Right Thing – even if that's switching on the kettle or brushing your teeth?

Jesus, please walk closely to me all day today.
Keep showing me just the Next Right Thing to do. Amen.

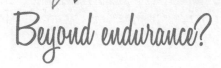

Beyond endurance?

Then he went on alone into the wilderness, traveling all day.
He sat down under a solitary broom tree and prayed that he
might die. "I have had enough, LORD," he said. "Take my life …"

1 Kings 19:4 NLT

FEBRUARY 24

Elijah had had enough. He wanted to die. God had other ideas. Can you relate? Days when you think you can't go on?

Roman Emperor and philosopher, Marcus Aurelius, scribed this incredible wisdom a very long time ago: "Do not disturb yourself by picturing your life as a whole; do not assemble in your mind the many and varied troubles which have come to you in the past and will come again in the future, but ask yourself with regard to every present difficulty: 'What is there in this that is unbearable and beyond endurance?' … then remind yourself that it is not the future or what has passed that afflicts you, but always the present, and the power of this is much diminished if you take it in isolation and call your mind to task if it thinks that it cannot stand up to it, when taken on its own."

So on rough days when you default to Next Right Thing survival mode, take courage. The small brave steps you'll take today are not unbearable or beyond endurance.

When you've felt like you're done, how has God shown you that He is not?

God, be my present strength. Give me clarity and calm. Amen.

Your glory battle cry

He alone is my rock and my salvation,
my fortress where I will not be shaken.

Psalm 62:6 NLT

While it's not possible or fair to grade, equate or compare versions of hurt, you needn't look far to find people feeling the agony of sideswiping suffering that has hijacked any good they're intent on. You can probably fill in blanks I can't conceive of and I rage with you against your own heartbreaks.

Maybe your road has run out and you're on a precipice. Maybe you face a gradual but deceivingly long uphill and no one even knows how overwhelmed you feel or how you wake up each day wondering if you'll get to the end of it.

I pray that in the midst of your exhaustion, sadness or catastrophe, God will galvanize you to shield yourself, with truth and courage, from pain's enervating assault. I pray that you will not be thrown into panic or paralysis, but that staring down suffering will give you dauntless courage you didn't think was possible. May your heartache rise up in you as a battle cry for glory. May the sound fill the air, and change the world.

Are you willing to let God give you a new voice for the battle, to shout about His glory?

Lord, it seems impossible, but if You can turn my tears into triumph, I accept. Amen.

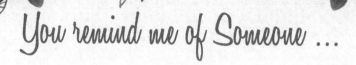

You remind me of Someone ...

Imitate God, therefore, in everything you do, because you
are His dear children. Live a life filled with love,
following the example of Christ. He loved us and offered
Himself as a sacrifice for us, a pleasing aroma to God.

Ephesians 5:1-2 NLT

Forgiveness makes you look like Jesus.

I have a friend with an inner elixir of sorts that makes her more beautiful each year. She has a sense of fun that can transform a tedious event into a laughter riot. Her smile can restore people's hope in humanity. She has profound intuition, wisdom way beyond her years, and unwavering compassion. She is one of those people where I can't decide – is she more beautiful inside, or out?

Some years back, she was deeply hurt. Hurt enough to give her every reason to be abidingly bitter. Instead, she forgave. And so instead of magnifying the heartbreak she carries, she chooses to live a full, beautiful, meaningful life, free of obsession and self-induced depression. People watch her life in wonder, because she trusts God and His best for her, and she is bent on mirroring His glory.

Do you know someone who is quick to forgive, and reminds you of Jesus? What would it look like for you to be that person today?

Jesus, I want people to watch the way I manage my relationships and my resentment, and I want it to make them think of You. Amen.

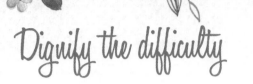

Dignify the difficulty

Dear brothers and sisters, when troubles come your way,
consider it an opportunity for great joy. For you know
when your faith is tested, your endurance has a chance to grow.

James 1:2-3 NLT

No one hopes to get hurt. No one plans for the pain of being sinned against. And yet realistically, it's impossible to walk from cradle to grave without hurting others, and being hurt.

So when it happens? See it as an opportunity to showcase your total trust in God. Sure, you may question His plans and purposes for you in allowing this knife between your ribs. Sure, you're going to feel angry and upset. But in you – image-bearer, God-chaser, Jesus-lover that you are – there will be a surprising spring of freshness and freedom. You will dignify the difficulty. You will make it inexplicably beautiful, and you will inspire the instinctive admiration of your accidental or deliberate spectators. When there's someone you need to forgive, wear your wounds quietly, with grace and tender patience. Offer broken heart sacrifices before your Father in secret, and in so doing broadcast how blessed it is to surrender all to a wise, loving, powerful God.

Could you be brave enough today to move from bitterness to beauty?
Would you let the caustic comments slide, and be your best self?

God, I hate that I have to face what I'm facing. But please enable me to forgive, and please use my forgiveness to spread beauty. Amen.

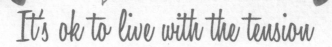

It's ok to live with the tension

Oh, how great are God's riches and wisdom and knowledge! How impossible it is for us to understand His decisions and His ways!

Romans 11:33 NLT

Internet search engines run our culture, and they'll convince you that you can know everything about everything. But they're not God. Praise Him that you can never know everything about the everywhere, every time God of eternity past and future. Because it wouldn't be worth worshiping a boxed god – small enough to fit into a search engine – devoid of massive mystery.

And the truth is that it's ok not to have all the answers to everything. It's ok to live with the tension of the questions, and the tension of the truth. Like, how it's true that Jesus can heal and it's true that He doesn't always heal, and it's also true that in Him all things hold together (Colossians 1:17). Which means that He holds that tension for us. You can rest in Him because the tension is fixed by the sureness – the certainty – that we have in His sovereignty, His omniscience and His love.

Tension creates beauty. Like how we can't hang fairy lights without tension. The tension is how we string up the splendor.

Do you tend to carry all your questions? Would you let Jesus take the tension?

Lord, my brain short-circuits when I think of Your hugeness. Thank You, great God. Amen.

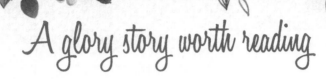

A glory story worth reading

I know that You can do anything, and no one can stop You.

Job 42:2 NLT

God could take away the hassles and hardships you're dealing with this week. He can do anything, and no one can thwart His purposes. There's deep peace to be unpacked from that simple truth.

And sometimes, He does take away the hassle or the hardship. Sometimes there's miraculous healing and divine intervention and incredible relief and release from angst. And sometimes, He doesn't, and there isn't.

If you're like me, you've wondered why God doesn't answer your prayers to alleviate your suffering or iron out the complications of a frenetic life. After all, He would take so much glory from a miracle – an intervention – a rescue operation on you.

It's ridiculously hard to see when you're in it, but the fact that God *doesn't* always answer your prayers for a lighter load means that He's stretching and strengthening your faith. He's doing more in you than the miracle would have done. He's writing a real page-turner – even *more* of a glory story than you could dream up.

Do you trust that God can do anything – including restore your soul – even though He hasn't (yet) alleviated your pain or dissolved your difficulties?

God, write a best-seller with my life. Take Your glory. Amen.

MARCH

Slay dragons, scrub dirt

None will see or know
Your wrestling in wee hours
Wrestle anyway.

Here be dragons

How do you know what your life will be like tomorrow?

James 4:14 NLT

Medieval explorers drew dragons on maps to show hazardous or uncharted territory. If there be dragons, you wouldn't be going there and you wouldn't be discovering the splendor of new lands. Those dragon drawings were really just a picture of fear: fear of change, fear of unknowns, fear of *new*. It was fear that kept the explorers away.

All sorts of mystery dragons may be pacing the borders of your life. Changes you wouldn't have planned for or ever expected. Challenges you feel ill-equipped to tackle. Those dragons can hem you in. Hot breath withering dreams and diminishing influence. You know you need to hunt them down. But you're too scared so they huff and drool and flick their tails. They feast on your time and your potential, stopping you from being and doing all you could and should.

You may not know what your life will look like tomorrow. You'll never predict all the changes and challenges that for sure are coming. But God knows. And He's infinitely bigger than your biggest fear.

Are you afraid of who or what may be lurking in the gloom ahead?

Jesus, help me to remember that dragons lose their fierceness when dragged from the shadows. You are the light of the world! Amen.

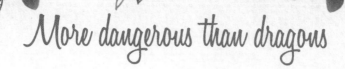

More dangerous than dragons

"Blessed are the pure in heart, for they shall see God."

Matthew 5:8 ESV

We can slay our dragons. We can axe the external pressures that stop us from using our time and our potential to change the world. But the truth is we don't have all that many enemies outside of ourselves.

It's easy to blame the dragons for keeping us from the spilling-over life Jesus promises because we get to be the victims. It's easier to be a victim than to be a world changer. So we keep blaming the dragons.

And sure, the dragons lurk. But there's something more sinister than fire and fangs. Something more destructive than people or circumstances that beat us up unbidden. It's what happens on the inside of you and me that ultimately affects how we use our years, abilities and opportunities for the Kingdom. And because we want to live the full life – the best life, the God life – we need to be honest with ourselves and find the courage to deal with the dirt in our hearts because there's a link between moral purity and knowing God. It quite takes my breath away – what Jesus said – that the pure in heart are blessed, because they'll see God.

Is there sin stuck stubborn in your heart – stopping you from being the most excellent, most beautiful you?

God, I want to see You. Purify my heart! Amen.

You got cockroaches?

Create in me a clean heart, O God,
and renew a right spirit within me.

Psalm 51:10 ESV

Sometimes when I snuggle my boys at bedtime one of them will ask me, "Mom, you got any cockroaches?"

We've adopted the metaphor from a Christian animation for kids in which Jesus shows this kid that his heart is crawling with cockroaches, feasting on the goo of nastiness, jealousy, anger, and all sorts. The kid is grossed out by the cockroaches – he wants Jesus to get rid of them – which He does, with His supercool love machine – and the kid's heart turns sweet and delicious with marshmallows.

So I ask the boys when I kiss them good night or during quiet moments over peanut butter toast: "Any cockroaches? Marshmallows?" Lately, they're asking it right back at me. We share hurts and frustrations, anger or fear. Incidents and accidents and questions about God, life and the universe. We talk it over. Pray.

I ask my boys about their hearts because I want to know what they're hiding. More than that, I want *them* to know what they're hiding. And you and me, friend, we need to know what we're hiding too.

Are you honest – with yourself, with others, with God who knows anyway – about what's really going on in your heart?

Father, I want the filth and the muck out of my heart.
Help me to be honest about what I'm hiding.
Forgive me, and cleanse my heart. Amen.

Intentional scrubbing

Wash me clean from my guilt. Purify me from my sin.

Psalm 51:2 NLT

If you're not good at leaving your comfort zone, don't do what I'm about to suggest. Don't do it if you have secrets – stuff no one knows and stuff you've half-forgotten because it's buried so deep and you plan to keep it that way. Don't do it if you enjoy nursing old hurts – bringing them out every now and then and stroking them just enough to keep you angry.

But if you're tired of heaving around a heavy heart; if you're spiritually short of breath because actually you're not just unfit, you're sick; if there are days when you feel ugly and guilt-tinged; if you're willing to accept that the common denominator in all your relationships is *you*; if you want to live free, love and be loved – then maybe you need to commit to the difficult, liberating process of scrubbing out your heart. Ask God to shine light on patches of your life that are damaged – even a little – by guilt, anger, greed and jealousy.

Do you dare to be intentional about this? Would you actually make some pen-and-paper lists of people you've wronged and people you need to forgive? Would you be honest about how jealousy or pride has stained your heart?

Jesus, all this dirt is piling up and making me sick.
Please give me the strength to get scrubbing.
And thank You for Your gift of forgiveness! Amen.

I owe you

> "So if you are presenting a sacrifice at the altar in the Temple and you suddenly remember that someone has something against you, leave your sacrifice there at the altar. Go and be reconciled to that person. Then come and offer your sacrifice to God."
>
> *Matthew 5:23-24* NLT

When I started the heart scrubbing habit, there was a lot to scrub. Years of grime. I started by making a list of the people I'd wronged. People I thought about with a twinge – or truckload – of guilt. I asked God to bring people to mind, and He did. An old varsity friend. An ex-boyfriend. I wrote down the names. Then I got in touch.

I realized how much easier it is to fess up privately to God. It took courage to own the hurt I had caused others. I asked forgiveness. I didn't make excuses or mention the thing(s) they may have done to me. I took responsibility for my slice of the relational pie. And I knew I wasn't responsible for their reaction.

It may be uncomfortable for you to make contact with someone – maybe after years – to ask forgiveness. But you'll be amazed at the grace that comes your way. Gathering the guts to risk and be vulnerable can unleash understanding, reconnection, affirmation and freedom.

Who's on your list? Do you dare to get in touch – ask forgiveness – come clean?

God, I want to do what I can to make right with the people I've hurt. Make me brave. Amen.

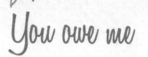

You owe me

Get rid of all bitterness, rage, anger, harsh words,
and slander, as well as all types of evil behavior. Instead,
be kind to each other, tenderhearted, forgiving one another,
just as God through Christ has forgiven you.

Ephesians 4:31–32 NLT

If you've written an I-owe-you list, maybe now it's time to write a you-owe-me list. The names on that list answer: Who am I angry with? Who has taken something from me that they had no right to take (like my lane in the traffic, my innocence or dignity)? Who ignored my requests or ignored me entirely? Who disrespected me? Who cheated on me? Who purposefully left me out, to hurt me? *Who do I need to forgive?*

Write down the names, if you know them. From the rude cashier at the drive-through to the coach who humiliated you on the field. Be honest with yourself about the angry memoir you've been writing in your head. You needn't call or email the people concerned. Those who've hurt you may not even know, and don't actually need to know. This is for you to take to God. Wrestle your anger to the ground in His presence. Sob, probably. Then remember how much you have been forgiven – and *pray*.

Until you can forgive. Breathe. Say with lightness: "They owe me nothing."

Who owes you? Will you be brave enough to cancel the debt?

God, there are people I need to forgive.
Loosen them from my heart, so I can be free. *Amen.*

I owe me

But people who long to be rich fall into temptation
and are trapped by many foolish and harmful desires
that plunge them into ruin and destruction.

1 Timothy 6:9 NLT

It's easy to see greed in others, and really difficult to see it in ourselves. Culture also preaches that we owe it to ourselves to give in to our desires for whatever, whenever, however.

It takes courage and clear intention to ask God to show us where greed is clogging our arteries, or where we're lying to ourselves about how much we deserve. When we have more month than money, do we doubt that God will provide for us? And when we have more money than month, do we hoard fearfully or spend hedonistically, when we could give generously?

You could check your priorities by asking yourself if you *give* before you *save* before you *live*. But of course we're not always greedy for only money. Sometimes we're greedy for food, fame, attention, or sympathy. Paul wrote to Timothy that those who are greedy fall into traps. So the challenge is to figure out if, or where, you're trapped.

Is God spotlighting an area of your life where you could be more generous this week? Or maybe a way for you to steer clear of the temptation to spend too much?

God, I'm so grateful for what You've given me to enjoy.
Keep me free from thinking I deserve all this.
Keep me quick to be generous, and beautifully responsible. *Amen.*

Grace rain

The LORD observed the extent of human wickedness on the earth, and He saw that everything they thought or imagined was consistently and totally evil.

Genesis 6:5 NLT

This passage of Scripture goes on to detail the flood God sent to wipe out the wickedness. These are uncomfortable verses. Not the sort of thing you'd read at your child's dedication, or a wedding or funeral. People generally don't like the idea that they're dirty and need cleaning, or broken and need fixing.

But until we realize our desperate need to be saved, we won't seek the Savior. There's dirt and debris heaped in our hearts and we're powerless to clean it all up. We're born broken and we can't fix ourselves or our kids or anyone else – which should heighten our relief and joy in knowing that God didn't leave us bent low in the muck. He made a miracle plan to restore and renew us, even refreshing our desire to do good.

So for you – beautiful believing woman – this hard truth should be thrilling. Because sure, you were dirty and broken too, yet you were, are and will be *never* without hope because Jesus took your dirt to the cross. He was broken on your behalf. And you've been cleansed and recreated by the grace flood of His blood.

Are you ok to be honest with yourself about human nature – yours in particular?

God, I want to stand in the grace rain and get myself uncomplicatedly drenched. Amen.

No prizes

"Then your Father, who sees what is done in secret, will reward you."

Matthew 6:4 NIV

One of the reasons we put off cleaning out our hearts is probably because there's no obvious or immediate tangible benefit. A clean heart doesn't dramatically Botox the outside of your life. You won't win any prizes for doing it. You won't get thousands of likes or retweets. No one will know that you have brought your dirt before the Holy God who knows it already, completely.

Yet the most important things – the things of inestimable and eternal value – are the things done in secret before God alone because with no one looking on, you are your most honest. Your worship is truest. And the God who sees what is done in secret will reward you.

Head into today content with the truth that your soft, surrendered heart won't earn awards, but know that there will be evidence in your life of your vulnerability before your heavenly Father. An undeniable dawning of light and wholeness. A new peace and perspective. Rising courage and excellence. Greater good. More startling beauty.

Will you go before God in secret, today?

Father, help me feel satisfied that You see everything I do in secret and that You reward me above and beyond earthly accolades. Give me a glimpse of the lasting change You're shaping in my heart. Amen.

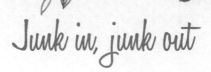

Junk in, junk out

Guard your heart above all else,
for it determines the course of your life.

Proverbs 4:23 NLT

No one teaches us to break commandments or evade the law. It comes naturally, and we're really good at it (Romans 3:10). But we can get ourselves even dirtier – and make it even harder to mop up the mess – by seeking out extra dirt to heap onto the rubble we're amassing.

If you're serious about taking on this dare – serious about cleaning out your heart by owning your junk – you need to be sure that you're not just adding to the muck. Pause. Try to figure out where you're gathering extra dirt. The Internet? A series you're watching? A friend you're hanging out with?

Jesus said that you'll speak from what fills your heart (Matthew 12:34). What goes in, comes out. If you want truth, excellence and beauty to come out of you – and I know that you do – then that's what you need to be putting in.

If you squeeze a toothpaste tube, toothpaste comes out, because that's what is inside. When life squeezes you tight – when you're pushed to react or decide – what comes out of you?

God, guard my heart. And grow my
desire to fill it with what's healthy. Amen.

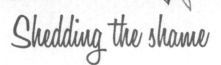

Shedding the shame

> People who conceal their sins will not prosper, but if
> they confess and turn from them, they will receive mercy.
>
> *Proverbs 28:13* NLT

Repentance tends to be shrouded in shame. I guess because repentance is an admission of guilt – wrongdoing – sin – and that makes us feel ashamed. And yet shame carries the sense that you're the only one and the whole world is pointing fingers, and so in a weird way, there's *no* shame in repentance. Because *all* have sinned and fallen short of God's holy standards (Romans 3:23). Friend, it's just not true that you're alone in your insufferable humiliation. You're not. In fact, trying to stick it out alone – hiding your sin and hanging on to it in secret – that's what's going to make it cling and cloy.

In David's great psalm of repentance, after committing adultery with Bathsheba (Psalm 51), he writes, "Oh, give me back my joy again," and "Restore to me the joy of Your salvation." And in another psalm he writes, "Yes, what joy for those whose record the LORD has cleared of guilt, whose lives are lived in complete honesty!" (Psalm 32:2). The result of repentance isn't shame. It's joy.

Is there unconfessed sin in your life that is stealing your joy? Will you shed that shame by bringing it into the light, and allow God to restore your contentment?

God of grace, I revel in Your mercy.
You are my joy, my peace, my freedom. Amen.

It's what we fight for

So if the Son sets you free, you are truly free.

John 8:36 NLT

Freedom is the endeavor of life. We fight for it from birth to death. Babies yell red to be free from the high chair at dinner. Kids skive to be free from school. Adults lie and manipulate to be free from responsibilities and poor-choice consequences. The ultimate civil punishment is to take someone's freedom of movement and choice. We want free rides, free time and free stuff.

And for sure when it comes to freedom, I'm like, "Pick me!" I want the kid-me inside the grown-up-me to be free to run and climb and shriek happy and learn and think and worship unashamed. I want to be free to be all I was created to be. I'm guessing that's what you want too.

But the truth is that even if you had the best, the freest, the fairest education and you've been set free to explore unthinkable opportunities and live in the freest and fairest and most benevolent of all democracies – still you will never be free and you will never maximize your time and live out loud your astounding potential if your heart is locked up behind anger, bitterness, resentment or hurt.

Because you won't ever be free if you don't ever forgive.

Do you really want to be free – not just physically or intellectually, but emotionally, spiritually and socially?

Jesus, help me fight for freedom by forgiving, the way that You freely forgave me. Amen.

No time to pray

But the LORD said to Joshua, "Get up!
Why are you lying on your face like this?"

Joshua 7:10 NLT

Joshua rips his clothes and bows facedown in the dust before God in prayer, because Israel has been thrashed in battle. Astonishingly, God says, "Get up! Stop praying!"

Israel's defeat is the result of one man – Achan – violating God's command that Jericho – the miracle acquisition – should not be plundered. So when Joshua prays earnestly for God to restore Israel's victory, God tells him to stop praying – get up – and sort out the real problem.

God had given clear instructions to His people in this situation about what was right and what was wrong. There was no need to pray about it. They just needed to do the Next Right Thing, and obey.

The same is true for us. You don't need to pray about something that God has covered in His Word. You don't need to pray about being faithful to your husband, not defrauding your boss, or being gentle towards your teenage son. Scripture is full of how-to-behaves for all those situations. And for sure, you don't need to pray about cleaning out your heart. You need only act on God's commands. Be brave. And just do it.

Are you stalling by "praying about it" when you know you really need to "just do it"?

Jesus, I don't want to discuss the same things with You, over and over. You've given me clear commands – all the coaching I need. Amen.

Prayer doesn't undo your doings

> Then David got up from the ground, washed himself,
> put on lotions, and changed his clothes. He went to
> the Tabernacle and worshiped the LORD. After that,
> he returned to the palace and was served food and ate.
>
> *2 Samuel 12:20* NLT

David and Bathsheba's first son dies as a consequence of their adultery. David fasts and prays while the child is ill, but as soon as the baby dies, he responds with remarkable calm and acceptance. He says to his baffled attendants, "I fasted and wept while the child was alive, for I said, 'Perhaps the LORD will be gracious to me and let the child live.' But why should I fast when he is dead? Can I bring him back again? I will go to him one day, but he cannot return to me" (2 Samuel 12:22-23).

David doesn't try to pray his way out of a situation that he behaved his way into. He understands that God isn't mocked. He repents (Psalm 51). Then he presses on – deeply aware of God's unmerited favor – and behaves better.

Prayer isn't a wand that can magic away the aftereffects of unwise choices. Of course, we *must* talk to God about everything. Even – especially – our mishaps and mess ups. But we also need to be brave enough to answer for our actions.

How can you live beautifully and excellently today by facing the truth and taking responsibility?

*God, help me accept the consequences
of things I know You've forgiven me for. Amen.*

How your changed heart can change the world

Since you have heard about Jesus and have learned the truth that comes from Him, throw off your old sinful nature and your former way of life, which is corrupted by lust and deception. Instead, let the Spirit renew your thoughts and attitudes. Put on your new nature, created to be like God – truly righteous and holy.

Ephesians 4:21-24 NLT

It's true that changed people change a nation, and changed nations change the world. And the only thing that changes people is changed hearts. And the only One who can change hearts is Jesus. Economics, education, medical care: all good and necessary. But even in the freest and fairest and most affluent spots on the globe, those things can effect skin-deep changes; maybe even sway the culture. But they have no power over the hearts of people.

It's from changed hearts – hearts turned soft by turning to Jesus – that behavior changes. Deeply. Intrinsically. And that changes how people live, love and work to build families, finances and infrastructure.

Friend, you *know* Jesus. You can tell the beautiful stories of changing grace because you're living them. He has crafted a heart change in you, and that makes you part of world change.

What do you think might happen if the Christians in your country prayed like never before for new attitudes, new actions?

God, I don't feel like I'm making much of a difference on this planet. But I'm trusting You to change me, to change the world. Amen.

Quiet convictions

I lie awake thinking of You, meditating on You through the night.

Psalm 63:6 NLT

If you're determined to clean out your heart – to be bravely, brutally honest about the things you carry with you that no one else sees but that unmistakably and inescapably influence your attitudes and your actions – then you need to capture some time to *be*. Still. Unhurried.

I find that God speaks to me when the house is quiet and I'm wiping a counter or folding a tablecloth. It's often in those moments that a thought dawns slow but clear: *"You spoke too harshly."* Or, *"You shouldn't have joined in the gossip."* Those kinds of thoughts. Quiet convictions. Maybe for you it's lying in the dark when the day's busyness settles and sinks and truth distils – floats to the top of your consciousness. Pay attention. What is God saying? What is He showing you about your heart? Don't drown out what you know the Holy Spirit is whispering.

How can you manage your schedule to make sure that at some point in the day or the week you are quiet enough to sense the pressure of God's love?

Jesus, sometimes I rush too loudly. I don't want to hear what You have to say because I know it won't be easy. Forgive me. Help me to be brave enough to slow down and listen. Amen.

What about them?

Why are evil people so happy? Your name is on their lips,
but You are far from their hearts. But as for me, LORD,
You know my heart. You see me and test my thoughts.

Jeremiah 12:1-3 NLT

It's hard to feel motivated to deal with your sin when you look around and see how many other people are wallowing in theirs. And getting a free massage. And a cocktail. In fact they're laughing so loudly you can hardly hear yourself pray.

Take heart. Because God sees yours. And He sees every other heart, everywhere, every time. You'll never know what another person's heart looks like on the inside, and probably, you wouldn't want to know. Thank God that it's not your place or your problem to understand the weight of sin or suffering that another person carries.

You are also, thankfully, not responsible for their outward behavior or their real or contrived self-satisfaction. God will hold you accountable only for your own heart and how you managed it. He'll do the same for everyone else, and He'll do it with perfect justice (2 Thessalonians 1:6).

Could you make today spectacular by living from a heart of truth, courage, excellence and beauty – rather than fretting over the lies, cowardice, mediocrity or malice emitting from others?

*God, thank You that You and I only really need to
discuss what's going on in my heart. You have all
the information on everyone else.* Amen.

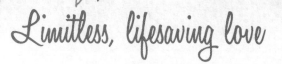

Limitless, lifesaving love

> Can an Ethiopian change the color of his skin?
> Can a leopard take away its spots? Neither can you
> start doing good, for you have always done evil.
>
> *Jeremiah 13:23* NLT

These were harsh words for Jeremiah to deliver. Harsh words to hear. They came from a God who loved His people furiously and relentlessly – people who had forgotten their faith and drifted listless into sin. God was calling them back to Himself and making sure they understood how much they needed His righteousness, because – like you and me – they had none of their own.

Just as it was for those Israelites, it's uncomfortable for us to hear God's Word sometimes because it tugs at us sore where we've coasted from the truth.

And yet, who ever saw a mom stand by as her toddler ran into a busy road? I'm pretty convinced that every mom would grab her child – probably yell – maybe even bruise him in her love-grip because she would do anything to keep him from harm. How much more would God do for us – to draw us to the safety of Himself?

Do you believe that God is for you, not against you?

Thank You, God, for Your formidable love. Thank You for the radical lengths You go to – and have done, throughout history – to draw us to Yourself. Amen.

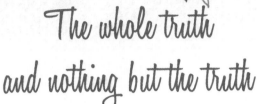

The whole truth
and nothing but the truth

Keep me from lying to myself;
give me the privilege of knowing Your instructions.

Psalm 119:29 NLT

We're so good at talking to ourselves. We can convince ourselves of anything, and talk ourselves into or out of whatever we really want. Like, despite what the scale screamed in shock, you tell yourself that refusing dessert at the dinner party will hurt the feelings of the hostess. Or, despite what you know happened the last time you invited him in for coffee, you tell yourself that *this* time you can handle it.

Maybe if you could do one thing differently today it could be this: Don't lie to yourself. At every opportunity, invitation or decision, in every conversation and interaction and in the midst of every common or complex task, determine that the narrative in your head will be completely honest. You can't fool God, and there won't be lasting change on the inside of you until you stop fooling yourself. Tell yourself the truth about you, and then seek the truth of God that equips you to live wisely wherever you find yourself.

Could you create excellence, beauty and positive change today, just by telling yourself the truth instead of justifying what is risky or reckless?

God, forgive me for treating You like an idiot – as if I could seduce You the way I seduce myself. I want to come clean and start telling You and me the truth. Amen.

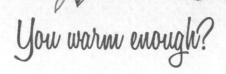

You warm enough?

And the LORD God made clothing from
animal skins for Adam and his wife.

Genesis 3:21 NLT

Growing up, and going out, my mom would always ask me if I was warm enough or if I had a sweater. It would irritate me. I vowed I would allow my own kids one day to decide for themselves if they were cold or not. Of course, that hasn't happened. I ask my boys *all the time*. If they're warm enough. If they shouldn't perhaps put their sweaters on before we leave. The mom-love has put me on nurture autopilot. I love them, and I will keep them warm. Like it or not.

It moves and amazes me how, after Adam and Eve plunged all of history into cataclysmic depravity, God made them clothes. He was interested in them, and concerned about their day-to-day well-being. Sure, there was a message in the clothing about shame. But even so – He could have left them naked and ashamed. They deserved it. Instead He pursued them, to cover their disgrace. That's the persistent, unyielding love of a Father. And that's the way the Father loves me, and you.

When do you feel most exposed – uncovered – unsafe? What truth about God can you tell yourself?

Father, thank You that You never leave me out in the cold.
Your love finds and covers me. Thank You that opening my
heart to You doesn't mean it will freeze over, but rather that
You will warm me with Your grace. Amen.

Keep a short account

Finally, I confessed all my sins to You and stopped trying to
hide my guilt. I said to myself, "I will confess my rebellion
to the LORD." And You forgave me! All my guilt is gone.

Psalm 32:5 NLT

If you read this psalm you'll see that David had been holding out on
God. He simply declined to confess his sins. It's not clear if he was
afraid or too proud or in denial – but he hung on to his sin until it
made him sick. When he finally admitted that his sin was just that –
sin – he was free.

Because embracing repentance frees us to move on unfettered
from the sad sticky tangles of self-pity, resentment, jealousy and all
the other junk that makes us ugly on the inside and eventually on
the outside. Admitting our disobediences to God leaves our hearts
in that soft, supple place of gentle, steadfast Christ-likeness.

Would you talk to God about it today, and be free already? Don't
hold out.

If not you, is there someone close to you whom you suspect is hanging on to a grudge or habit – and keeping their sin on life-support?
Could you pray for them today, or encourage them to take it to God,
and be free?

*God, thank You that my guilt is gone. I wish I'd confessed it all long
ago. Help me from now on to keep a short account of my sin.* Amen.

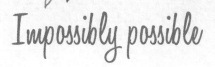

Impossibly possible

For He has rescued us from the kingdom of darkness and
transferred us into the Kingdom of His dear Son,
who purchased our freedom and forgave our sins.

Colossians 1:13-14 NLT

You and I will never completely wrap our heads or hearts around redemption until we meet our Redeemer, face-to-face.

It seems too staggeringly good to be true that God loved us so much that, for the sake of our good and His glory, He was pleased to crush Jesus, who understood our suffering and temptation (Isaiah 53:10, Hebrews 4:15). It seems too incredible that Jesus was obedient even to death (Philippians 2:8). That by His stripes we are healed (Isaiah 53:5). That even in His agony He had compassion (Luke 23:34). That He nailed our filth to the cross (Colossians 2:14). That the tomb is empty (John 20:1). That death has lost its sting (1 Corinthians 15:55). That we are free indeed (John 8:36). And that when this blink-of-an-eye life is done we will spend eternity with Him (Ephesians 2:6).

Would you take a minute today just to marvel at the second chance we've been given? The wonder of it.

Which aspect of Christ's sacrifice and victory over death most stirs your heart? Could you make someone's day more beautiful, by sharing that truth?

*Jesus, thank You for making the impossible
possible in my life. I stand amazed.* Amen.

Death to life

For the wages of sin is death, but the free gift
of God is eternal life through Christ Jesus our Lord.

Romans 6:23 NLT

If you're a parent you'll know how much it sucks to realize that your kids haven't only inherited your good qualities – like your smile and sense of humor, or your husband's eyes and easygoing outlook. They've also inherited your dirt. You've seen how your instinctive me-me-me rebellion manifests in them and you desperately want them to understand that sin causes death.

Obviously – eventually – we'll all physically die because of a decision involving two people and some fruit long ago. But there's more to it. Death follows sin *every time*. It's always the wage you pay. The death differs, depending on the sin. It could be the death of your health. Or the death of a relationship, or someone's trust. Maybe it's the death of a job, a dream, your finances, your waistline, your reputation, or your desire for what's natural and good.

We need to drum it into our hearts and minds that none of us is above the ultimate consequence of wrongdoing: *death*. But that there is a way out – an escape – a free gift that's ours for the taking: *life*.

Have you owned this dazzling truth – that God has given you life, instead of death?

God, may I never treat my sin lightly. You paid an infinite price to cover it. And may I never take for granted Your gift of life. Amen.

Hidden hooks

The serpent was the shrewdest of all the wild animals the Lord God had made. One day he asked the woman, "Did God really say you must not eat the fruit from any of the trees in the garden?"

Genesis 3:1 NLT

If you accept that sin results in something as dramatic as death, then surely you'll recognize it? Surely you'll see death coming? But that's the terrifying thing. Sin is insidious. Even beautiful. It promises that it's ok, as long as you're not hurting anyone. It somehow makes you forget that *you* are someone, and it will definitely hurt you. It starts with a thought, the way it did with Eve when the snake suggested that maybe she – or God? – didn't have the story straight about the tree. The thought lingers. Nibbles. Then comes back for bigger bites if you let it.

Paul warned the Corinthian believers about Satan's angel-of-light disguise (2 Corinthians 11:14). So don't be surprised when sin shows up as something delectable. It's how Satan hides the hook to bait you into disaster. If you taste what's on offer, you can be sure that he's got more where it came from.

Be brave. Stand on truth. And thank God for the insight and discernment He gives when we stick close to Him.

Can you think of a time when you were tricked – when you didn't see the hook?

God, don't let me be fooled into feeding an appetite that will only grow into something dangerous. Help! Amen.

Sin is not the boss of you

Sin is no longer your master, for you no longer live
under the requirements of the law. Instead,
you live under the freedom of God's grace.

Romans 6:14 NLT

It's not trendy to talk about sin much at all anymore. But we *so* need to get it that if we weren't in dire need of redemption, God would not have sent a Redeemer. In which case, why Jesus? Our faith would be lame and laughable and it would make more sense to join a country club.

Friend, you need to cling to Jesus because you need Him more than air. He holds grace in one hand and freedom in the other. Grace says He owes you nothing but He calls you beloved and offers you forgiveness and eternal life anyway.

And freedom says that sin is no longer your master. You're liberated from its grip. Released so that you can stop trying so hard and failing even harder, and let Christ live His life through you. For sure, the consequences of sin may be strung across your life every which way, but grace cuts the trip wire so you can run free.

"Sin is not my master." Could you try saying that a couple times today, to some old habits dying hard?

Jesus, You and You only are my Master. You broke the power of darkness over me, so help me to stop saying "Yes, sir!" to sin. Amen.

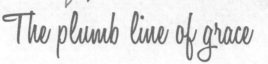

The plumb line of grace

Then Jesus stood up again and said to the woman, "Where are your accusers? Didn't even one of them condemn you?" "No, Lord," she said. And Jesus said, "Neither do I. Go and sin no more."

John 8:10-11 NLT

We live in a world of reactionary pendulums swinging out of whack. Even amongst believers, the pendulum swings from legalistic attack to laissez-faire acceptance, neither of which reflects the power of changing grace.

We're not just recipients of a no-worries, whatever-floats-your-boat kind of lenience. Grace is so much more than benign tolerance. And grace doesn't leave us condemned – trapped in a tick-box regime. Grace isn't a pendulum; it's a plumb line suspended dead center – the accurate measure of truth.

Grace said to seething Pharisees, goading Jesus to enforce the law to stone the adulterous woman: "All right, but let the one who has never sinned throw the first stone!" (John 8:7). Grace turned the accusers sheepish. But grace didn't say to that woman, "Never mind. Carry on!" Jesus loved her far more than that. He lavished upon her acceptance, cleansing and hope. And then, because He wanted her to be free, He said, "Sin no more." Which He wouldn't have said if it wasn't possible, because grace powers heart change – life change – world change.

Today, how can you lean into grace and away from legalism (earning God's favor) or liberalism (excusing sin)?

God, I'm in awe of Your grace. It enfolds me, and refuses to leave me as I am. Amen.

Scrutiny for the win

Search me, O God, and know my heart; test me and know my anxious thoughts. Point out anything in me that offends You, and lead me along the path of everlasting life.

Psalm 139:23-24 NLT

If you have a couple of extra minutes today, read all of Psalm 139. It's pure poetry and astounding reality: a deep assurance of how intimately God knows us, and how fearfully and wonderfully He made us. Allow the psalmist to remind you that, because you were created incredibly and intentionally, God will use you in distinctive, remarkable ways, according to your gifts and passions and opportunities, to plough Kingdom ground, and to change the world.

But it's no accident of literature that this fearfully-and-wonderfully-made psalm closes with the verses above: this beautiful prayer for close examination. Because, to be a world changer? You need to embrace how God knows you and how He has molded you – not just your talents and flairs, but all your physical, emotional and intellectual quirks, and your obvious or inevitable shortcomings. Bow low before Him. Surrender your spiritual deficiencies to the scrutiny of the Spirit and as He convicts and forgives and restores, your life will be different. And so will the world.

Are you willing to submit yourself to the Holy Spirit's gentle, relentless conviction?

God, You had me in mind before You set the clock of history. I can't fathom Your great love and Your detailed plans. Search me. Dig up any heart dirt that lurks. Amen.

Younger the older you get

But when God our Savior revealed His kindness and love,
He saved us, not because of the righteous things we had done,
but because of His mercy. He washed away our sins, giving us a
new birth and new life through the Holy Spirit. He generously
poured out the Spirit upon us through Jesus Christ our Savior.

Titus 3:4-6 NLT

The bonus by-product of cleaning out your heart is that it makes you younger. More beautiful than Botox. A heart alive to God is refreshed, rejuvenated and replenished. Bits of your soul that had been subject to atrophy are drenched in newness.

It's one of the wondrous ways in which God's truth turns upside down the trends plotted by statisticians. Sure, year by year we'll find more and more gray hairs in the mirror, but if Jesus is the center of our lives – if in Him we live and move and exist (Acts 17:28) – then equally, year by year, our spiritual vision will sharpen and our soul energy will be restored. We will remind people less and less of our naturally aging selves and more and more of Jesus.

How are you aging on the inside?

God, help me to look after the body You've given me. But help me not to be too hung up on keeping it all gorgeous. Make me so exquisite on the inside – so like You – that people will end up seeing it on the outside, to Your glory. Amen.

Soul auction

But as for me, I know that my Redeemer lives.

Job 19:25 NLT

The word "redemption" isn't Christianese. It has to do with slavery. A slave trader could buy back a slave – *redeem* that slave – and give him his freedom. We were slaves to sin and we didn't have the means to buy ourselves out of the deal. Jesus put in the highest bid. He paid for us with His blood. He bought us back to set us free.

And I'm all about the freedom so I keep going back to what Jesus said – that the truth would set us free (John 8:32). And freedom born of truth slashes the fear ropes that cut deeper than our wrists and into our souls. We live out that freedom through the paradox of being bound to Christ for eternity in the perfect love that casts out fear (1 John 4:18).

You are free, because you cost a lot. That's the gospel.

Could you jot down – on your phone or in a journal – the ways in which you are free? Are there whole areas of your life that God has bought back – redeemed – for your good and His glory?

God, thank You for redeeming me! I want to rest in Your unthinkable, unmerited favor so that I will not be bound by sin or religion. Thank You that Your sacrifice for me binds me forever to You. Amen.

Gravity

Because of the joy awaiting Him,
He endured the cross, disregarding its shame.

Hebrews 12:2 NLT

It's a paradox to me that defying gravity in outer space is a pinnacle of human endeavor, and yet our forays into the universe are what most make me feel the smallness of our planet, and the smallness of us.

Of course, gravity can also mean *seriousness*. Like, the gravity of the cross – the grave filled. A heaviness. Because of the joy ahead of Him, Jesus submitted Himself to the bonds of earthly gravity and He carried the heaviness so that condemnation didn't sit heavy on any of us.

And another paradox: the gravity of the cross weights my life in truth – pulls it down solid into significance. And the gravity of the cross is my lightness of being – the levity of life. The heaviness – the severity – of the sacrifice means that we can "strip off every weight that slows us down, especially the sin that so easily trips us up" (Hebrews 12:1). Heavy truth. Weightless grace. We dare not un-tether ourselves from either.

As you walk on green grass or cracked concrete today – feet gravitated to earth – would you remember that you are secure, and free?

Jesus, You conquered the grave!
I could never praise You enough. Amen.

Clean-heart habit

Put me on trial, LORD, and cross-examine me.
Test my motives and my heart.

Psalm 26:2 NLT

I do my best work when I've decluttered. I take toys back to the playroom. I close all the tabs and docs and apps that I can. And peace settles. Thoughts clear. Productivity soars. I do what needs doing when I've cleared the litter of life from my mind and my desk and the floor at my feet.

It's the same with my heart. And yours.

Friend, when it comes to your sin, take no prisoners. Do a ruthless declutter. Be honest. Repent. Because all the tarnished bits of you rendered useless under grime will suddenly gleam valuable. And because cleaning out your heart unleashes energy and stretches time. You'll use your best gifts and do your best loving and leave the best legacy if you've tidied up inside of you.

You won't regret starting a clean-heart habit. Once you've operated industrial-strength degreasing equipment, it will be easier to wipe crumbs off the counter day by day. Because a once-off clean out is not enough. You can scour out the stuff that seeps foul from the past, but that doesn't make you immune to grunge that gathers every day. Dust settles and sticks and dirt attracts dirt. You have to make heart scrubbing a no-arguments daily habit. Like brushing your teeth. Like, you'll feel gross all day if you haven't done it.

Do you dare?

O God, cleanse me. Amen.

APRIL

Character, calling and simple success

"It is not the critic who counts; not the man who points out how the strong man stumbles, or where the doer of deeds could have done them better. The credit belongs to the man who is actually in the arena, whose face is marred by dust and sweat and blood; who strives valiantly; who errs, who comes short again and again, because there is no effort without error and shortcoming; but who does actually strive to do the deeds; who knows great enthusiasms, the great devotions; who spends himself in a worthy cause; who at the best knows in the end the triumph of high achievement, and who at the worst, if he fails, at least fails while daring greatly, so that his place shall never be with those cold and timid souls who neither know victory nor defeat."

– *Theodore Roosevelt*

Don't miss your calling

Let me hear of Your unfailing love each morning, for I am trusting You. Show me where to walk, for I give myself to You.

Psalm 143:8 NLT

From this psalm it's clear that David isn't hedging his bets when it comes to wisdom and direction for life. He doesn't have a Plan B. He prays confidently, convinced that God will hear and answer. He is certain and satisfied that God will come through for him with the unfailing love and the step-by-step guidance he's asking for. And he prays like this – believes like this – *each morning*.

It's fascinating that David – the great shepherd king whose heroism is still carved deeply in the hearts and history of his people – doesn't ask: "O God, what is my calling? Show me the great work of my life." He simply prays: "Show me where to walk." He understood the crux of calling: that if you miss the daily call on your life, then for sure you'll miss the big call – the life's work – the calling.

You need to stay close enough to God, *each morning*, to hear His voice, calling you. It's all those yeses to His call, all those mornings, that add up to a most excellent, most beautiful life's work.

Are you straining to see the big thing you'll do with your life, and looking right past the Next Right Thing, right in front of you?

God, don't let me miss my calling.
Show me where to walk today. Amen.

Context + Character = Calling

When the training period ordered by the king was completed,
the chief of staff brought all the young men to
King Nebuchadnezzar. The king talked with them, and
no one impressed him as much as Daniel, Hananiah, Mishael,
and Azariah. So they entered the royal service.

Daniel 1:18-19 NLT

Daniel and his friends arrived in the royal court under unique circumstances. They had a specific and intriguing context. More than that, they had character. It was the combination – when and where God had placed them in time and space, and the work that God had done in their hearts to form their characters – that shaped their calling.

Your context and character will influence and inform your calling, because you're a holistic being and these elements are part of the story God has written for you. That's pretty exciting – knowing you've been positioned ideally for God to use you. It's also a relief. You can stop trying to figure out God's will for you, because as long as you're living a saved and Spirit-filled life – which means as long as you can trace a growing pattern of head and heart changes that make you more like Jesus, and as long as you're seeking to live in gratitude, worship, prayer and obedience to God – then you're exactly where you should be, and who you should be.

What's your story? What's your strength?

God, please give me wisdom around my context and my character, so that I can get busy living my calling. Amen.

Be tough

"Don't be afraid," he said, "for you are very precious to God. Peace! Be encouraged! Be strong!" As he spoke these words to me, I suddenly felt stronger and said to him, "Please speak to me, my lord, for you have strengthened me."

Daniel 10:19 NLT

Daniel had an incredible calling on his life. As a result he was engaged in a fierce spiritual battle. He didn't even really know how fierce. But he committed to praying and staying humble (Daniel 10:12), and because of that, he stayed strong.

There's a calling on your life too. The living God has mapped out your destiny. He delights in using you to accomplish His Kingdom purposes. He loves emboldening you to fulfill your potential, for His glory. But you'll need to be tough. Paul said it well to those Corinthian Christians who heard the call and fought to live it: "We are pressed on every side by troubles, but we are not crushed. We are perplexed, but not driven to despair. We are hunted down, but never abandoned by God. We get knocked down, but we are not destroyed" (2 Corinthians 4:8-9).

Don't be surprised by opposition. Rather, stay strong. Be at peace. Be encouraged. Be brave. Answer the call, whatever it is, and know that you are very precious to God.

What scares you about obeying God's call?

Lord, keep me strong. I want my life to be a beautiful answer to Your call. Amen.

Be tender

Instead, be kind to each other, tenderhearted, forgiving
one another, just as God through Christ has forgiven you.

Ephesians 4:32 NLT

Otosclerosis is the hardening of the bones in the inner ear and it results in impaired hearing. There's no cure, but the condition can be treated with a hearing aid. The same kind of thing can happen to the hearing of our hearts. Less and less resonance gets through to a hardening heart. The sounds of grace, hope and joy grow faint. The still, small voice of God, calling you, becomes muffled – then muted.

The great relief is that there's mercy and healing for the spiritually deaf. Hardening of the heart can be reversed and restored. Paul shared the remedy with the Ephesians: kindness and forgiveness, always remembering the kindness and forgiveness that God has shown you. Because it's in keeping a soft heart towards others and a soft heart towards God that you'll pick up every reverberation, note or nuance of your calling. As much as you need a strong spirit to be all God made you to be, you need a soft heart.

Are there singular events or whole seasons of your life that caused you to harden your heart? If you surrender those controlling memories, what do you hear?

*God, please soften my heart so that I can
hear the hearts of others, and hear You.* Amen.

Succinct success

... the LORD has told you what is good, and this is
what He requires of you: to do what is right, to
love mercy, and to walk humbly with your God.

Micah 6:8 NLT

So here's a crazy idea about success: It isn't hard. You needn't slave over it or scramble towards it. It's also not necessarily the triumphant soaring or sweeping victory that the world promises. It may be noticeable; it may be entirely hidden. It's never complicated; always simple.

Because success in God's dictionary is defined by obedience. And obedience isn't an arduous, religious obligation. It's the love response – the relieved, relaxed answer – of a heart restored by grace. Because when God says He's paid the price for your sin – that there's nothing to do to earn His love – then there's nothing more obvious than for you to give Him your very best yes. Obedience is a pure joy reaction born of freedom from law.

And obedience is not a rung in the go-getter ladder to success. It simply is success. Because doing the will of God – His way, in His power, and for the honor of His name – is all we're ever called to do.

Can you trust God today for the measurable results you're looking for, and just take the next step of obedience?

God, help me to be satisfied with the sweet, succinct
success of simply obeying You, even when it doesn't
make sense or when it doesn't feel like progress. Amen.

Beautifully inconspicuous

Work willingly at whatever you do, as though you
were working for the Lord rather than for people.

Colossians 3:23 NLT

Anonymity – being ignored, overlooked, misunderstood or taken un-seriously – can be a gift, when it comes to fulfilling your God-mission in this life. You'd think that obscurity would be counterproductive, and yet there's a transcendent freedom in being played down. It allows you to get busy doing what you're called to do because you're not waiting for somebody else's go-ahead nod. You're not waiting to be empowered or energized by the consent of the crowd. It's massively liberating to realize that your mandate is from the living God and you live your gifts brave by the authority He gives.

Of course, it makes for a far richer life if you get to share your capacity and live out your calling within community. But what if the community is overlooking the potential God has given you and the areas of influence in which He has positioned you? Don't let that stop you from doing what you do, and doing it well.

Could you go about your business today, confident and content that you're obeying directives from the King?

Jesus, I want to do what I do, for You. Help me not to be bothered by who does or doesn't notice or care. Hide me in the quiet, concentrated work to which You've called me. Amen.

Hidden

It is God's privilege to conceal things ...

Proverbs 25:2 NLT

It seems from the Scriptures that God glories in hiddenness, and in revelation. Like, He will hide people or display them as and when He deems it right, in this life or the next. Joseph was hidden in prison before being made prime minister. Moses was hidden in a desert before delivering his people. David was hidden in caves then crowned as king. Elijah was hidden by a brook then restored to boldness. Paul's seismic activism for the gospel began after three years of hiding in Arabia.

And Jesus – master-teacher – rewriter of destiny – the God-man – was hidden in a corner of history where there were no auditoriums. No big-screen live-streams. He was hidden amidst small crowds on grassy hillsides and in homes on narrow streets. He bore the Biggest Name and He lived the smallest life. And then He was revealed. Raised up to die, then raised up to live.

What a wonder to know the truth that, though your life is on the down low, the great, hidden work you do is part of something cosmic – something Kingdom.

Are you content to stay hidden until God says otherwise?

God, even in the hiddenness and the waiting, help me to lean hard into the truth, to live bravely and excellently, and to create beauty wherever and whenever I have the opportunity. Amen.

Labeled

And when you believed in Christ, He identified you as His
own by giving you the Holy Spirit, whom He promised long ago.

Ephesians 1:13 NLT

To change the world, you need to maximize your time and potential.
So the enemy will do what he can to make you feel that your efforts
are futile. He knows that if you're thinking, "What's the point?
They don't get me," you're likely to give up, give in or give over
and abandon the truth you're doing, saying or believing because
others' misunderstanding makes you feel inadequate. The enemy
knows that if you've been labeled *substandard* and shelved, then
it's hard for you to believe that you've something worthwhile to
offer the Kingdom.

A wise person reminded me that only the manufacturer, owner
or purchaser of something gets to stick a label on it. Only God
made you. Only God bought you with His blood. You belong to
only God. So if God has labeled you *adopted by the King* and
clothed in royal robes – do you dare argue with that?

When you understand the dazzling truth label stuck all over you,
it won't matter so much how you're perceived or appreciated. The
certainty that Almighty God overlooks nothing – that He sees every
intention of your heart – will bring sure peace. Quiet confidence
and constant courage. Delight and lightness of being.

What labels has the world stuck on you?

*Father, thank You that You have
tattooed Your love all over my life. Amen.*

Secret weapon

But you belong to God, my dear children. You have already
won a victory over those people, because the Spirit who
lives in you is greater than the spirit who lives in the world.

1 John 4:4 NLT

It's important to follow the straight path of your calling by straight-ening out what's crooked in your heart. You need to forgive. And it helps to remember that the power to forgive is in you because the power of the living God is in you.

Next time you're engaged in conversation – in real-life or in your head – with the person you're fighting to forgive, remember what John said, that "you have already won a victory over those people." Let the small talk you're pretending your way through be drowned out by the din of earthmoving equipment in your heart as the might of God shifts the grudge:

Dig. Loosen. Release. Let the person go.

Because we should cling to the truth that if we don't transform our pain, we will transmit it. Finding the courage to forgive can change *your* world, and dozens – maybe hundreds – of personal worlds set free by forgiveness will change the world at large. Forgiveness is our most powerful secret weapon for living full and free.

The victory is already yours. Will you forgive?

*God, help me remember that it's futile trying to forgive in
my own strength. Fill me and empower me to forgive. Amen.*

Reaping irresponsible

When Adam sinned, sin entered the world. Adam's sin brought death, so death spread to everyone, for everyone sinned.

Romans 5:12 NLT

If you look at the facts, you could say that it's really not fair, that we and all creation sank into sin – because of Adam. And you'd be right. It's not fair that we reap what others have sown. But like so much of reality Earth-side: it's not fair, but it's true. The beauty and the cruelty of community is that we're connected. Your decency affects me positively, and mine affects you. Your irresponsibility affects me negatively, and mine affects you.

It's not fair that, possibly, your journey towards fulfilling your calling has been altered and affected by the poor choices of your parents or friends or governing authorities. Know that they will be held accountable for their decisions and how they played out in your life, and the lives of others. And in the meantime, become intolerant of irresponsibility in yourself and those around you. Urge those in your areas of influence – starting with you – to spread radiance, not rot.

Have you been waylaid – losing sight of where you're headed – because you've reaped what others have sown irresponsibly?

God, You know the facts. You see every thought and intention, and You judge righteously. Help me to accept that You see the unfairness leveled at me, and that You will plead my case. Help me to move on and take responsibility for the things I can. Amen.

Own it

For we are each responsible for our own conduct.

Galatians 6:5 NLT

You've probably experienced the frustration of cleaning up the mess made by someone who bought into the selfish leaning of our culture that it's all about getting ahead, regardless of the consequences. (Maybe, like me, you've even been the one making the mess?). Because almost every stream of media and influence will tell you that it's ok to do whatever it takes, heedless of right or wrong, to make sure that you're ok, and that you get what you want.

And yet you don't have to be super smart to notice that irresponsibility is never neutral. Someone else will always end up taking care of your carelessness. It's not an option to say, "I'm not hurting anyone." It's not an option to brush something off with, "It's not my problem." Because if you don't take responsibility for your decisions – your actions and attitudes, your relationships, your money or morality – then all those decisions eventually become someone else's responsibility. There's a braver, more beautiful way to live than that.

It's hard to recognize recklessness in our own lives, but could it be that you've let something slide, ignoring the possible penalties?

God, help me to own what's mine to own. Help me face up to my responsibilities in a society that baits me to abdicate my calling to do what's right. Amen.

Happiest you

Then God blessed them and said, "Be fruitful and multiply.
Fill the earth and govern it. Reign over the fish in the sea, the
birds in the sky, and all the animals that scurry along the ground."

Genesis 1:28 NLT

We're inclined to groan under duty. Like, at best it's arduous and unpleasant; at worst it's evil. And yet God gifted humankind with responsibility *before* our fall into sin. It's not a curse. He placed on people the holy mantle of caring for the world He had made us, to honor Him. Created in the image of God whose sovereignty takes full responsibility for every atom in the universe, we're made to take responsibility too. We're designed for it. It suits us. That's why you probably don't know any irresponsible people who are also truly happy.

And if you're honest? You'll know that when you're taking charge of what's been allotted to you – dealing excellently with your inbox, your kitchen or your kids – you're most gratified. You're happiest.

Which of the enormous or minuscule responsibilities that form part of your daily life give you the most satisfaction? Are there some responsibilities that stress you out? Could you trust God to help you wear them beautifully?

Creator God, thank You for showing me that taking responsibility for my life is good for me, and glorifies You. Show me where and how I can step up to what's required, knowing that You will equip me for the tasks You give. Amen.

Later and greater

Don't be misled – you cannot mock the justice of God. You will always harvest what you plant.

Galatians 6:7 NLT

You reap what you sow.

That isn't fatalism or karma. It's just the straightforward out-working of a practical principle that God designed to bring order and predictability to the universe and daily life. So, if a kid keeps pulling the cat's tail, he'll get scratched. He'll reap what he sowed.

The intriguing thing about sowing and reaping is that once we've sown, there's always a delay of sorts (a few seconds, a few decades). We reap *later*. And there's always an exponential result. Like, the bleeding scratch on the kid's face is far more painful than a few tugs of the tail. It's a worse payoff. We reap *greater*.

Mercifully, the same is true for sowing goodness. You may have to wait a long time – even a lifetime – for the harvest to come in. But if you've sown in trust and obedience, then you'll reap more than you could possibly have dreamed up.

Has this principle played out in your life? Have you reaped a rich legacy because you had a parent or grandparent who sowed into your life, years ago, through faithful prayer?

God, forgive me for all the ways that I've sown unwisely. It has cost me, and it has cost others. Help me to be intentional about what I plant, so that I can be sure of an ample harvest – later, and greater. Amen.

Dissolve your stress in a tall glass of humble

True humility and fear of the Lord lead to riches, honor, and long life.

Proverbs 22:4 NLT

When we're most stressed, we're certainly not living the rich or honorable life that Solomon describes (in the sense of peace and emotional well-being). Sustained stress will also ensure that we probably won't live a long life.

And stress – the too-much-to-do and not-enough-time kind of stress – can reveal our pride. We stress when stuff doesn't work out because we think we deserve for everything to go our way. Or we worry that we don't have what it takes. It irks us when we feel forced to drop some of the balls we're trying to keep in the air, because we'd quite like to be known as someone who can keep right on juggling.

It's in stressful situations that it helps me to remind myself that pride can be thinking too much of myself, or thinking too little of myself. The point is that I shouldn't be thinking of myself at all. I need to humble my very ordinary, finite self and remember that I'm not the center of the universe, and that sure, I can do anything. But I can't do everything, which is, really, rather a relief.

What's at the root of your biggest pressure points?

God, humble me. Help me to depend on You.
Trying to be a hero and killing myself in the process
doesn't achieve much, or glorify You. Amen.

It's Who you know

"Yes, I am the vine; you are the branches.
Those who remain in Me, and I in them, will produce
much fruit. For apart from Me you can do nothing."

John 15:5 NLT

Tolkien, in a theological essay, wrote that what makes the Gospels so wondrous is that they contain the elements of fantasy, myth and fantastical folktale – and yet they're true. They are the very best kind of dream – rooted in reality but with pinch-myself splendor and too-good-to-be-true certainty and veracity.

Just by *knowing Jesus* whose life was swathed in authentic legend and whose death set you free, you're living the dream. You're living in the surety that God imagined you from eternity past, fashioned you just so in the womb, wired you complexly, and is shepherding you on a wholly unique journey that will awaken in you wholly unique dreams. You can trust Him not to waste a moment or a mistake. You can trust Him to accomplish the good work that He started in you. You can trust Him to hold your fragile hopes. You can trust Him to use your best dreams for His best purposes, and for His glory.

Are you convinced that you've got the very best connection in the business of living your dreams?

Jesus, I want to know You and remain in You. Thank You for this one slice of history – the life I have to live. Help me to live it well. Amen.

Aroma

Now He uses us to spread the knowledge of
Christ everywhere, like a sweet perfume. Our lives
are a Christ-like fragrance rising up to God.

2 Corinthians 2:14-15 NLT

God created something in the brain that responds to smells. No other sense triggers the same emotional intensity. Just a whiff in a mall or on a beach or at a school concert can take you back in all but body to a Christmas, a kiss, or a holiday. Scents have an irresistible power to unleash feelings. We don't choose to remember with nostalgia or pleasure or grief when we pick up a memorable scent. We just do.

Maybe that's why Paul says we should be an aroma in this world, because that would make it impossible to ignore us. How world changing would it be if we were to walk into a room and the fragrance of us carried people straight back to the foot of the cross (perhaps gladly, perhaps kicking and screaming). They would have to admit that Jesus is for real.

What do you think your life would look like, if it also smelled like Jesus?

Jesus, help me to follow You – and my calling in You – the way I follow the smell of fresh bread, cinnamon or ocean salt. I want to walk so closely to You that Your aroma gets all over me, and others catch the scent. Amen.

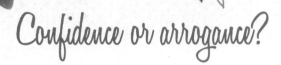

Confidence or arrogance?

So humble yourselves under the mighty power
of God, and at the right time He will lift you up in honor.

1 Peter 5:6 NLT

I cheerlead my little boys. A lot. They bring me a scribble and I gush like it's the Mona Lisa. I encourage their every exploration into life. Because growing confidence in young men is crucial to the Kingdom.

But I would be doing them no favors if I didn't point out that confidence has a tipping point. Unchecked, it can landslide into arrogance. I want them to understand the destructive potency of pride because they will never be all God designed them to be – never live out their callings for their good and His glory – if they spend their time hung up on themselves. They will burn up their potential trying to generate neon signs flashing their own names. I want them to know how they're not designed to shine their own light but to mirror God's. The same is true for me, and you.

Have you believed the world's lie – that it's all about you finding a way to shine your own light? How could you, today, find a way to reflect the light of God?

God, I'm determined to live excellently for You, with confidence in Your strength. But give me wisdom to discern between confidence and arrogance. Convict me when the first slips into the second. Keep me humble as I answer Your call. *Amen.*

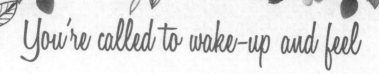

You're called to wake-up and feel

So be on your guard, not asleep like the others.
Stay alert and be clearheaded.

1 Thessalonians 5:6 NLT

I'm quick to point fingers at others treading water languid in slow burning pots. Proverbial frogs that won't jump because complacency has them drugged and drowsy. It's much harder to see where or how I am the frog who should be leaping shocked and sickened out of the nearly boiling water.

The enemy uses culture and conformity to get us drifting indolent into night. Because the tragic truth is that culture acclimatizes to imperceptibly escalating temperatures of deceit and depravity in all the cut corners of the globe. Culture acclimatizes to all that sickens – in slick malls and parliaments, on dusty streets and porn sites. And all that sickens, sickens slowly. Degree by rising degree.

We'd do well to feel sickened too by the wave of complacency that has washed up even amongst us – the people of hope. So believing woman? You who are a child of light and day because you don't belong to darkness and night? You who have aligned your destiny with the King? Wherever in the world you find yourself – shake yourself up so you can *feel* again. Awaken to what God is doing, and calling you to do too.

Is there an area of your life in which the heat has been slowly – barely noticeably – increasing?

Jesus, keep me from complacency,
so that I can answer the call to action, or reaction. *Amen.*

You're called to rise up and see

But those who trust in the Lord will find new strength. They will soar high on wings like eagles. They will run and not grow weary.

Isaiah 40:31 NLT

We need this every day – this reminder that God engenders strength in His beloved. He makes us soar on eagles' wings.

We need the reminder that eagles know the danger of the downward spiral – how sin sides with gravity and wings can crumple. But eagles have vision. Experts say if you swapped your eyes for an eagle's you'd see an ant in the dust from ten storeys up. Things straight in front of you would appear magnified and inconceivably colored.

Eagles scrutinize – swoop – soar. Because real vision is brave. It sees possibilities beyond problems. It sees the truth that God is biding His time (2 Peter 3:9). He still holds this bent-out-of-shape biosphere spinning slow through the stars. He hasn't ended it all as He might have given the mess it's in. He has us here still – we who are desperate to be the difference in congress or constitution, classrooms and clinics, in long queues of short tempers, in all the Third World worry, in all the First World waste. He has us here still because He's not done rolling out His plan for redemption.

Will you hope in God for new strength and fresh vision?

God, help me to trust You so that I'll be strengthened to soar. Give me clarity and foresight as I strive to answer the call. Amen.

You're called to make it count

"Wherever your treasure is,
there the desires of your heart will also be."

Matthew 6:21 NLT

To answer the call of God on your life, decide what you treasure. Decide what you *value*. Because your values will determine your priorities, your priorities will determine your capacity, and your capacity is the strength out of which you will live where you live and fill your days with ways to sow hope.

Keep listening for God's voice – for how He is calling you to make your life count. You'll recognize His voice because it's always the voice calling you to invest in people – in their soul needs, their whole needs – rather than in pleasure, possessions, and prestige. He calls you not to regurgitate what's brewing bitter in you but to drink in and pour out again the riches of faith, family, friendship and eternal future. Because these are the things that really matter, in this life and the next, and because He calls each of us to leave the glitter of His glory on every life we love and on everything we touch or try humble – wherever in the world we are.

What do you value most? Does it show?

*Father, I want to risk living a life
that will count now and in eternity.* Amen.

Keep casting the glory vision

So whether you eat or drink, or whatever
you do, do it all for the glory of God.

1 Corinthians 10:31 NLT

Here's a thought to clear the murk of conflicting callings and concerns: Until we realize that God's priorities are His glory, and the spread of His Kingdom, we're going to be miserable, and confused.

If we can just view sufferings and victories and delays and opportunities and all the crazy complexities and straight-line simplicities of life through that big picture lens, so much of the small picture comes breathtakingly into focus and there's joy, gratitude and a clear way forward. All our pursuits – the stuff into which we're pouring our time, energy and resources – will be ultimately unfulfilling unless we're using those pursuits to pursue the big picture. And if your calling – or if what God seems to be doing, or not doing, in your life – is unclear, make sure that your small daily investments of time, energy and resources are spent on His glory.

Could you buy into God's priorities today by courageously and generously spending your time on His glory?

God, help me not to lose sight of the big picture. Keep me casting the vision that this life is about making Your presence known. Help me today and every day to do what love requires of me, so that others catch that vision and You are glorified. Amen.

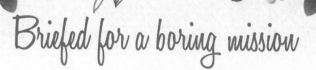

Briefed for a boring mission

"If you love Me, obey My commandments."

John 14:15 NLT

A time may come when you'll be called away from the frontlines of combat and briefed for another (less exciting) mission. Like, you'll be peeling potatoes in the mess tent far back from the action while others brave the battles.

And that bothers you. You feel wasted. What you'll be doing just doesn't seem important. Yet the truth is that wars are lost and won in the barracks. What happens in the background is life-or-death crucial to what happens on the front. It's also true that every season prepares you for the next, so this time is training you for something, and God's strategies are better than yours. You know that He knows you. He wouldn't have put potential in you if He didn't plan to use it in the battle to make His glory known. He planned today before there was a universe. He sees the hours and the things He has appointed to fill them. He can use, for the Kingdom cause, your offerings of minutes and days. They may even win the war.

Do you really believe what you say you believe – that although your duties have shifted you're still contributing to God's work – and that the payoff really will be magnificent and eternal?

God, help me to humble myself, get on with it, and enjoy what You've called me to do and be in this season. Amen.

You don't have what it takes, but He does

And this same God who takes care of me will supply all your needs from His glorious riches, which have been given to us in Christ Jesus.

Philippians 4:19 NLT

When you're bent on fulfilling your calling, the world will cast doubt where you're trying to cast vision. It's then that you need to trust that God sees, knows and works, for your best and the fame of His Name. Stake a truth claim in your heart instead of giving heartland over to the lies of the enemy.

Like, maybe you're told that your small life doesn't count and you won't amount to much. That you're not gifted enough, passionate enough or connected enough. That you don't have what it takes to leave the legacy of a life's work.

Then you're told that it's all about your big life. That you deserve more and shouldn't be satisfied with less.

The truth is way more extreme. Your bigness doesn't even come into it. And you're much smaller than you imagine. *And much more precious.* The truth is that no matter the role or task, big or small, you're not supposed to be up to it. Give God your everything – which amounts to very little. He will multiply, strengthen and equip – and be glorified.

Would you live today differently if you believed that you're infinitely precious to God, and that He can empower you to fulfill your calling?

God, You are enough for me. And in You,
I'm enough too. Thank You. Amen.

He dares you

"Now I say to you that you are Peter (which means 'rock'),
and upon this rock I will build My church, and all
the powers of hell will not conquer it."

Matthew 16:18 NLT

I wonder if Jesus terrified Peter when He said to him, "I'll build my church on you." Peter is the rough-around-the-fishing-net guy who was the pebble that became the rock that spread truth to continents. Jesus was calling out Peter's potential and sealing it with a promise – yet I wonder if Peter felt pushed? Stretched beyond capacity? Dared unfairly?

Jesus knew what He had put inside of Peter. Just like He knows what He's put inside you. It may be that you think you don't have any more to give. Except that, you probably do. And God dares you into scouring your soul for greater potential to lay down on His promise to protect, establish, promote and provide. Sometimes the way He calls it from you can feel fierce. Yet as pressures rise, you're compelled to become more and more the woman He made you to be.

Do you feel challenged by God to fulfill a calling that feels impossibly, overwhelmingly too big?

*Jesus, sometimes the powerful interest that You
take in my life is intimidating. Help me to trust that You
are always at work, leading me and loving me.* Amen.

He delays you

Forty years later, in the desert near Mount Sinai, an angel appeared to Moses in the flame of a burning bush.

Acts 7:30 NLT

I like how Elisabeth Elliot talked about being sick. She said she wasn't laid aside by illness, but called aside to stillness. Because somehow when our plans short-circuit and there's disappointment or delay, God does deep things that just don't settle and sink in when we're caught in the frenetic mêlée of normal life. When Jesus shows up in the waiting, we're never the same again.

Moses was seriously delayed. Forty years in an Egyptian palace separated from his people. Forty years in the wilderness looking after his father-in-law's sheep. Forty years wandering to the brink of promise. That's a lifetime of delay. Yet Moses was the friend of God who stood *sans*-sandals on holy ground and raised his staff above parted waters and saw the glory till his face shone. It would be a mistake to think that all the days of delay in Moses' life added up to time wasted. It would be a mistake to think that about the delays in your own life too.

As you pursue your calling, does it seem to you as if God is taking His time – and wasting yours?

God, thank You for this delay. I know You must have an excellent reason for stalling my dreams. Help me remember that You are never slow, idle, or forgetful, but always right on time. Amen.

Know thyself. Don't box thyself

O LORD, You have examined my heart
and know everything about me.

Psalm 139:1 NLT

There are heaps of personality classification trends. We're educated to package people and you've probably been told that you're a typical firstborn or lastborn, melancholic or choleric. You've probably drawn those kinds of straight lines around others too.

And it's all good. Boxing people (in categories – not with gloves) helps us to understand behavior and predict reactions. It helps us to tolerate – even embrace – differences we encounter in others. It also helps us make peace with ourselves. You can begin to accept who you are and how you are – seeing your strengths as signposts to your capabilities and calling. It's a beautiful thing – a great relief – to release yourself to be happily just who God made you to be.

But boxing (in categories – and with gloves) can also be dangerous. Profiling can predetermine your behavior if you believe you should think, feel or enjoy something because it's what your personality type *should* think, feel or enjoy. Don't be too hung up on what's "typical". Because actually, the only thing that's typical about you is you. There are you-shaped gaps that only you can fill. God knows you better than anyone, and it's in getting to know Him that you see yourself as He does – and as you should.

How do you think God might describe your personality?

*God, it's just amazing to think that there are no
two people on the planet who are exactly alike.* Amen.

What did you do with what wasn't yours anyway?

"After a long time their master returned from his trip and called them to give an account of how they had used his money."

Matthew 25:19 NLT

Life's not fair, and the parable of the talents illustrates that point pretty well. It's not fair – in the one-for-me-one-for-you sense of the term – that the three servants in the story have differing levels of ability and are given different amounts of money in accordance (Matthew 25:15). I mean, they didn't choose their giftedness or lack thereof, right? Yet it's clear that God isn't all about fixing the unevenness of life. Rather, He shows us how best to leverage the opportunities that we have been given.

Coming to terms with what you have going for you (or not going for you) – relationally, financially, athletically, aesthetically or intellectually – is easier when you remember that those talents and resources weren't yours to begin with. They belong to the Master and He will hold you accountable for what you did with *His* prospects. You're to give back to Him everything that He has given to you. It's so freeing to know that it doesn't actually matter how much you've been given. It only matters that you ask yourself – and ask God – how best you can use it for His glory.

What's the truth about the opportunities you hold? How can you courageously leverage them to create excellence and beauty?

God, I'll serve You with everything You've given me. Amen.

Excuses, comparisons or complacency

"Then the servant with the one bag of silver came and said, 'Master, I knew you were a harsh man … I was afraid I would lose your money, so I hid it in the earth. Look, here is your money back.'"

Matthew 25:24-25 NLT

This parable is about one-bag people, two-bag people and five-bag people. I heard a preacher say once that one-bag people make excuses ("I can't be expected to make anything of my life because I got a raw deal"). Two-bag people compare themselves to others ("It's unfair that I wasn't given what *she* was given," or "At least I'm making more of my life than *that* one-bag person"). Five-bag people take what they have for granted ("I can afford to waste a bit, or relax a bit, because I've got it all going on for me …").

These are all dangerous responses because each one indicates a waiver of responsibility. To live a life of excellence and beauty requires the courage to leverage fully what God has entrusted to you. You don't need to know if you fall into the one, two or five-bag category. All you need do is your very best, with the bags in your hand.

Do you ever make excuses and comparisons, or find yourself growing complacent?

God, give me the wisdom to know how to take seriously, and live beautifully, what You have entrusted to me. Amen.

Living for something bigger than you

"The master was full of praise. 'Well done, my good and faithful servant. You have been faithful in handling this small amount, so now I will give you many more responsibilities. Let's celebrate together!'"

Matthew 25:21 NLT

The servants who were given two and five bags understood stewardship. They also understood that a life of meaning and purpose went way beyond just themselves. It went way beyond what would even have seemed possible. They worked for an expansion of influence that would ultimately reflect on the Master, not them.

There's a reason we don't read books or watch movies about characters who live for themselves. We're drawn to heroes – world-changers – who know that they're far too small a thing to be living for. They answer the call to something higher – something bigger.

You could live like that too. You could live for something higher and bigger than your bank account or the letters behind your name, greater and wider than what's trending on Twitter or on the catwalks. Embrace the fact that any extra that you've been given is a responsibility from God to be managed for the sake of others and His glory.

What distractions draw your eyes down to the small, and keep you from looking up to the Big God you serve?

God, I don't want to live for small stuff, small statuses, small pleasures, small me. I want to live for enormous, Almighty You. Use me to rock my world. Amen.

Be humble, and unafraid

Humble yourselves before the Lord, and He will lift you up in honor.

James 4:10 NLT

Pursuing your calling can be scary. What if you fail?

Here's a better question: What if you humbled yourself?

Because really, it's our pride that makes us afraid. Humility means asking yourself, "What's the worst that can happen?" and courageously ploughing on. Humility means you keep telling yourself that obedience to God is the goal – not pleasing people or protecting your social prospects. Obedience is the end result. The tick of success. If God said, *follow this dream,* you follow it. You make it your spirit-and-truth worship (John 4:23). You trust God for wisdom. You ask Him to arrest your heart to honor only Him. You surrender your flaws. Cling to His perfection. You let every next decision be a brave yes to truth, excellence and beauty.

Then, when your dream turns to real? There might be wild cheering. There might be awkward silence. (Expect the *thwack-drip* of egg on face.) But for sure, there will be satisfaction, and cosmic success. Because God doesn't define you by the apparent triumph or failure of what does or doesn't survive in the big out-there, or by what people think of your dream-chasing. He delights in the simple everything of your obedience. Nothing more, nothing less.

What terrifies you about where God is leading your life?

God, humble me so that I can fearlessly answer Your call. Amen.

MAY

Billboards, bank accounts and deep peace

"As long as you are proud you cannot know God. A proud man is always looking down on things and people: and, of course, as long as you are looking down, you cannot see something that is above you."

– *C. S. Lewis*

The big three

For the world offers only a craving for physical pleasure, a craving for everything we see, and pride in our achievements and possessions. These are not from the Father, but are from this world.

1 John 2:16 NLT

The world can hiss about keeping up and giving in. It knows how to needle your ego and ignite your indulgence. It murmurs at your neck – sweet-talking you with foul breath to believe you need to *feel* more and *have* more and *be* more. John knew just how the world worked. He knew how it could lure us with three big temptations:

Pleasure. Possessions. Prestige.

Which are all good things. Good things from a good God because His plans are wondrous and mysterious and kind. He delights in us, for His glory. He gives us ice-cream and sex and satin skirts and long beaches at sunset and plane tickets and lucky parking spots and promotions.

But it wouldn't be wise to ignore the truth that pleasure, possessions and prestige can avalanche catastrophically across the path of life. And surviving the landslide demands the courage to make God our chief pleasure, to trust Him with and for our possessions, and to enjoy as our highest prestige our joint-heir position in the Kingdom.

What do you crave?

Almighty God, I don't want the empty promises of the world. I want the fullness of life in You. Amen.

Pleasure

I said to myself, "Come on, let's try pleasure. Let's look for the 'good things' in life." But I found that this, too, was meaningless.

Ecclesiastes 2:1 NLT

I'm an *experience* person more than a *thing* person. If I had to choose between an immense shopping spree and an overseas trip, the overseas trip would win every time. So it's easy for me to get sucked into pleasure – pursuits that take time, emotion, intellectual energy and sometimes money. I fantasize about facebooking sensational events. I want to drink sublime cappuccinos and meet fascinating people and exhaust my adrenal glands.

Maybe you can relate? Too often we *want* certain experiences, so we convince ourselves that we *need* them. But the truth is that if we want to change the world by living out the potential God has given us in the time He has fixed for our lives, then we must find the courage to ask ourselves honestly – for every bridge swing and every slice of cake: "Is this worship?" It could be worship. It *should* be worship. Because God created all the intensities of pleasure. And because reflective reveling – enjoying stuff and knowing it comes from God – glorifies Him.

What really blows your hair back? In the quiet of your own heart – amidst the thrill or hilarity or delicious wonder – could you live it as worship?

God, when I'm relishing an amazing experience, let it immediately remind me of You! Amen.

Possessions

I also tried to find meaning by building huge homes for myself …
I collected great sums of silver and gold … I had everything a man
could desire! … But as I looked at everything I had worked so
hard to accomplish, it was all so meaningless – like chasing the
wind. There was nothing really worthwhile anywhere.

Ecclesiastes 2:4, 8, 11 NLT

If you have kids, know kids or remember being a kid, you under-stand the powerful anticipation and exhilaration of birthdays and Christmas mornings. Presents. Stuff. Things. Objects of burning desire. Which get lost, forgotten, broken or boring after, sometimes, a couple hours.

And even all grown-up, you know that things don't satisfy. Your kitchen remodel or new wardrobe or keys to a dazzling new ride – these things don't guarantee that you'll never have a bad day. They won't fix your marriage or bring you peace in the small hours of the night when your teenager hasn't come home. Things are great. They're fun and for sure they can make us momentarily – even seasonally – happy and hopefully deeply grateful. But as solid as they are, they don't fill the soul spaces that yearn for the solid truth of an everlasting Savior.

Do you ever catch yourself saying or thinking, "If I just had one of those …"?

O God, I don't want my hope to be eclipsed by bling or big bucks.
Keep me trusting in You alone, and never in my stuff. Amen.

Open palms

"For all the animals of the forest are Mine,
and I own the cattle on a thousand hills."

Psalm 50:10 NLT

My reaction when things are damaged, broken or stolen reveals how I don't always have my priorities straight when it comes to things. Which are, after all, just things. No matter how much they cost. Things given for our good – our use and pleasure – but still just things. Like, when my kid dipped my cell phone in my coffee, I didn't show the grace that I'd offered when he submerged his shoes in the bath.

Sure, we should respect property. But we should also remember that it's good to work, better to work to have, and best to work to have to *give*. We should live as stewards not scrooges. Generous, not thoughtless. It takes courage not to clutch possessions, but rather to unfurl fingers that hold things in a frantic attempt to hold happiness.

Try to picture balancing – carefully, in open palms – all the things you own, knowing they could be taken from you at any time. Picture holding out your things for the God who owns the cattle on a thousand hills and everything else, because it'll remind you that, really, your things weren't yours to begin with.

Do you take a philosophical stance when it comes to earthly things, or do you get mad when someone messes with your stuff?

Jesus, help me to take responsibility for what's entrusted to me, holding it loosely. *Amen.*

Prestige

"Everything they do is for show …"

Matthew 23:5 NLT

Maybe you've experienced real or perceived loss of prestige. Giving up a career to stay home with kids. Or leaving your kids to go back to work. Maybe you've been retrenched, or had a lateral company or ministry move that may as well have been a demotion.

It's tough. You've stepped off the soft safe carpet of belonging in a career community or friendship clique. And often, with the loss of job or social status there's a deeper loss of prestige tied up with what people think of you.

Perhaps much of your identity – your deep satisfaction that you're a worthwhile member of society – is fused with what you do, or did. You've been chasing results, measurable success and the admiration and affirmation of friends, family or colleagues. And suddenly you feel bereft of worth. Desperate to explain and justify. And *please* people.

Which is *not* what you believe, right? Because your life is about pleasing God, not people.

Friend, leave the cathedrals of grand ideas. Go deep and daily into your cloistered heart. There, remember that the truest thing about you is that you're Christ's beloved. *That's* your prestige. From being loved flows your love for Him. From your love flows obedience. And obedience just asks, "What next, Lord, to please *You*?"

What do you think God would write on your résumé?

Jesus, help me to find my worth in You,
not in my skill set or others' perceptions. Amen.

Good might not be good enough

We justify our actions by appearances; God examines our motives.

Proverbs 21:2 MSG

I want to confront and conquer social pressures in my life because I don't want to waste time chasing things and experiences and status instead of chasing my unique calling. And even chasing good stuff – like wanting to be healthy, wanting to be well-educated, or wanting to change the world – isn't good enough. Because if my motive for chasing those things isn't rooted in wanting to chase God – to follow hard after Him – then anything else I chase, no matter how noble, adds up to idolatry.

There might be really good things in your life too – things you're running after to secure and enjoy. A husband, a baby, a promotion, an investment or adventure. Yet it's true for you too that you'll miss wide-open opportunities to live bold and bright if you're tunnel-visioned by pleasure, possessions and prestige, in whatever shape or form or handheld device they come.

What are you pursuing right now? Are your motives God-centered, or you-centered?

Father, show me my heart. Help me to distinguish between good things and God things. I don't want to waste my time hurtling after junk. Amen.

How to know what you're worshiping

Son of man, these leaders have set up idols in their hearts.
They have embraced things that will make them fall into sin …

Ezekiel 14:3 NLT

Maybe you're not affected by stuff, titles or cool happenings. Maybe you don't think you're chasing pleasure, possessions or prestige. It may still be worth scrutinizing the subcutaneous motives that fire your life. Like, ask yourself this: Would your identity or sense of worth change if there was a change – for better or worse – in what you wear or do or drive, in where you shop or live or study or travel or work, or in what others say about your ideas and decisions?

Or maybe this: What is it you talk about most? Where and how do you spend the most time and money? What motivates your outfit, your diet, your route to work, your calendar, your decision to move cities or not, or the school you've chosen for your kids?

All these things make up the necessary stuff of life. But all this necessary stuff can switch insidiously into the object of our worship. With God on the throne, the necessary stuff just takes its right and necessary place.

What does how you live say about your priorities? If you asked a close friend to make a list of what she thought was most important to you, what do you think she'd write down?

God, forgive me for living a life scattered with mini-gods that mean nothing. I bow before You only. Amen.

Breathless

"Seek the Kingdom of God above all else, and live righteously, and He will give you everything you need."

Matthew 6:33 NLT

You'll know if you're chasing pleasure, possessions or prestige by the feeling of restless, relentless panic. The soul breathlessness. You'll chase because you want to *capture* – a thing or a position or another person's high opinion. Initially, it feels sophisticated and cutting-edge. Then it just feels addictive and mandatory and scary. And then it makes you tired. And desperate. And mad.

Because you'll realize you're no longer the charioteer wielding the whip. You're the horse being flogged.

So maybe, stop. Stop it. Stop chasing the degree, the marriage partner, the skiing trip, the ministry, the compliment, the exclusive invitation or the cloth you're trying to cut bigger. The pressure of trying to please people – the ruthless carrot dangling of socioeconomic ambition – will leave you drained and disappointed, feeling inadequate and afraid.

Of course, it's not wrong to get excited about doing a PhD or walking the Inca Trail or dishing up seconds. Relish the good things God gives – the daily bread and the dessert – for His glory. But be aware that like all good things, they'll enslave you if you let them. Check your intentions before tucking into whatever is on your plate.

Are you emotionally out of breath? Why?

Jesus, I want to catch my breath. I'm tired of running after stuff and status. I want to seek You first. Amen.

Talk to God

But in my distress I cried out to the LORD; yes,
I prayed to my God for help. He heard me from
His sanctuary; my cry to Him reached His ears.

Psalm 18:6 NLT

When the social, emotional, financial and other pressures overwhelm you, talk to God about it. When the world sneers condemnation and fear, let Him whisper conviction and faith.

A friend of mine describes how sometimes you can feel like a soda can at the bottom of the sea and the pressures of life are the deep waters getting deeper. Only God can maintain your internal pressure so that as external pressures increase, you can hold steady and strong without being crushed on the ocean floor.

Ask Him to help you recognize the pressure for what it is. Ask Him to reveal your motives for chasing what you're chasing. He knows your heart anyway, but tell Him how tough it is because of how badly you want it. Tell Him that you want to *want* to stop chasing it. Then try to leave it with Him.

Have you been avoiding God because you feel too frazzled to discuss anything with Him? Are you so overwhelmed that you feel alone – as if God can't possibly understand what you're experiencing?

God, this is me crying out to You. Help.
You know my heart – how desperately I want this stuff.
But I do want to want Your will. Amen.

Culture shock

> For the word of God is alive and powerful. It is sharper than the sharpest two-edged sword, cutting between soul and spirit, between joint and marrow. It exposes our innermost thoughts and desires.
>
> *Hebrews 4:12* NLT

We love pop culture because it's cutting-edge and cool. We want to stay current – keep abreast of the latest in fashion and devices, schooling, socializing and avant-garde ideas. And as believers, that's ok. While we're not called to embrace or participate in every aspect of culture, we're called to meet with a world engaged in it. If we fail to recognize the trends and obsessions of that culture, we may miss opportunities to translate truth into the midst of it.

But it can be exhausting and intimidating trying to keep up. So there's strength and solace in what the writer of Hebrews says about abiding, immutable Christian culture: we have God's Word. And it's so cutting-edge that it's never so last season. It transcends time and place, culture and community. Its relevancy supersedes what's splashed across media platforms as the definitive *now*.

Because ultimately, culture only effects skin-deep changes. The Word of God changes hearts and lives, for eternity. So don't be scared of how culture shifts and sways inconstant. You've got the living God's living Word.

Does the velocity of cultural change freak you out?

Lord, thank You for the constancy and consistency of Your Word – for how it weighs in significantly on every question of culture, and brings life. Amen.

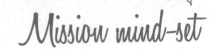

Mission mind-set

Not that I was ever in need, for I have
learned how to be content with whatever I have.

Philippians 4:11 NLT

It's interesting – and intriguing – that missionaries in far-flung places don't expect comfort. They seldom ask for or assume that they will have the luxury of amenities and modern conveniences. They don't expect these things, and so they're content without them. Their focus is on their purpose – why they're in that far-flung place, in the first place.

But here's the thing: you're a missionary too. God has called you into active, full-time service in the field, whether you're living in First World suburbia or Third World slums. The challenge we face in the Western world, however, is that we expect amenities and conveniences and luxuries. We want things to be slick and fully operational. Our happiness depends on it. Depending on where we live, the fickle things that make us comfortable (or not) generally only make us complacent (or frustrated) – not necessarily content.

How would your contentment levels change if you focused on your purpose – why you're here – instead of on the things that would make life easier for you?

*God, help me not to get wrapped up in the here and now,
but to be content with whatever You give. And God, never
give me so much comfort that I stop depending on You. Amen.*

Rich

"I'll say it again – it is easier for a camel to go through the eye of a needle than for a rich person to enter the Kingdom of God!"

Matthew 19:24 NLT

Jesus doesn't hate rich people. He certainly wasn't saying that rich people can't go to heaven. When His disciples questioned Him – worried – He explained that salvation is out of reach for *any* human being, rich or poor, but He goes on to say to them, "Humanly speaking, it is impossible. But with God everything is possible" (Matthew 19:26).

There's hardly a standard definition for wealthy, and wherever you are on the sliding scale of economic success it's possible for you to serve God. But you need to know how secure – or insecure – you would feel if your possessions or investments were taken away.

Maybe the point that Jesus was making is that it's harder than we may even realize for us to trust in Him alone, because we have money to trust in. If or when our money is taken away from us, He really is our only option, and our real wealth.

What would threaten your sense of daily security? Do you believe that God provides for your needs?

Jesus, please give me the wisdom to manage or multiply the resources You have blessed me with. And keep me from ever looking for peace and safety in money. Amen.

Trapped

"And you will know the truth, and the truth will set you free."

John 8:32 NLT

You don't have to be in prison to feel trapped. You can feel trapped by a culture or a country, a family, a friendship, a job or a deadline. You can feel financially trapped, or trapped by the expectations – real or presumed – of those around you.

Jesus has told you the truth: His sacrifice on your behalf means that you get to walk free. Knowing this truth sets you free from the cloying lies that cling and tell you that you're owned, stuck or restrained by your circumstances. Feeling trapped is just that – a *feeling*. A feeling that has come over you because you've forgotten you're saved by a sovereign God who sets you free and who is so much bigger than the limits currently imposed on your life. He can move, change and channel you in any new direction He chooses. He may not do this with the timing or techniques you think He should, but you can trust Him to make something beautiful of your life. You're free.

What is pinning you down, emotionally or spiritually? How can you loosen the bonds by telling yourself the truth?

Thank You, God, for the freeing power of Your Word.
Help me to climb up onto safe truth where lies
can't get to me, or hold me down. Amen.

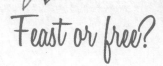

Feast or free?

"Don't store up treasures here on earth, where moths eat them and rust destroys them, and where thieves break in and steal. Store your treasures in heaven, where moths and rust cannot destroy, and thieves do not break in and steal. Wherever your treasure is, there the desires of your heart will also be."

Matthew 6:19-21 NLT

The world breathes lies 24/7 about what will satisfy and fulfill you. Advertisers and advocates for every endeavor will tell you that you're free to be happy, and they know just the way.

Jesus tells you something different. He tells you that freedom is the peace, confidence, security and calm authority of knowing who you are in Christ. Because of His death on the cross, God has set you free. He wants to keep you that way.

Don't let pleasure, possessions or prestige seize you and sink their teeth into you. Don't be dragged to their lair and pressured to feast on things that will leave you hungry. It's a free world and you're free to do anything. You're free to get tangled and trapped, and you're free to choose to use your freedom to stay free.

Have you ever been enslaved by the very thing that started out as an expression of your freedom?

God, thank You for my earthly resources – which, really, are Yours. Help me to invest intentionally, excellently, and in eternity. Amen.

Lifestyle or legacy?

I cry out to God Most High, to God
who will fulfill His purpose for me.

Psalm 57:2 NLT

When billboards and spin doctors scream about success, it helps to remember that what really matters in the end isn't lifestyle. It's legacy. Because as believers living for God's glory to complete His mission on earth, knowing that this life is not the end, we're ultimately faced with these two choices – lifestyle or legacy – when it comes to what we're going to do with the rest of our lives.

Lifestyle is about earthly comfort. It has you making decisions out of anger, fear or hedonism. Choices that aren't necessarily wrong, but choices that also don't necessarily reflect God's heart for you. All they really reflect are your priorities, and the things that you call comfort.

Legacy is about eternal consequence. It has you making decisions out of obedience to God's call on your life. Choices that elevate your relationship with God and others over what's easy, safe or comfortable. Choices that foreground Kingdom work and how you can sow seeds for a harvest you may never live to reap.

Are you building your life around the scaffolding of lifestyle, or legacy?

God, shine a light on what motivates my decisions
and my way of life. I want to build a legacy that glorifies
You, not a lifestyle that promotes me. Amen.

Fitting your will into your way

Fools think their own way is right, but the wise listen to others.

Proverbs 12:15 NLT

There's no doubt that some of the trends and traditions draped over our lives by society can smother our good judgment. But we may also be complicit in the plot – stifling our own insight and discernment.

The truth is that you can sell yourself any idea. You can even do it biblically – for or against the same concept. You can twist and tug, cajole and convince, until the Scriptures mean exactly what you want them to mean and you've talked yourself into how right it is to do the thing you want to do. You can do this about money, ministry, relationships, careers, emigration – anything.

That's why it's crucial to walk closely to God in prayer and in His Word – so closely that His light shines on the way you're walking and shows up the truth of your situation, and of your heart. It's also crucial to seek the counsel of wise people – not just the companionable conspiracy of your one confidant who you're pretty sure will tell you exactly what you want to hear. Be brave enough to lay down your agenda, and seek God's, honestly.

Are you currently convincing yourself that a particular course of action is definitely God's will?

Father, I don't want to shame Your name by being a fool. Give me ears to hear truth and wisdom. Amen.

It is what it is

"I am leaving you with a gift – peace of mind and heart.
And the peace I give is a gift the world cannot give.
So don't be troubled or afraid."

John 14:27 NLT

The mantra *It is what it is* may have morphed into a cliché, but it makes a lot of sense when you're under social pressure. It's one of those paradoxical philosophies that seems at best laissez-faire, at worst fatalistic, and yet it actually manifests as optimism. It turns the obstacle into a springboard. It brings acceptance, which births restoration – even hope. It doesn't change your problem, but it may help to change your perspective.

You can apply it to almost any less-than-ideal circumstance. Like, it seems your best friend falls pregnant every time her husband walks past her in the lounge. You've been trying for years, unsuccessfully. *It is what it is.* Your sister seems to earn more money than the president. You sure don't. *It is what it is.*

You get the idea. The scales of life this side of eternity are never going to balance. God never promised us that they would. He did promise us His peace.

Are you wrestling with one of life's inequalities? How can you lay it down – because you can't make the unevenness, even – and trust that God sees it, and that He can give you peace?

Jesus, thank You for Your incomprehensible gift of serenity.
What deep relief and quiet perspective You bring. *Amen.*

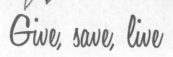

Give, save, live

"And I have been a constant example of how you can help those in need by working hard. You should remember the words of the Lord Jesus: 'It is more blessed to give than to receive.'"

Acts 20:35 NLT

Pretty much every media source out there will reach through the screens in your world, tug at your handbag, and tell you to *spend*. It's an epidemic: gathering stuff, guzzling food, buying thrills.

There's a wiser way. Jesus taught that it's way better to give than to receive. He also promised abundant life – a *blessed* life. And if He said that we're more blessed when we give than when we receive, maybe He was giving us the key to a supernatural dynamic that happens when we give. A paradoxical filling up and spilling over that occurs when we put ourselves second to meet someone's need. When we give generously, save responsibly, and then spend wisely and joyfully, there's blessing. Not a health-and-wealth plastic gospel of expediency, but rich peace.

Is there someone who keeps on coming to mind – someone who could use your practical or financial help? Could you restructure your budget so that you're free to give gladly?

Provider God, You've given me so much. Open my eyes to the needs around me and give me the wisdom to manage my money to meet them. Amen.

Pressured to stay or go

Build homes, and plan to stay. Plant gardens, and eat the
food they produce. Marry and have children. Then find
spouses for them so that you may have many grandchildren.
Multiply! Do not dwindle away! And work for the peace
and prosperity of the city where I sent you into exile. Pray to
the Lord for it, for its welfare will determine your welfare.

Jeremiah 29:5-7 NLT

In a global culture of flux and sway where nothing's forever and
there are always new pressures urging us to dig in or uproot, God's
command to His people – exiled and captive in Babylon – brings
peace. He had plans to rescue them and we love those words a few
verses on: "He knows the plans He has for us, plans for a future and
a hope" (Jeremiah 29:11).

But the challenge, really, is to trust God with your life, *today*.
Until He moves you – Home Forever or another home-for-now –
plant your gardens. Eat. Fall in love and make babies. Pray for your
city. Live your God-glory story well. God's people in Babylon were
the very best kind of free, even though by definition they weren't
free at all.

Are there cultural or political pressures that steal your joy – rob
you of contentment? Can you position yourself to be actively open
to God's leading, and also actively present, practical, positive and
productive where He has you?

*Heavenly Father, help me do the best that I can,
as and when You guide and lead me.* Amen.

Why them not me?

I am counting on the Lord; yes,
I am counting on Him. I have put my hope in His word.

Psalm 130:5 NLT

To find peace and perspective, you may need to be brave enough to admit that God seems to love some people more than He loves you. He's blessed them. Set them up for success of some sort. He hasn't done the same for you. And you're jealous. You feel like Job, moaning about how the wicked prosper and saying, "My complaint is with God, not with people" (Job 21:4). Maybe you're not dissatisfied with your life; you're dissatisfied with God.

Like, you're jealous of other people's successes, followings, families or financial gains. You're going, "What about me, God? Why aren't you making it happen for *me*?" There are – will be – always – people beating you at the game, outplaying you one way or another. But it may be especially hard to watch others' success when you're doing everything you know to be right and still the big breaks aren't coming. And convincing yourself that God is just suspending success to teach you a bunch of important stuff doesn't necessarily make it easier.

Today's the first day of the rest of your life. Start telling yourself the truth: *you can count on God.*

Are you mad at God for the way He has blessed someone else?

God, forgive me for being disgruntled by what You're doing in others' lives. I only want Your perfect plans for me. Amen.

Divine compensation

The LORD says, "I will give you back what you lost
to the swarming locusts, the hopping locusts,
the stripping locusts, and the cutting locusts."

Joel 2:25 NLT

Locusts are probably not your biggest problem. But I love how God's call to repentance and His promise of restoration, given through the prophet Joel, show us so much of His character.

On the epic scale of history, it is and always has been God's plan to reconcile humanity to Himself, and to restore relationships between God and people, and people and people. That's why Jesus told His disciples, "Your love for one another will prove to the world that you are My disciples" (John 13:35).

Take courage from the truth that no matter what has been wrongfully – ruthlessly – ripped from your life, in Christ you're a new creation and God will restore you wholly and completely.

That restoration will definitely be eternal. Yet the wonder is that so often God replenishes, reinstates and rebuilds our lives this side of eternity too, in excellent, beautiful ways we might not even have hoped or imagined.

Looking back, can you already see how God has repaid you – restored or reestablished things in your life that you once thought were destroyed forever?

God, You know what has been wiped out of my life, and the effect it's had. Help me to trust You for restoration. Amen.

Let God vindicate

Dear friends, never take revenge. Leave that to the righteous anger of God. For the Scriptures say, "I will take revenge; I will pay them back," says the Lord. Instead, "If your enemies are hungry, feed them. If they are thirsty, give them something to drink …" Don't let evil conquer you, but conquer evil by doing good.

Romans 12:19-21 NLT

You probably don't (often) picture taking violent revenge on someone who has hurt you. But maybe you picture a social situation in which all the attention turns to you and before an audience of adoring fans, you're vindicated. Your offender is overtly or subtly shamed, and feels abysmal. Everyone thinks you're awesome.

Or maybe that's just me. The point is, there's great relief for us in knowing that we don't have to worry about finding ways to assert or defend ourselves, to prove or protect or wield any sort of vengeance. God has promised that He will do that, in His infinite wisdom, power and mercy. All we have to do is lavish love on those who have injured or affronted us. We can staunch the searing pain by launching a love offensive. Blind the darkness with blazing, burning compassion.

Can you change the battle plan of a certain relationship by mobilizing your troops of kind words and good deeds?

God, thank You that I can leave vengeance up to You. Your ways are so much mightier and more effective than mine. Amen.

Just enough for just today

*Yet true godliness with contentment is itself great wealth.
After all, we brought nothing with us when we came into
the world, and we can't take anything with us when we leave it.*

1 Timothy 6:6-7 NLT

I once spent a weekend with an elderly lady in Harare, Zimbabwe. Her family farm had been taken years before, and the Zim dollar took the rest. Her husband fell critically ill a few days prior to my arrival. Still, she insisted I stay, as if I were doing her an enormous favor. She was irrepressibly positive, eager to serve and put herself second. She looked for the best in every person and situation.

This woman had every right to be angry. Yet she couldn't talk enough about the kindness of God and His provision in all sorts of ways. "We want for *nothing*!" she exclaimed, her eyes ablaze with Jesus.

I was gutted by our conversations. Convicted, challenged, encouraged and almost envious of this woman so fully alive to the joy of God and spreading it through her uncomplaining, spirited demeanor. She was part of an impoverished, displaced generation. Yet instead of being bitter she determined to trust God, allowing the light of Christ to shine through her in a warped world.

What has been taken from you? Can you find peace, knowing God knows about it, and knowing you have just enough, for just today?

God, help me to let go of bitterness, and be content. Amen.

Happy in the here and now

So if we have enough food and clothing, let us be content.

1 Timothy 6:8 NLT

The world's lie is that we're missing out because everyone else has a better life. We should know better – we should *feel* better – yet we battle discontent almost every day.

So friend, almost every day you need to remind yourself that God made you *just so*. He placed you here, set you on this journey and loves you unimaginably. And the stories you're living are yours to tell – not the stories of another life that looks better, richer, fuller, more successful, more influential or more fun.

Comparison constantly ogles at what God is doing for others. Comparison forgets that the Kingdom is a co-op, not a competition. Comparison steals your dreams. It punctures your confidence, embezzles your energy and joy, and ruins relationships. It marshals minions of pressure and tension. You find yourself closing up, pretending, boasting, avoiding, seething, making stupid financial decisions and generally spewing the dirt of a dissatisfied heart. Because comparison spawns discontent, and jealousy.

And yet if I'm writing this and you're reading this, and we've eaten in the last twenty-four hours and we've got clothes to wear today? Then we can unwrap the God-gift of contentment. Serenity. Satisfaction. Perfect peace.

What is it you want so badly? Will it bring you supreme contentment, or is it possible that you could have that already?

God, thank You that I'm fed and clothed. It's enough. I'm content. Right here, right now. Amen.

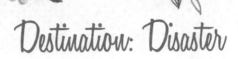

Destination: Disaster

For wherever there is jealousy and selfish ambition,
there you will find disorder and evil of every kind.

James 3:16 NLT

Some years ago a friend of mine bought the company she was working for. She wore her rapid rise to beautiful boss intoxicatingly – like expensive perfume. And I was driving my boys to swimming lessons and wracking my brain for ways to make chicken more interesting.

I was jealous. I knew I had heart scrubbing to do. So I rolled up my sleeves, sunk fists into suds of Scripture, and found that God's Word is littered with the debris of lives devastated by comparison. I'm talking real disasters. Saul compared his popularity to David's, then tried to kill him (1 Samuel 18). Jacob's less loved sons compared themselves to Joseph and, again, tried to kill him (Genesis 37). Sometimes the comparison catfight went both ways. Rachel compared herself to (pregnant) Leah; Leah compared herself to (gorgeous) Rachel (Genesis 29-30). The Pharisee compared himself to the tax guy (Luke 18). Epic fail. Jesus' disciples even jostled for favorite (Mark 10).

The reminders helped me see the truth that comparing ourselves to others makes us either bitter or arrogant. Either way, not pretty, and pretty disastrous. True beauty is a courageous commitment to stay out of the envy danger zone.

Are you avoiding the disaster of jealousy, or heading straight for it?

Jesus, don't let me forget that comparison is a minefield, and a girl can get blown up. Amen.

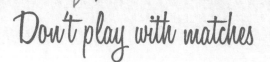

Don't play with matches

Anger is cruel, and wrath is like a flood,
but jealousy is even more dangerous.

Proverbs 27:4 NLT

We're wired to avoid physical danger. We teach our kids to keep safe and we safeguard our stuff. But we don't always see how dangerous the unseen elements of envy can be. How destructive it is to resent people – sometimes whole groups of people – and how the flames of hostility eventually spread from our hearts to our facial expressions, conversations and communities.

And yet it's *so* hard. It's so hard not to be jealous when someone gets what you want, especially when what you want is a good thing. Like a job that pays the bills. A baby. A break. How do you lay down those desires as pleasing burnt offerings – sacrifices of trust – so that jealousy doesn't run rampant and leave your life in ashes?

Start praying. Tell God how messed up you are. How mad you are that He hasn't hooked you up with the life you want. It's far, far better – far *safer* – to take your burning embers straight to Him before they fall on dry ground to smolder and spread.

Will you be honest with God about who you're jealous of, and why?

God, I know this jealousy is too dangerous
for me to handle on my own. Help! Amen.

Congratulations beats comparisons

Be happy with those who are happy …

Romans 12:15 NLT

The only way to beat this cutthroat culture at its games of comparison is to find ways to celebrate those people whom you envy. Brag about how awesome they are. Commend their particular victories and successes. Celebrate God's best for them, for His glory. Thank God for what He is doing for them or in them. Fling your joy, not your spite. Rejoice with a genuine, generous hug or text or phone call. Or catch yourself saying something nice – something warm and kind – about that person, behind their back.

And remember: *God doesn't love them more than He loves you.* Remind yourself that He has promised His best for you too, and that you wouldn't want anything other than that. If what He has done or allowed or given in another person's life were really the very best thing for you – the thing that would make you more like Christ – then He would have set things up just the same for you.

Will you always *feel* like celebrating? Definitely not. But do it anyway. Outwardly and inwardly. You can *decide* to celebrate. Force it without being fake. And trust that right feelings will follow as your heart catches up to your head.

How can you send legitimate joy in someone's direction today, instead of pitching a backhanded compliment?

God, keep me from scorn and sarcasm. Help me to celebrate Your goodness to those around me. Amen.

Stay in your lane

Pay careful attention to your own work, for then you will get the satisfaction of a job well done, and you won't need to compare yourself to anyone else.

Galatians 6:4 NLT

When you've prayed, and celebrated, hear what Paul says to the Galatians and stay in your lane. At times in my life when pride has risen selfish and cruel, I've tried to scrape together the courage to put on blinkers, refusing to look right or left. I've remembered that this is my race and that no two races are the same. God has different Kingdom plans for different people. He has shaped each of us for His purposes.

That's cause for even more celebration – and relief. I've let the truth wash clean over me: you don't have to be anyone but you. That's why God made you *you*. There are you-shaped spaces that only you can fill. Get busy filling them.

You should also know that there's stuff going down in the lives of the people to whom you're comparing yourself. You wouldn't necessarily like that stuff. Like yours and mine, their lives aren't perfect. Let's remember: we should be kind, because every person we meet is fighting a hard battle.

Would you decide today to look straight ahead at the course God has you running, instead of getting tripped up trying to see what's happening in someone else's lane?

God, help me to do the things
You have called me uniquely to do. Amen.

Follow Me

Peter turned around and saw behind them the disciple
Jesus loved ... Peter asked Jesus, "What about him, Lord?"
Jesus replied, "If I want him to remain alive until I return,
what is that to you? As for you, follow Me."

John 21:20-22 NLT

When jealousy distracts you with shiny objects or flashy people speeding past, preach truth to yourself: Following Jesus is all you're expected to do. Peter – miffed, glancing back at John – asks the resurrected Christ, "What about him, Lord?" And Jesus' words put him – put me and you – gently in place: "If I want him to remain alive until I return, *what is that to you?* As for you, *follow Me.*"

Focusing on just that – just following Jesus – helps to keep you running in your own lane. To follow someone, you have to keep on looking straight ahead. If you glance from side to side and something else grips your gaze, you'll lose sight of who you're tracking. They'll get ahead of you. You won't see which turn they took. Don't worry about the people on either side of you – or just ahead or just behind. Follow Jesus. The rest will be what it will be, and all will be well with your soul.

Are there days – or particular situations – where you find yourself worrying about what God has planned for someone else, rather than just following Him into His plan for you?

Jesus, keep me fixed on following You. Amen.

Power of the paradox

Remember, dear brothers and sisters, that few of you were wise in the world's eyes or powerful or wealthy when God called you. Instead, God chose things the world considers foolish in order to shame those who think they are wise. And He chose things that are powerless to shame those who are powerful. God chose things despised by the world, things counted as nothing at all, and used them to bring to nothing what the world considers important.

1 Corinthians 1:26-28 NLT

The world swaggers proud and spreads dirt about big living and small living. It tells us that we need a Big Life. Big name. Big bank account. Big office. Big ministry. Big boobs. But God is all about paradox. Using the weak to show He's strong. Going lower for greater glory.

We're also quick to look at others and think we should be doing what they're doing, their way, to get their Big Results. And sure, it's good to follow good examples, but you can only be you. If God wanted us all to be identical, He could have made us that way. It's likely that God wants to do something totally fresh in your life – even through your unique weaknesses or disadvantages.

Friend, the world would change if we were brave enough to use our time and potential to live small lives for His Big Name.

How does God display His magnitude through the circumstances that make you feel small?

Great God, I bow low. Amen.

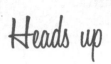

Heads up

I look up to the mountains – does my help come from there? My help comes from the Lord, who made heaven and earth! He will not let you stumble; the one who watches over you will not slumber.

Psalm 121:1-3 NLT

Whether you're commuting in subways or slicing snacks for your toddlers, you'll face the taunting, teasing pressures of culture. And unless you're intentional about seeking the truth and mustering the courage to live by it, you'll be tricked to look up to the billboards for help, rather than finding your peace, perspective and purpose in Jesus.

C. S. Lewis said that if you aim at Heaven you'll get earth thrown in, but if you aim at earth you'll get nothing. Don't just lift up your feet to be swept away helpless by the mess and mêlée of society or circumstances. Put your feet firmly on the Rock that's never shaken. From there, lift up your eyes and remember that your help comes from the One who made the seas and the stars. He watches over you unblinkingly, and with great love.

Do you know someone who needs to hear this truth? How can you encourage her today?

God, I look to You for help. Keep my eyes on eternity, so that I'm not enticed to throw myself into things that won't last. Amen.

JUNE

Lay low, sing loud

"Most of the things we need to be most fully alive never come in busyness. They grow in rest."

– *Mark Buchanan*

Busy doesn't change the world

It is useless for you to work so hard from
early morning until late at night, anxiously working
for food to eat; for God gives rest to His loved ones.

Psalm 127:2 NLT

Maybe, like me, you wake up tired?

You surface through the dark into morning. Fumble for phone alarm. Snooze. Snooze a little longer. Reach for morning mugs because, *coffee*. And maybe like me you think about how today really started hours ago, when midnight ticked into the first unfilled seconds of an untried day, and how still there wasn't enough rest in those dark hours to recover from the life stuffed into yesterday.

The voices in your head will get louder with the lightening sky – shouting at you to get busy and busier if you want to change the world. But in the kitchen quiet of a new day, may you be beautifully bolstered by the counter-culture truth that *busy doesn't change anything*.

Because if you really want to change the world by living fully – if you really want to taste life as you swallow it down slow – you need to be awake. Alert. Work is a gift and rest is a gift. They were both given before the fall and called *good* (Genesis 1-2). Lived right, there's no guilt in either.

Are you sacrificing rest for the kind of busy that makes a noise but doesn't really make a difference?

*God, thank You for the gift of sleep.
I need it desperately. Help. Amen.*

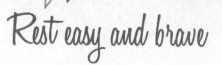

Rest easy and brave

Then Jesus said, "Let's go off by ourselves
to a quiet place and rest awhile."

Mark 6:31 NLT

It takes courage to rest in a world that tells us to go faster and push harder because it's a world that relegates rest into the shame-on-you categories of laziness, procrastination or distraction. Sure, you don't want to be leaking priceless time from the seams of a stitched-tight day because you're stuck on a Pinterest board. You want to amplify moment by full-bursting moment the hours you have so that they aren't frenetic – just *full*.

But rest is part of the fullness. Even Jesus – perfect Son of God – rested. Rest was one of the first things God modeled for His children, because kids copy: "On the seventh day God had finished His work of creation, so He rested from all His work" (Genesis 2:2). He didn't *need* rest. He wasn't tired after speaking out the universe. He was making a point. Declaring something holy. He commands us to rest and if we're going to be effective instruments of change in His hands, we'd be blessed to obey.

"It was evening, it was morning." The next day (Genesis 1). What would it look like for you to live a Genesis day – moving from rest into work?

God, make me brave enough to rest in preparation for work so that my rest is a mindful laying down of me for the coming work of God, rather than a collapsing – a petering out. Amen.

Return

This is what the Sovereign LORD, the Holy One of Israel, says: "Only in returning to Me and resting in Me will you be saved. In quietness and confidence is your strength. But you would have none of it."

Isaiah 30:15 NLT

I'm guilty of seeing rest as squandered time. Hours that could have been used constructively – lost forever to sleep. Yet I should rather see rest as vital if I'm serious about giving a good account of spending my time and potential on God's glory.

I need to learn how to rest well so that there's nothing in rest that whispers, "Slacker!" Whether it's sleep, laughter, or a slow stirring of Sunday soup – resting well should energize me and increase my capacity and effectiveness for Kingdom influence.

But we *don't* rest like we should, because it's hard.

It takes discipline to put down the device and say no to distraction. It takes courage to argue that we're kidding no one saying that it's downtime when really it's waste of time. It takes brutal honesty to see the stuff crowding our lives – Facebook pages – headspace – vying for our attention and affection, and making us tired. It takes energy to simplify spreadsheets, schedules and supper menus so that we can build the beauty of rest into days lived long and loud.

Do you dare to turn to God, and get some radical rest?

God, help me to embrace rest as crucial to my quietness, confidence and strength. Amen.

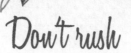

Don't rush

The LORD replied, "My Presence will go with you, and I will give you rest."

Exodus 33:14 NIV

I'm pretty sure that as my kids grow they will carry clear childhood memories of me *rushing* them, every day, into and out of the car or the bath or the front door. I rush them because I forget God's presence with us. I forget that He will give us rest. I forget that I can in fact listen and laugh and let them finish their sentences. Because at the end of my life it won't mean much if my kids say, "Wow, Mom got such a lot *done* every day!"

But the enemy fights for our time – our rest. He wants us to think we're falling behind. We need to shut out the lie that busyness equals success. That we must always carry the demeanor of being rushed and run off our feet. As in, "Sigh. I'm such a martyr. And so productive!" We need to stop groping guilty for an airtight alibi when people ask, "So what do you do all day?" We need to rest, and rest in the truth that there's time enough each day to do God's will.

How can you rest well so that you have strength and focus – emotional and physical energy – to do a few things with purpose and intent, rather than three dozen things halfhearted and haphazard?

God, help me to slow down and draw strength from resting in Your presence. Amen.

Day off

"You have six days each week for your ordinary work,
but on the seventh day you must stop working, even
during the seasons of ploughing and harvest."

Exodus 34:21 NLT

Sabbath is an old word, for an old idea. Jeremiah pleaded with the people: "This is what the Lord says: 'Stop at the crossroads and look around. Ask for the old, godly way, and walk in it. Travel its path, and you will find rest for your souls'" (Jeremiah 6:16).

Maybe you wonder if you're the only person who feels *this* overwhelmed. Because the feverishness of life can have you at the crossroads and caught in the headlights. Take it from the prophet and go back to some old ideas, like: *Take a day off.*

The idea of a Sabbath wasn't old to the 24/7 slave nation of Israel – men, women and children who had been sweating under Egyptian whips, day in day out of unending shifts, for as long as any of them could remember. Rest was a radical command. And like it was for those Israelites who couldn't believe there'd be food on Day 7 when they weren't working for it, rest is the ultimate act of faith. In resting, we *have* to trust God to provide.

Do you trust God enough with your life, to take a day to relax – refresh – recuperate?

*Thank You God for lovingly providing for all my needs –
so much so that You want me to take a day off.* Amen.

Stop trying so hard

Truly my soul finds rest in God; my salvation comes from Him.

Psalm 62:1 NIV

The Sabbath – and the concept of rest in general – counters legalism and all forms of tick-box righteousness. The Sabbath says, "Down tools. Stop trying so hard."

The Sabbath is also common sense for finite creatures needing to be intermittently refueled by food and sleep and hugs and eye contact and something hysterically funny. The Sabbath is a good habit – a beautiful, God-honoring thing. And though it doesn't have to be a sunset-to-sunset set time – because trains need to run on Sunday mornings and kids with high temperatures on Sunday nights need emergency rooms – it's possible to isolate some sacred time to desist from checking emails and doing to-do's and filling up a day with obligation.

Maybe, this Sunday, you could make space for inviting people to come rest with you despite the fact that you didn't make a single bed before leaving for church and the house is just your holy mess. Maybe you could make space for contemplative tea under trees. Or ridiculous lawn wrestling. But decide not to make space in the rest for restless guilt.

Could you live into the idea that you need rest to be the best version of yourself, and that rest mirrors the astounding truth that God did the work of your salvation?

God, thank You that I don't have to work for my salvation. I can rest in what You did for me. Amen.

Peaceful sleep

You can go to bed without fear; you will lie down and sleep soundly. You need not be afraid of sudden disaster or the destruction that comes upon the wicked, for the Lord is your security. He will keep your foot from being caught in a trap.

Proverbs 3:24-26 NLT

To make for peaceful sleep tonight? Give God the hours of today. Give Him your budget and bank accounts. Give Him your energy and ideas. Give Him all your friendships and relationships and ask Him to play Tetris with your schedule so that there'll be rest enough.

The day will pick up speed and hurtle on unstoppable; but afternoon will wane mellow and night will fall. Teeth will be brushed. Beds will beckon. And whether you're snuggling close for bedtime stories or hands around mugs for sips of something sweet – may you feel full with the wondrous refuge of night when streets sleep and the planet spins slow to face out at a different part of the universe.

And I pray that as you rest God would whisper wisdom and that dreams might be born in the quiet. I pray that as stars move across the sky towards a new day there would be new mercies. New possibilities for changing the world.

What can you do today to ensure that you sleep easy tonight?

God, thank You for the refuge of rest. Help me to be awake well, so that I can be asleep well too. Amen.

Rebel without a rest

God's promise of entering His rest still stands, so we ought
to tremble with fear that some of you might fail to experience it.
For this good news – that God has prepared this rest – has
been announced to us just as it was to them. But it did them
no good because they didn't share the faith of those who
listened to God. For only we who believe can enter His rest …

Hebrews 4:1-3 NLT

There's a warning and a promise attached to this idea of entering God's rest. Both are a pretty big deal and all over Hebrews chapter 3 and 4: there's rest and blessing for those who believe, and don't rebel.

This suggests that we won't experience deep soul rest unless we're at peace with God. Rest begins with belief: that God is who He says He is, that He can be trusted, that He is good and powerful and wise and loving, and that He can save us even when we're bent on our own destruction. If we deviate from those core beliefs by veering off into brash or even unspoken rebellion, we forfeit the incomprehensible peace of living safe in the hands of our Heavenly Father.

To breathe deeply and sleep deeply too? Settle your beliefs.

Are you holding onto something in your life – doubt, or an old habit, addiction or relationship – that is keeping you from real rest?

God, I believe, and I want to enter Your rest.
Keep me from rebelling! Amen.

The stress decision

… the report of His power spread even faster, and vast crowds
came to hear Him preach and to be healed of their diseases.
But Jesus often withdrew to the wilderness for prayer.

Luke 5:15-16 NLT

Jesus knew all about stress. And He knew how to handle it. He withdrew to pray. Which challenges me to ask myself, "How am *I* handling stress? How much am I praying and resting – if at all?"

Life is a frenetic bourgeoning of activities and obligations and online distractions and it's easy to use busyness as a cover – to shroud ourselves in a feel-good aura that says, "I'm so busy I must be successful!" It's easy to develop a messiah complex, assuming that people desperately *need* us to be doing all the things we do.

The truth is, we're least like the Messiah when we're frazzled and overwrought. And most of the time? We *decide* to be busy. As hard as it may be to find time for rest and prayer, you and I could make the brave choice not to wallow self-pityingly in our tub of decisions. We could choose to work excellently and rest excellently, the way Jesus did.

Do you feel guilty saying no to an invitation in favor of resting – as if you have to defend your decision to take time out? Could you create margins today, to refuel?

*God, give me wisdom to make time to rest and pray
as I fill up the hours of fast-flying days. Amen.*

Rest your restless thoughts

You will keep in perfect peace all who trust
in You, all whose thoughts are fixed on You!

Isaiah 26:3 NLT

If you're at all competitive or goal-oriented, you may need more rest than most. Constantly checking your progress, and the progress of strangers and friends, is exhausting.

Rest in the truth that there will always be people behind and ahead of you. Your journey is your journey. Swallow all the right thinking you can. Like, "Don't think you are better than you really are. Be honest in your evaluation of yourselves, measuring your-selves by the faith God has given us" (Romans 12:3). So, don't be arrogant, but back yourself and fail forwards. Fix your thoughts on God. Risk. And rest.

Rest in the truth that no one can steal your dream and that God has prepared your good works (Ephesians 2:10). He will lead you into living each one, His way, in His time, in His strength, and for His glory. Rest by surrendering to the agenda of the God who holds all of time, and holds you.

Could you set reminders to take a few five-minute breaks today, to fix your thoughts on God and His purposes for you, instead of allowing your thoughts to wander restless and resentful to what's happening in other people's lives?

*God, help me to enjoy where I am, and to
rest in Your plans for me. Amen.*

Rivers through the wasteland

"For I am about to do something new. See, I have already begun!
Do you not see it? I will make a pathway through the
wilderness. I will create rivers in the dry wasteland."

Isaiah 43:19 NLT

Through Isaiah, God was promising the Messiah, and salvation, restoration and eternal rest for His people. He was doing something new. Interestingly, the people weren't aware that He was at work. "Do you not see it?" He asks them.

God did something new in your life through Jesus. He made a pathway through the wilderness for you. He made rivers of rest and renewal flow through your wasteland. But it's possible that you don't always see it. It's possible that you still feel like you're in a dry, wild place. You may still feel tired, and without the capacity to extend grace or any sort of generosity of spirit to people around you.

Could you start telling yourself the truth? That God has made a pathway through your wilderness and that there are rivers watering the wasteland? He sees your fatigue, but He will sustain you, and use the new life He's growing in you to give shade and rest to others.

Would it change how you live today if you remembered that God has renewed, refreshed, restored and rejuvenated you?

God, thank You for doing something new in my life –
for replenishing my thirsty soul, and giving me rest. Amen.

See a doctor. Get some rest

If you think you are standing strong, be careful not to fall.

1 Corinthians 10:12 NLT

If you're human, you've probably discovered that your greatest strength is always what most quickly becomes your greatest weakness. Like, the gentle introvert can become the withdrawn misfit. The confident leader can become the domineering dictator. You'll also know that, more often than not, stress and fatigue are the weights that tip the scales in favor of our flaws.

Take ambition, for example. Managed well, it's essentially a good thing. It's what drives you to keep on becoming everything God made you to be. It's an overriding-undergirding desire to live out loud, outside of yourself, all the best bits of you that God has stuffed into your DNA.

Left unchecked? It goes viral – in a bad way. Ambition is dangerous when your ego becomes more important than God's glory, and when things don't happen as quickly as you'd like them to, in the direction of your dreams.

It's then that you need to take time out to rest. Give yourself space for serious soul-searching and self-medicating on Scripture. Allow God to do some heart surgery to realign your motives, and to renew your strength.

Are you sick? Suffering from a Double-Edged Personality Disorder?

Jesus, You are the great Physician. You understand my ailments like no other. Heal me. Give me rest. Amen.

Give the reins to the One who reigns

"Be still, and know that I am God! I will be honored
by every nation. I will be honored throughout the world."

Psalm 46:10 NLT

Two of the biggest enemies of rest are our craving to be in control and our inability to be still. The Amplified Bible renders Psalm 46:10 like this: "Let be *and* be still, and know (recognize and understand) that I am God." I would find deep rest if I followed this simple instruction more often. If I let go and acknowledged that God is God, and I am not.

Really, you should enjoy the staggering relief of knowing that you're not holding the reins of your life or the universe, but that God is. You can relax and enjoy the rhythm of the ride because you know the God who reigns – the holy King of matchless worth. Calling to mind amidst the crazy of life that He is powerful, good, all-knowing and ever present, and that He forged your life and is the front-runner of your journey – all this will allow you to rest in peace.

What truths about God's character could you hold close today, to stop you from turning into a control freak?

*God, it's so freeing to hand over the reins to You,
and to rest in Your powerful love.* Amen.

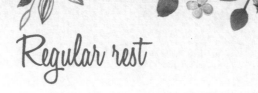

Regular rest

In peace I will lie down and sleep,
for You alone, O LORD, will keep me safe.

Psalm 4:8 NLT

Some of the best advice I was ever given about rest was to make it regular – on a macro and micro life level.

Like, schedule evening downtime. Don't check emails or Twitter or anything else for an hour or so before you go to sleep. Those emails – those Facebook posts – those to-do lists – will still be there in the morning. There's no point inducing tossing and turning because you're worried about something you can't fix or control at that time of night anyway.

Take a day off once a week – and don't feel guilty for investing that time in people, or in quiet. Even if you don't have anything planned, it's ok to plan to do nothing. Or to plan to lie down on some grass and look for poodles in the clouds.

Build in ninety-day rest periods throughout the year – a couple of days of intentional, deep rest. You'll slot back into the stream of life soon enough, and you'll be stronger, healthier, more alert and more at peace for the time you stood on the banks to catch your breath.

Is there really anything stopping you from committing to regular rest?

God, I pray that You would teach me to rest, so that I can live more courageously, more excellently, and more beautifully. Amen.

Sleeping through the storms

Suddenly, a fierce storm struck the lake, with waves breaking into the boat. But Jesus was sleeping.

Matthew 8:24 NLT

Jesus wasn't fast asleep because He didn't care about His disciples or the imminent danger. He wasn't asleep because He was irresponsible. When it was time for Him to act, He did – decisively and powerfully. But He slept in that boat on that lake during that storm, because He knew that His Father was wide-awake (Psalm 121:4).

When the storms of life rock your boat – as they will – God will give you the clarity, wisdom and extraordinary strength to act – to take responsibility for what you need to when the time is right. But He will also give you the grace to sleep. To take the rest that you can, when you can, and allow Him to stay up all night to dwell on your circumstances. Resting doesn't always make sense when you're in the throes of a crisis or emergency. It can feel counterproductive – like sliding two steps back – losing ground you should be gaining. Fight that feeling of panic. Because rest is part of the paradox of God's perfect plans. Those two steps back will give you three steps forward – maybe more.

Could you schedule in some early nights this week, and let God work in the darkness while you stock up on sleep for body, mind and soul?

Thank You, God, that because You never sleep, I can. Amen.

Slow down for the season

He will feed His flock like a shepherd. He will carry the
lambs in His arms, holding them close to His heart.
He will gently lead the mother sheep with their young.

Isaiah 40:11 NLT

Isaiah expresses so beautifully the tenderness of a God who
wouldn't dream of hurrying little ones, who won't be hurried.
When our boys were tiny and we were up at night – a lot – I hung
my sanity on two big hooks: the fact that God's mercies are new
every morning (Lamentations 3:23), and the prayer that my tender
Shepherd would give me (and my lambs) as much sleep as I needed
each night to do His will the next day.

But really, that's true of any and every season of womanhood.
Whether you're single or an empty-nester, you can rest in God's
fresh, daily, sufficient grace, and you can trust Him to meet your
physical and emotional need to rest. His Father-heart won't demand
a pace that's faster than you can manage, for the season you're in.

What are the demands of the stage of life that you're in? How do they
dictate your pace? How much rest do you need?

God, You know exactly where I find myself on the timeline
of my life. Help me to live this season well, and to remember
that what's really important – like rest, or taking slow time
to build relationships – seldom feels urgent. Amen.

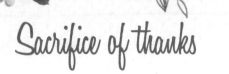

Sacrifice of thanks

Make thankfulness your sacrifice to God …

Psalm 50:14 NLT

When God was preparing His people to enter the Promised Land, He instituted the morning and evening sacrifice (Exodus 29:39). It was a laying down of the difficult things, and also a way of thanking God – giving glory back to God – for the wonderful things.

And sometimes thanksgiving is just that: a *sacrifice*. An offering – a giving up and laying down of something. And sacrifices can be hard to make. Like, if a doctor tells you that you need to give up sugar, it may be seriously tough for you to say no to cake. But once you're in the habit of it, and once you begin to see the benefits, it gets easier. It's the same with thanksgiving. You won't always *feel* like giving thanks. It may be difficult to muster gratitude in a heart laid low by worry. But if you make the morning and evening sacrifice of thanksgiving your habit – over breakfast or dinner, or by keeping a gratitude list – the thanksgiving gets easier and easier.

Can you thank God for something today, even though there's a nagging issue or some unresolved stress in your life?

God, it's a costly offering – and difficult to lay down – but I want to give my thanks to You, for all You are and all You have done. Amen.

Unstoppable

Since everything God created is good, we should
not reject any of it but receive it with thanks.

1 Timothy 4:4 NLT

It's Christmas in just over six months. What if you started a thanks-giving habit – kept a list of all the gifts you'll receive between now and then?

Disclaimer: You'd better know upfront that it will change your life.

Some weeks the thanksgiving might be easy. You won't be able to scrawl fast enough the blessings you see, smell, taste or touch. Some weeks you'll need to wrack your tired brain for scarce moments of joy. But you'll learn how to give thanks even for lousy things – because they'll have first passed through the hands of God, and they have purpose.

You won't realize how much a gratitude list changes you, until you stop. Because you'll realize that you *can't* stop. You'll have been searching so hard for goodness and the grit of glory that you'll have forced a beautiful habit that teaches you to live in the moment – and to live each moment as a gift.

What do you hear – see – smell right now? Could you thank God?

God, how amazing that I don't have to wait for once-a-year gifts under a Christmas tree because daily there are things to unwrap at the foot of the tree – the tree that held You, my Savior, so that I could be held by You in eternity, and in the here and now. Amen.

Travel light

Enter His gates with thanksgiving; go into His courts with praise. Give thanks to Him and praise His name.

Psalm 100:4 NLT

It's a beautiful image – entering into the King's court – His presence – to praise and thank Him. I love that we're called to enter just as we are. And perhaps there's a lesson there – that when the posture of our hearts is praise and thanksgiving we needn't drag baggage into every conversation, or dredge up memories unless they're poignant, helpful or beautiful for the moment at hand. For sure, we shouldn't be living in denial of past or present pain, but it's easier to kneel free at the feet of the King if we're not clutching cases bulging bitter.

Be brave enough to travel light. Because to live the moment at hand we don't need much more than an open heart. We'd do well to remember that no matter how easy, carefree, tragic or frightening any given moment might be, that moment still holds the gift of the greatest story ever told: of a King born low to live astounding love beneath stars He flung. To die a promised death nailed to a tree He seeded. To rise so that we could be free.

What might it look like, for you today, to leave some baggage behind and thank God, as you are, empty-handed, open-hearted?

God, I'm so honored by Your invitation to enter Your presence and bring You my gratitude, even in this moment. Amen.

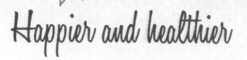

Happier and healthier

You have turned my mourning into joyful dancing.
You have taken away my clothes of mourning and
clothed me with joy, that I might sing praises to You and
not be silent. O Lord my God, I will give You thanks forever!

Psalm 30:11-12 NLT

The optimism bias is a well-known and well-researched concept, and affirms that those who hold the resilient belief that the future will be better than the past enjoy improved physical health and emotional well-being. The truth about thanksgiving is that it's the heavy grace that tips the happiness scales. Thanksgiving keeps us from blaming others (or God or the government or the neighbor's cat). And that keeps us happier because blame is just another way of saying to the person or thing that we're blaming: "Here! Take my happiness. Hold onto it."

As you forge a thanksgiving habit, don't go it alone. Find yourself a gratitude partner and share the wellspring that will rise up in you. Be courageously accountable to one another. Even spurring each other on to give thanks for three things a day will likely require a disciplined, excellent effort. It will also open your eyes to wonder.

Do you want to be healthier, happier and live longer? Thought so.

Jesus, I want to be the best, most beautiful and most effective version of me. Strengthen me to keep on giving thanks! Amen.

How you see the half

For His unfailing love toward those who fear Him is as great as the height of the heavens above the earth. He has removed our sins as far from us as the east is from the west.

Psalm 103:11-12 NLT

We're halfway through the year – halfway through a journey of truth-seeking and courage-mustering and learning to live brave and beautiful. And maybe it's good – halfway – to remind ourselves of how wholly we're forgiven and restored.

Halfway, it's also good to remember that how you see the half makes all the difference. For you, is the year running out, or filling up? In a wholly broken world full of half-hearted half-truths and people half-desperate half-disbelieving with broken-in-half hearts because half their hopes have been taken and tossed – how you see the half is the difference between fullness and futility. And the fullness floods in when we remember that we have been wholly forgiven because there are no half-measures with God and although all our lives we're only halfway to somewhere and the best is yet to be, knowing how to see the half is what fleshes us out whole again.

Are you disappointed, or encouraged, by where you are halfway into this year?

O God, thank You that we're not done. That the best is yet to be. And that, though this side of heaven I'll only ever be halfway along to where I'm headed, You have wholly restored me. Keep me resting grateful in You. Amen.

Fake it till you make it?

Be thankful in all circumstances, for this is
God's will for you who belong to Christ Jesus.

1 Thessalonians 5:18 NLT

Some people, if you ask them, "How are you?" they answer, "God is good!" I always want to say, "Yes. I know God is good. But how are *you*?" Because it feels like they're giving me a shiny happy cop-out and I want real.

But Paul writes to the believers in Thessalonica that they should be thankful *in all circumstances*. So is this his vibe too? Suck it up and just say thank you? Should you say, "Thank You, God, that I was abused as a child. Thank You that my car was stolen. Thank You for my postpartum psychosis. Thank You that I lost my job"?

Jesus gave thanks the night He was betrayed (1 Corinthians 11:23–25). He could taste the approaching agony. But in those dire circumstances, He didn't thank God for the betrayal. He thanked God for the bread.

Because there's always something – something? – to give thanks for. And even if you've scoured your circumstances for a glimmer of grace and found none – even if there is nothing left to be grateful for – God is in the circumstances and God hasn't changed. You can give thanks for that.

Could you etch out a bit of thanksgiving today, even if you're not at all grateful for the heavy things you hold?

*Lord, I'm grateful every day for Your
changeless character, and for hope.* Amen.

Momentum

To all who mourn in Israel, He will give a crown of
beauty for ashes, a joyous blessing instead
of mourning, festive praise instead of despair.

Isaiah 61:3 NLT

Gratitude is powerful because it mobilizes you through difficult times. It gives you the momentum you need to move through pain. Like, you may not want to give thanks for a tragedy you're facing, but you could probably give thanks for all the meals that family and friends bring to stock your freezer. Or you could give thanks for the sensitivity and gentleness of a doctor delivering a diagnosis, or for the school teacher who turned a blind eye to your kid's undone homework because she saw the crazy in your eyes and knew not to go there.

And in time, it may become easier to thank God for His perfect plans, for His love, power and wisdom in your life. It may take years but eventually you may well move from sorrow to resignation to acceptance to embrace. To deep thanksgiving – the kind that thanks God for the whole journey, even the toughest parts. Because what we reap in growth and grace from years in the valley is irreplaceable. Priceless.

Can you look back on something shocking, traumatic or painful in your life, that now you wouldn't actually swap for anything?

God, it feels impossible to even begin to dredge up some kind of gratitude for where I find myself. But I'm clinging to You. Bring beauty from these ashes. Amen.

Beauty hunting

The heavens proclaim the glory of God.
The skies display His craftsmanship.

Psalm 19:1 NLT

When my visually impaired son put a leaf under a magnifier for the first time – tore it in half and saw the fibers inside – he was awestruck. I was ashamed. Because I'm so used to seeing God's fingerprints smudged beautiful over all creation that I've become a little desensitized to the miracle. There is so much of God's glory in what gets yawned at as normal.

So I'm challenging me and I'm challenging you: before the sun sets and today is gone, notice something you've taken for granted. Hold for a moment something you've rushed past. Were you aware of God's work in challenging and changing you? Have you stopped to take grateful, awestruck note of His preposterous blessings – His favor and goodness in everything from hot tea to raucous laughter to the hope of heaven? How have you seen Him reaching into a concrete, hurting, hoping world to leave His divine, eternal marks of majesty?

Thank Him for places that exist – simultaneously with, and despite, your frenetic reality – like a mountain pass, somewhere faraway, quiet under snow. Thank Him in the busyness for rich reminiscence. Slow time and sand castles and stargazing. Thank Him for holding all things together – galaxies and ordinary lives.

Would you go on a beauty hunt today?

God, please open my eyes to the beauty that surrounds me and that exists all over the world, declaring Your glory. Amen.

Open your hands

I will exalt You, my God and King, and praise Your name forever and ever. I will praise You every day; yes, I will praise You forever. Great is the LORD! He is most worthy of praise! No one can measure His greatness.

Psalm 145:1-3 NLT

Have you experienced God's blessings to be so magnificent – so unexpected – so heavy to carry – that you panic? I can feel overwhelmed and uneasy and the gratitude comes out hot, stomach-flipping and pinch-myself surreal in a terrified sort of way. Maybe we need to learn to unclench our fists in thanks even as we're asking amazed, *why me?* Unfold our fingers for torrents of beauty and grace.

Then of course, we can also get ourselves so steeped in First World blessings that we grow dissatisfied, discontent and disconnected from the Giver of the gifts. Sometimes there really is more chance of stuff going right than wrong. Sometimes God just blesses – for no obvious reason and against all odds. Whichever side of the equator you find yourself today – whether you're giving thanks for the stark branches of a cold bright dawn, or for the vivid green of summer warmth – there's splendor all over this tough-beautiful world of ebb and flow if we'll just see it, and receive it.

Do you ever feel guilty for how God has blessed you? Or do you feel entitled?

Father, I don't deserve all Your goodness to me, but I want to open my hands and heart, and accept it gladly. Amen.

Cheer up! Get up! He's calling you

> When Jesus heard him, He stopped and said,
> "Tell him to come here." So they called the blind man.
> "Cheer up," they said. "Come on, He's calling you!"
>
> *Mark 10:49* NLT

The God's Word Translation of this Scripture has Jesus' disciples saying to the blind man, Bartimaeus, "Cheer up! Get up! He's calling you." And I sure need those words poured quietly and daily into my morning coffee. Because they're just the thing to keep me in the trade winds and out of the potential doldrums of self-absorption. And they're just the thing to help me not to blink, to help me not to miss a thing, and to help me to polish the ordinary things in each day until the extraordinary shines and I can give thanks.

The disciples' mandate also reminds me that, although some days it's hard to stop in the moment and shut off the outer or inner noise because I'm scared to hear the quiet, giving thanks weights the silence. Fills it eloquently. Makes me brave to cheer up, get up, and get busy living fully.

Do you need to pull yourself up by your bootstraps today – and answer the call to rejoice in your King?

God, help me not to wallow or self-obsess. I want to get up and cheer up and thank You for all You've done, all You've promised, and the daily magnificence of Your presence in my life. Amen.

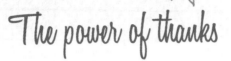

The power of thanks

Let us come to Him with thanksgiving. Let us sing psalms of praise to Him. For the LORD is a great God, a great King above all gods.

Psalm 95:2-3 NLT

Thanking God is to jealousy, anger, greed and other dark things of the heart, what paper is to rock, or rock is to scissors. It beats them, every time.

There are dangerous consequences to the thankless life – misery will sink you if you let it – but thanksgiving lifts your head because thanksgiving puts God back on the throne. It acknowledges Him as the sovereign source of life and the Giver of all good gifts. Thanking Him – the Potter – for how He made your jar of clay (Romans 9:20-21), for how much He loves you, for where He has placed you, for the wealth of people filling your days, for opportunities to trust Him in the face of others' strengths and your weaknesses, and for the chance to be happy with those who are happy and to weep with those who weep (Romans 12:15) – all that gratitude ushers in the power of deep peace and quiet contentment.

What damaging emotions are fermenting in your heart? What can you thank God for – right now – to gain the upper hand and live victoriously over anger, jealousy, greed or other sin?

Lord, don't let me be beaten up by negativity.
Help me to give thanks. Amen.

Thanking God for deadlines, delays, and other difficulties

The Lord isn't really being slow about His promise, as some people think. No, He is being patient for your sake. He does not want anyone to be destroyed, but wants everyone to repent.

2 Peter 3:9 NLT

When I dropped my smartphone, cracked the screen, and had to go without it for a full 48 hours while it was in for repairs, I did *not* feel like giving thanks. And yet C. S. Lewis put it so well, saying: "We ought to give thanks for all fortune: if it is 'good', because it is good, if 'bad', because it works in us patience, humility and the contempt of this world and the hope of our eternal country." It struck me that smartphones will come and go, but the things of unfathomable and eternal importance are my relationships – with God and others.

It seems ridiculous to thank God for delays, inconveniences and other stressful, unfair and uncertain bits of life happening. But it makes perfect sense to thank Him when you remember that He sees things that you don't. He knows things that you don't. And He loves us in a way that we can't actually begin to appreciate.

Are you grateful for the roadblocks God sent across your past path, to protect or empower you in ways you couldn't see at the time?

God, help me to trust You, and to give thanks sincerely for the ways You work in my life, for my good and Your glory. Amen.

Making art

And as God's grace reaches more and more people, there will be great thanksgiving, and God will receive more and more glory.

2 Corinthians 4:15 NLT

Grace. To thanksgiving. To glory.

For us to live that grace-thanks-glory progression – to create beauty – maybe all it takes is looking up from the sludge of life long enough to celebrate how the suffering of Jesus has set us free. Maybe the aesthetic appeal of each new day would change if we opened our heart-eyes to His mercies: new every morning for this world, new every morning for you and me.

Because to live the wide-eyed, beauty-hunting, thankful life is to *make art* with the words or songs or plates of pasta or text messages or other random materials of any given day. Any ordinary magical day. Thanksgiving has a way of transforming what is bland into what is noticed, treasured and laden with splendor.

Your day probably looks very ordinary, or very stressful. It doesn't look like a gallery. But could you give thanks for just one thing? Could you display it in a different light – hang it up as art?

God, open my eyes to the ways in which
Your grace and goodness surround me, so that I can
give thanks, and paint today on canvas. Amen.

Flavor and fragrance

Let all that I am praise the Lord; with my whole heart, I will
praise His holy name. Let all that I am praise the Lord;
may I never forget the good things He does for me.

Psalm 103:1-2 NLT

Michel de Montaigne said that, "The most evident token and apparent sign of true wisdom is a constant and unconstrained rejoicing ..."

So friend, you'd be wise to laugh more. Turn up the music that makes you drum your fingers on the steering wheel. Buy someone chocolate, just to be awesome. Look out of a window for five full minutes and thank God for three things you see, even if the day ahead of you feels unplayable. Lick the baking bowl and run through sprinklers with kids.

Because I think what De Montaigne was getting at is that when we're wise about watching and listening and feeling for beauty it flavors and fragrances our worlds and each exquisite moment is allowed to exist just then, for what it is, without being frayed at the edges by gnawing worries or squashed by adjacent less exquisite moments. We'll catch ourselves in pockets of peace here and there on each humdrum or frenetic or orderly or unraveling day going, "Right now? I am outrageously happy."

What thanksgiving habits have shaped and deepened your gratitude over this month? Will you keep on keeping on giving thanks?

*God, I want gratitude to be something that colors
and characterizes my whole existence. Amen.*

JULY

Strong spirit, soft heart

"To forgive is to set a prisoner free and discover that the prisoner was you."

– *L. Smedes*

Just right

For the whole law can be summed up in this
one command: "Love your neighbor as yourself."

Galatians 5:14 NLT

Personal relationships are never perfect, and seldom evenly matched or seamlessly reciprocal, all the time. In our connections with friends, family, colleagues or acquaintances, it can feel as if we're getting too much or too little. Our expectations are uncomfortably exceeded, or not quite met. That's the ordinary ebb and flow of ordinary humans with diverse emotions and circumstances. And the sooner we make peace with that – and extend to others the grace we desperately need ourselves as imperfect and sometimes erratic contributors to relationships – the happier we'll be.

But we can still do our best to make our connections as beautiful and as God-glorifying as possible. Excellent relationships don't just happen, and constantly managing our interactions takes courage, deliberate selflessness, and the discernment to read people just right – to gauge their surplus or their deficit – and to meet them in the midst of their story.

How could you intentionally be the Goldilocks factor in someone's day today – not too much or too little, too soft or too hard, too hot or too cold – but just right?

God, I'm asking for exceptional insight into the people You've placed in my life to love, so that I can love them well. Amen.

Soul sisters

Your faithfulness extends to every generation,
as enduring as the earth You created:

Psalm 119:90 NLT

Women innately, instinctively long for soul mates, and yet we spend a lot of our lives feeling alone. We waste great chunks of valuable time nursing hurts inflicted by other women. And even amidst the throngs of our extensive social, career or family networks, we can believe ourselves to be isolated, even friendless. We can also deceive ourselves into believing that we're the only ones who feel this way.

The psalmist declares that God's grace is enough, even for us. His grace extends even to the women of our generation who so often experience the soul-terrifying sensation of being lonely in a crowd. What's more, the wonder and the great relief is that God's grace is *changing* grace. It can change us into a generation that knows well how to love the souls of our sisters. After all, the courage, effort and vulnerability it costs us to love people – this is the stuff of life.

Are you willing to be the kind of friend to someone else that you'd love them to be for you? Will you listen first? Will you be kind, interested, inclusive and accepting?

Father, please bring to my mind someone who may be feeling cut off in some way. Show me who needs me to be a great friend today. Amen.

The weight of acceptance and rejection

> The LORD is for me, so I will have no fear.
> What can mere people do to me?
>
> *Psalm 118:6 NLT*

You and I are the sum of the acceptance and rejection we've received. Most of that acceptance and rejection happened when we were young – when our characters were supple and bent to the weight that others placed on us, for better or worse.

I know a teenage boy, for example, who overheard his preschool teacher telling his mom that "his lift doesn't go all the way to the top." His lift goes way higher than that because, as little as he was, he understood the slur on his intellect and it took him the better part of fifteen years to walk free from the lie.

The effect of rejection isn't the same for everyone. We respond to it differently because we all have different temperaments, contexts and characters. But no matter your story, you're exposed to the elements of criticism, opposition and rejection. They're outside of you, acting upon you.

The truth that makes you brave enough to carry the criticism is that Jesus already carried it all to the cross. God wholly embraces you. Strangely, the weight of that unthinkable acceptance allows you to travel light.

Do you really believe that, no matter what criticism, opposition or rejection has been dumped on you in the past, God utterly loves you?

God, thank You for embracing me and accepting me, absolutely and forever. Amen.

Really?

Fix your thoughts on what is true ...

Philippians 4:8 NLT

Criticism, opposition and rejection sometimes only exist in your head. They emerge from the trenches of your mind in the wee hours of the night when there's no one to turn on a light of truth. Which is ridiculous, right? To fear and feel scorned for things that may not even be – and probably aren't – real.

Tell yourself the truth. And what's true is that you can't know what's going on in someone else's heart or mind. You can't control it. There's no point wasting time and emotional energy worrying what someone else *might* be thinking of you. Probably? That other person is fast asleep.

If you're not very relationally gung ho – if you're prone to feeling spun out to the edges of the clique – ask yourself: Could my feelings be reactions to my perceptions, rather than the result of others' actual intentions? And when you know for *sure* that you're up against cattiness, exclusivity or the obvious blizzard in the room, take the weather with you. Keep smiling until you mean it – until it's *true* – because succumbing to cold gusts of bitterness that rejection blows through the soul withers your influence for Jesus. Keep the heart fires burning hot to melt the spite, trusting God to help you skate right over the ice.

Is the rebuff you're feeling actual or imagined?

Lord, I want to think on what is true.
Keep me from inventing relationship issues. Amen.

Take it like a king

If you listen to constructive criticism,
you will be at home among the wise.

Proverbs 15:31 NLT

The flames of criticism can be scorching. But they also burn off the superfluous so that you can see better the truth about you, and what to do with it.

Maybe you never expect criticism, whether nasty or constructive (and sometimes they're the same thing). Not because you think everyone should agree with you, but because you hate dishing out criticism yourself. Even when people ask for your honest feedback, offering criticism can be awkward and confrontational.

And yet when others' words slice you and pride sticks painful in your throat, you need to be able to swallow. You want to get it graciously right, so that, as Solomon said, you can be at home among the wise. Solomon also said, "A gentle answer deflects anger" (Proverbs 15:1). So maybe that's the key? When criticism is leveled at you, take a deep breath. Give a calm, quiet response, like: "Thank you very much for sharing that perspective; I really appreciate it." Make a calm retreat. And take another deep breath.

Solomon's tactic – a gentle answer – may just transform a critical (and critical) relationship you're managing. Are you willing to give it a try?

God, help me learn how to listen to criticism,
and how to respond in love. Amen.

Take it from your toughest critic

"I knew you before I formed you … Before you were born
I set you apart and appointed you as My prophet to the
nations … Don't say, 'I'm too young,' for you must go wherever
I send you and say whatever I tell you. And don't be afraid
of the people, for I will be with you and will protect you."

Jeremiah 1:5-8 NLT

Jeremiah, up against a nation that didn't want to hear what he had to say, went to his toughest critic – God. And God reassured him that, despite knowing the good, the bad and the embarrassing about Jeremiah, He had set him apart for a great work, and promised to equip and protect him.

Some say you're your own toughest critic. That's not true. We lie to ourselves all the time. Convince ourselves that we're not as bad as all that. Justify poor choices and excuse sin. Also, in our human frailty, we just don't see everything there is to be seen about us.

God sees it all. He sees you as no one else can or ever will. He sees your brilliance – He placed it in you – and He sees your sin, scars and suffering. There isn't a thing you can hide from Him. He also knows the extent of the antagonism you face, and His reassurance is to shield you and prepare you.

Are you making excuses because you're afraid to face opposition?

*Father, thank You for knowing me,
setting me apart and defending me.* Amen.

Take it like a prophet

Then I heard the Lord asking, "Whom should I send as a messenger to this people? Who will go for Us?" I said, "Here I am. Send me." And He said, "Yes, go, and say to this people, 'Listen carefully, but do not understand. Watch closely, but learn nothing.'"

Isaiah 6:8-9 NLT

God had a message for His people. He called Isaiah to deliver it, and Isaiah accepted the call. But like Jeremiah, Isaiah faced severe hostility from his people. God told him upfront that the nation wouldn't listen to Isaiah's message, but He called him to keep talking anyway. No matter how hard people's hearts were. No matter how few people listened. Isaiah kept being obedient. He kept going back, because God said so.

You may feel that the conflict or resistance you're facing isn't going anywhere anytime soon. It's enduring and relentless. But just as God sustained Isaiah for the call that was on his life, He will sustain you. Take heart. You are your bravest, your most beautiful, and your truest reflection of His grace in you when you keep on saying, "Here I am. Send me."

Does dealing with other people's disapproval or resistance feel futile to you? Can you trust that God is at work – and nourishing your needs – regardless?

God, it's exhausting being up against the reproach of others. It seems endless. Please uphold me. Amen.

Take it like a shepherd

You come to me with sword, spear, and javelin, but I come
to you in the name of the Lord of Heaven's Armies –
the God of the armies of Israel, whom you have defied.

1 Samuel 17:45 NLT

David was the sheep-watching baby brother of big brothers who didn't take him seriously, and didn't acknowledge him as the gifted warrior-poet that he was. They hardly noticed him, and when they did, they were critical of him – jealous, likely, of their anointed brother. When he brought them provisions on the battlefront they said things like, "What are you doing around here anyway?" (1 Samuel 17:28).

It was in bringing food to these brothers that David heard about the arrogance of the Philistine Goliath, whose condescending taunts incensed David. He didn't allow the rejection of his brothers to deflate the passion of his purpose, which was to defeat the enemy to the glory of God. He decided to be brave and vulnerable because the reward was great. He took on the giant, understanding that, although there is a time to be a lamb, this was the time to be a lion.

Is God calling you to be courageous in the face of criticism? Who might you need to stand up to – and how? Can you do so without in any way compromising your integrity?

*God of heaven's armies, make me brave to
fight for what is right, for Your glory.* Amen.

Take it like a poet

Examine yourselves to see if your faith is genuine. Test
yourselves. Surely you know that Jesus Christ is among you;
if not, you have failed the test of genuine faith.

2 Corinthians 13:5 NLT

Wordsworth, most celebrated of the Romantic poets, said that poetry was the spontaneous overflow of powerful emotion *recollected in tranquility*. He'd go walking and then, "Oh wow! Look at all those daffodils! I'm feeling so emotional right now!" He would go home, calm down, and write about it over a quiet cup of tea.

Criticism can spur us on to valuable self-examination. This is a really good thing, because conducting a regular soul search isn't just good advice. It's a command for Jesus-followers. So when you're at the brunt of some sort of condemnation, go home or find a quiet space away from the source of the censure. Calm down. Recollect the emotion in tranquility. Pray. Evaluate the origins of the criticism. Ask yourself the hard questions. Give yourself the honest answers. (And make tea.)

Can you put off replying to that email, making that call to that family member, or confronting that colleague in that meeting – until you've recollected your emotion in tranquility and looked at the facts with calm and clarity?

*Father God, I can't think straight or see through this
fog of hurt and anger. Quiet me. Compose me. Help me
to see the poetry You're writing, even in this.* Amen.

Not all bad

Wounds from a sincere friend are better
than many kisses from an enemy.

Proverbs 27:6 NLT

Hearing criticism is almost always really hard. And yet maybe you've journeyed with a friend who made some stupid decisions that threatened to blow up her life, and right before things exploded you were willing to speak up in warning or admonition at the risk of losing the friendship. Because you loved your friend so much, you wanted her to avoid disaster at all costs, even if that meant losing the friendship.

To live brave, beautiful lives, we need to be willing to take the same kind of treatment. It should shock us into rethinking a course of action – or repenting – if a friend is brave enough to risk hurting us in order to love us hard and honest.

Can you make a quick mental list of friends, colleagues, associates or family members who you know will only tell you what they think you want to hear? Who will tell you the truth? What can you do in this season to build your friendship with those truth-tellers?

Lord, please surround me with friends who love me enough to hurt me with the truth. And teach me how to be that kind of gentle, stalwart friend to others. Amen.

Totally known

O LORD, You have examined my heart
and know everything about me.

Psalm 139:1 NLT

Most of the humor in every romantic comedy or slapstick sitcom is based on the dramatic irony of misunderstandings. And misunderstandings make for cool dinner party stories. Usually there's no harm done. We love to laugh about how we all have preconceived ideas about everyone we meet, whether we mean to or not.

But sometimes misunderstanding can be a dragon to slay. This dragon is all about making you feel as if no one takes you seriously or really believes in you. It lures you into longing for acceptance, affirmation or affection. To be seen. To be heard. And like so many other external pressures of life, you can't control it. What people are determined to think of you (or not think of you) is their business. You can only try to understand how they are reading and interpreting you, and then manage your response, trusting that there is a God of all wisdom and knowledge, who knows every hidden and exposed part of you, perfectly.

Are you carrying some invisible scars from people who haven't known the whole truth, and so made you feel invisible?

Loving Creator, thank You that You see and know all the bits of me. My true worth and identity are wrapped up in You. I am so very happy to rest in that. Amen.

Relax

> "Love your enemies! Do good to them. Lend to them without expecting to be repaid. Then your reward from heaven will be very great, and you will truly be acting as children of the Most High, for He is kind to those who are unthankful and wicked."
>
> *Luke 6:35 NLT*

No matter how deeply you believe the truth about who you are in Christ and no matter how much you tell yourself that that's all that matters, it may still irk you when people don't appreciate you or understand you. And what bothers you is that many people – even people close to you – *never will.*

The good news is that despite this, you can relax into the love of your Redeemer who dealt with the sting of being overlooked on the cross. You can rest in the truth that you don't necessarily have to *solve* this thing. You'll understand that, for the most part, people don't mean to be mean and for sure they don't know how their words and actions – or lack thereof – are going to affect you. You'll have so much more grace for them, and grace makes you brave and beautiful.

Could you relax your grip on some of the tight hurt you're clutching? Whom can you love extravagantly today, despite how they've treated you?

Jesus, thank You for the peace and assurance
I have in Your love. Thank You that Your love allows
me to love others, regardless of how they see or snub me. Amen.

Reality check

The Lord hears His people when they call to Him for help.
He rescues them from all their troubles. The Lord is
close to the brokenhearted; He rescues those whose
spirits are crushed. The righteous person faces many troubles,
but the Lord comes to the rescue each time. For the Lord
protects the bones of the righteous; not one of them is broken!

Psalm 34:17-20 NLT

One of the beautiful spin-offs of being crushed in spirit is that it drives us back to God, usually on our knees. Being humbled – or worse, humiliated – by the betrayal or blasé indifference of others can be excruciating. And so very good. Because when you're face down in the mud you never think thoughts like, "I'm invincible!" or "I don't need God!"

The psalmist is totally real about the fact that we *will* face many troubles. It's what we do with those troubles – where we're brave enough to take them, and ourselves – that is the difference between victory and defeat, beauty and ashes.

Would you take your confusion, criticism, dishonor or disgrace before the throne of your living, loving God?

Father, I'm stunned, offended and kind of horrified.
This is crestfallen me, coming to glorious You.
Please hold me and hide me. Amen.

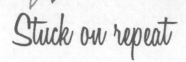

Stuck on repeat

Then Peter came to Him and asked, "Lord, how often should I forgive someone who sins against me? Seven times?" "No, not seven times," Jesus replied, "but seventy times seven!"

Matthew 18:21-22 NLT

Forgiveness is a good thing, sure. But who are we kidding? It's just about the hardest thing in the world. There's no forgiveness formula. No shortcuts to get you past the harm done or the time lost or the reputation damaged or the dignity stolen. There's no side road to get you past the rage.

Also, people keep hurting each other, right? You'll never reach some spiritual pinnacle and go, "Awesome. I've done all the forgiving I'll ever need to do." But you can get better at it – and quicker – with the practice that forms the habit that changes the heart.

I can tell you that sometimes forgiveness is a long, stuck-on-repeat process of going back to God again and again and dumping it all down – again – just to clutch it back close because it feels too hard to cancel the debt. But friend, keep up the rhythm of hitting repeat because the God who gives you strength wouldn't have told you to forgive if it wasn't possible.

Do you believe that God can supernaturally work something in your heart that empowers you to forgive?

God, I'm laying it down. Again.
Help me to forgive this person. Help me a year
from now, a week from now, five minutes from now. Amen.

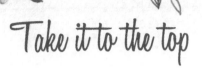

Take it to the top

"And forgive us our sins, as we
have forgiven those who sin against us."

Matthew 6:12 NLT

You've probably recited these words hundreds – maybe thousands – of times if you grew up in a churchy school or community. Jesus is teaching His disciples about prayer and this is a key concept – bringing to Him our own need for forgiveness, and the forgiveness we need to extend to others.

So when you know you should forgive someone and instead your thoughts keep drifting into imaginary tirades with them? Escalate your complaint and take those tirades up a notch. Take them to the very top. Take them to God. *Pray.*

Tell God about the hurt or anger. Yes, He knows. He saw the whole thing. He even saw it coming. But still, unravel your stories to the One who listens and loves and knows the nuances of every side to every story. Tell Him what happened and how you feel about it. Tell Him that you don't want to forgive the person but that you want to *want* to forgive. Kind of. Like the father of the boy with the evil spirit – how he cried out to Jesus, "I do believe, but help me overcome my unbelief!" (Mark 9:24).

Today, would you try venting to God about the person who has hurt or angered you, instead of venting to someone else, or making yourself sick with resentment?

*Lord, I'm going to tell You everything,
even though You know.* *Amen.*

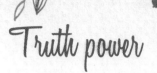

Truth power

"If you forgive those who sin against you, your heavenly
Father will forgive you. But if you refuse to forgive others,
your Father will not forgive your sins."

Matthew 6:14-15 NLT

Telling God what was done to you, and how you don't feel like forgiving but you know that it would be good to someday feel like
forgiving – that's the first forgiveness step. Then, be brave. Dredge
up the difficult Scriptures. Like the one that says, "Forgive others,
and you will be forgiven" (Luke 6:37). And another: "So watch yourselves! If another believer sins, rebuke that person; then if there is
repentance, forgive" (Luke 17:3). Pray into, over and through those
words until you start to *feel* them just a little – and find a way somehow to *live* them just a little.

The writer of Hebrews said God's Word is alive and powerful,
sharper than the sharpest two-edged sword, cutting between soul
and spirit, and exposing our innermost thoughts and desires (Hebrews 4:12). Don't underestimate the power of God-breathed
truth to start a heart revolution in you. Keep flushing out your
heart wounds with pure truth. It will sting, but it will bring healing –
remarkably, and more quickly than you think.

Which Scripture on forgiveness could you scrawl somewhere today,
allowing truth's power to take hold of you?

*Thank You for Your Word, God. It's hard to swallow –
and harder to digest – but I know it's good for me.
Use it to help and heal me. Amen.*

Life support

A jar of sour wine was sitting there, so they soaked
a sponge in it, put it on a hyssop branch, and held it up to
His lips. When Jesus had tasted it, He said, "It is finished!"
Then He bowed His head and gave up His spirit.

John 19:29-30 NLT

You probably have excellent reasons for feeling hurt, betrayed, angry or abandoned. Forgiveness isn't about minimizing your story of excruciating pain or entitlement to anger. Forgiveness doesn't deny the past. It just puts the past where it belongs, which is, behind you.

It may help you to forgive if you picture yourself standing with the people whom you believe owe you something – like a big apology. (And maybe chocolate.) Picture the truth that you are forgiven *much* and that all these other people have also been forgiven *much* and how if Jesus could look at them and say, "It is finished," then who are you to keep their sin on life support?

Most of those people, they're walking around in the world just fine. Light, free and unaware of your grudge. Oblivious to how you're inducing a coma in your own heart and quietly dying. The brave, beautiful thing to do is forgive.

What are you feeding the bitterness or fury to keep it alive?

Jesus, my sin and the sin of the person who sinned against me –
it was all nailed to the cross. You dealt with it.
It's finished. Help me to accept the relief of that. Amen.

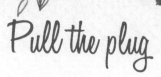

Pull the plug

Make allowance for each other's faults,
and forgive anyone who offends you. Remember,
the Lord forgave you, so you must forgive others.

Colossians 3:13 NLT

If the hard time you're having forgiving someone has their sin on life support then, instead of watching the machines beep incessant when it's in your power to switch them off, tell God that you're pulling the plug. *Clunk.* It will fall ugly-heavy from your heart. And live into the idea that you are free. You've let go. No one owes you. You've released the offenders to the God of everywhere-all-the-time justice whose grace in your life has surely been so extraordinary that the thought of withholding it from someone else is unthinkable.

But to forgive like this? You're going to have to be brave. Because if you're serious about cleaning out your heart, God will hold you to it. He will induce the beautifully unnerving heart palpitations of conviction, because He longs for you to be free.

Whom can you release today?

*O God, it's so hard. But I want to let this person go.
I can't cope with the weight of them in my heart
any longer. I release them to You. Amen.*

Relationship reigns

Then God said, "Let Us make human
beings in Our image, to be like Us."

Genesis 1:26 NLT

It's incredible and beautiful to think that what we call the Trinity – Father, Son and Holy Spirit – was in relationship before anything was created. What startling perspective it brings to understand that, since eternity past, the perfect unity of Their relationship has existed.

The implication is that a relationship is always more important than all the other tangible elements that make up reality. A relationship is always more important than doing stuff, or having stuff. God didn't *need* the world and He didn't *need* to create it. He desired fellowship with us, yes, but He was self-sufficient and fulfilled in the unanimous concord of His triune self.

It's a profound reminder of the importance of treasuring the gift of close relationships and chance interactions. It's a profound reminder of the importance of forgiveness which oils the machinery of those relationships and makes the world a beautiful place.

What would your life look like if all your stuff dissolved but your heart connections to other people were visible and tangible – bits of colored ribbon of varying lengths and thickness linking your heart to others?

God, thank You for showing us the importance of relationship. Help me to steward excellently all my relationships, and to make right with people when and where I need to. Amen.

Just miffed?

Always be humble and gentle. Be patient with each other, making allowance for each other's faults because of your love.

Ephesians 4:2 NLT

There's a difference between being sinned against and being offended.

Sin is choosing to do what's wrong, or choosing not to do what's right, according to God's law. When someone sins against you, it's their problem. God will hold them accountable, and they need to seek forgiveness from Him, and hopefully from you.

Offense is something different. Because if someone offends you, it's actually just your problem. The fact that you're bothered or put out because you've invited someone over and that someone has never invited you back, well, that's kind of your problem. Their refusal isn't listed as sin.

When you're offended, it helps to see what the other person has done or not done merely as information – about them or about the situation. Don't pick up that offense. It's not something you need to carry. It also isn't necessarily something you need to forgive. Make like Paul: be gentle and patient, and make allowances for each other's faults. And make like Elsa: let it go.

Is there someone in your life who regularly irritates you? Is he or she actually sinning against you, or do you just have different rhythms and values?

Lord, make me gentle and patient. Help me not to pick up offenses but rather to keep a sense of humor and brush them off bravely. Amen.

Stay in your vehicle

"Look, I am sending you out as sheep among wolves.
So be as shrewd as snakes and harmless as doves."

Matthew 10:16 NLT

Imagine a woman is raped. Her attacker is convicted, sentenced and jailed, because the law is in place to protect the innocent. Miraculously, the woman finds it in her heart to visit her rapist in jail. She extends forgiveness for the heinous thing he has done to her. Should the man be released from prison? No way. Should she ever trust him or make herself in any way, physically or emotionally, vulnerable to him? Forget it! Can she release him into the hands of the living God of perfect justice? Oh yes.

You may need to do those sorts of heart calculations almost daily, on a much smaller scale. You may never again trust the man who cheated on you, but you can forgive him. You may never fully trust the friend who gossiped about you, but you can forgive her. You can even love her – enjoy her – be warm and welcoming and genuinely kind. But careful.

These kinds of relationships are a bit like wild game viewing. Enjoy the splendor of the bush from a safe distance. Be at peace with the wildlife. But for goodness' sake, stay in your car.

In which relationships do you need to guard your heart? How can you still show love?

God, give me wisdom to know
when it's safe to open my heart. *Amen.*

Trash

When they came to a place called The Skull, they nailed Him to the cross. And the criminals were also crucified – one on His right and one on His left. Jesus said, "Father, forgive them, for they don't know what they are doing." And the soldiers gambled for His clothes by throwing dice.

Luke 23:33-34 NLT

We don't know for sure, but it's likely that the soldiers heard Jesus' words: "Father, forgive them …" You'd think that would have had some sort of effect. Like, make them feel really bad, or at least ponder if perhaps they had made a cosmic mistake. But no. They carried on gambling away His stuff.

Sometimes you'll pray for someone and genuinely seek their best – your child or spouse or colleague – and they will continue to treat you like trash. Please don't lose heart. Not only does God see your sacrifice and your pain, but He knows exactly what it feels like because He's been there, done that, got the scars. It may not feel to you as if He is intervening as you think He should, but know that you can trust Him. He loves you more than you can fathom. He cares about the heartache you carry. He will not leave you as you are, or where you are.

You do know that you're not trash, right?

Jesus, it helps me to know that You know what this feels like. Strengthen me to behave the way You did. Amen.

Confession session

Confess your sins to each other and pray for each other
so that you may be healed. The earnest prayer of a righteous
person has great power and produces wonderful results.

James 5:16 NLT

You, me and everyone – we sometimes need to confess our sins to other people. That doesn't mean draping dirty laundry for all to see. It just means that if we only ever keep dirty laundry scrunched up damp in the basket it will start to smell really bad. David wrote about the unpleasant effects of secret sin: "When I refused to confess my sin, my body wasted away, and I groaned all day long" (Psalm 32:3).

When you understand the importance of having just a couple of trusted people – your husband, a sister or a few close friends – that you can come clean with, you'll be welcoming a new kind of freedom into your life. There's great power in inviting others to pray into your broken areas, and doing the same for them. There's great power in vulnerability.

It may also surprise you to find that confessing your sin to others doesn't have to be scandalous or awkward. It could – should – be a natural element of an excellent, beautiful relationship.

Whom do you trust to be gentle with your open heart?

*Jesus, help me to be brave enough to include others in my life,
so that they can help me to become more like You.* Amen.

The wonder of wonderful friends

"There is no greater love than
to lay down one's life for one's friends."

John 15:13 NLT

Made in God's image, we're wired for friends. Our great King stooped to be our Friend, first. He didn't need us, but He made us even though He knew how we'd mock and cold-shoulder Him. The clay of our making was still wet yet the plan was in place for Him to send His Son, Friend of sinners.

Would you take some time today to thank God for friends, and for how He teaches you to be a friend? Thank Him for ridiculous fun and honest advice and being heard and seen and allowed to cry. Thank Him for kindred spirits and inner-circlers and long histories to cherish and new pathways to plough and spontaneous connections to enjoy.

You might also determine to make wise time investments, and brave heart investments. As you trust God to order your private and public world, ask Him to choose your friends. Trust Him to help you hold them loosely – palms open – so that you can live each friendship as worship. Trust Him with the place that each friend holds in the spaces of your life.

Are there friends whose voices you need to tune out, or tune in, depending on the influence they have on you?

Jesus, thank You for the wonder of wonderful friends, and for Your example of kindness, courage and sacrifice. Change me into the kind of friend that reminds people of You. Amen.

Undisturbed, undisturbing

Let your gentleness be evident to all ...

Philippians 4:5 NIV

There's nothing gentle about the world. There are very few soft landings and kind words. There is little genuine warmth. Gentleness is what can powerfully – stunningly – set us apart as believers in Jesus.

The loveliest explanation I've ever heard for Peter's instruction to have a "gentle and quiet spirit" (1 Peter 3:4) is this: be undisturbed, and undisturbing. The context of Peter's teaching is marriage, and yet we'd do well to make a habit of being undisturbed and undisturbing in all our personal relationships.

For example, if the pace changes or the road splits or life happens and there's distance between you and a friend, determine that it need be only for the greater growth of new seasons, and never for wound-licking and resentment. If scars are unavoidable, find healing in grace, not gossip. Don't poke or prod or drop snide asides: don't disturb. Don't be oversensitive or take things too personally: don't *be* disturbed. Be brave enough to be the gentlest version of you.

How could you be an excellent, beautiful friend today: undisturbed, and undisturbing?

Father, make me a soft landing for my friends. Help me to be a happy, uncomplicated person to know and love, to Your glory. Amen.

Coping when people change

Whatever is good and perfect is a gift coming down to us from
God our Father, who created all the lights in the heavens.
He never changes or casts a shifting shadow.

James 1:17 NLT

People change. It's nothing new and it shouldn't surprise you.
And yet you've probably been hurt or shocked or angered by
how someone has changed due to circumstances, age or lifestyle
choice. You may have hoped and trusted that they would change
well – grow better with time – and you've been disappointed.

Hug the truth that God never changes, and where others may
have cast shifting shadows – or blown hot and cold – His love for
you is constant. Get your security and assurance from Him and
not from an unrealistic hope that your relationships will always be
stable or that the characters of those around you won't change in
harmful ways.

Take courage from the truth that as you grow more and more into
the likeness of Christ, you'll take on, more and more, the stability
of His character.

Today, how can you decide to love unwaveringly the person whose
strange changes have hurt you?

Lord, thank You that I don't ever have to wonder how I'll be received
by You. Change me by Your grace so that I can show the same steady
mercy to others that I desperately need them to show me. *Amen.*

It's just my personality

Don't copy the behavior and customs of this world,
but let God transform you into a new person by changing
the way you think. Then you will learn to know God's will
for you, which is good and pleasing and perfect.

Romans 12:2 NLT

There's a difference between temperament and character.

Temperament – personality or disposition – is in your DNA. No one really taught you to be chatty, reserved, analytical or impulsive. It's just part of your unique makeup. It's what makes you, you.

Character – the quality of the fiber of your being – is often expressed through your temperament, but it's taught, learned, copied and grown. So, you discipline your kids for dishonesty or disrespect because you can't change their personalities, but you can prayerfully, intentionally shape their characters.

Sometimes we confuse the two, or make them synonymous. A nasty remark is excused: "Sorry. I say what I think. It's just my personality." Like it's ok because people can't help being mean; it's just who they are. Of course, it's absolutely necessary to be patient and tolerant with people and their quirks. But it's never ok to use our personalities as an excuse for sin. We can't change personality, but we can – we *must* – surrender our characters to changing grace.

Is God challenging you to submit to Him what feels natural and inevitable to your personality?

God, thank You for making me just as You did.
Show Your glorious self to the world through
the temperament You created in me. Amen.

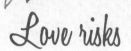

Love risks

"Your love for one another will prove to
the world that you are My disciples."

John 13:35 NLT

What if we all – in all our relationships – took a risk to let our love show, so the world would know?

Love risks being soft. See your offenders as brothers and sisters and remember that, like you, they know the freedom of the cross and God holds them tenderly. He is just as intent on their destiny as He is on yours. His love is relentless, unblinking and unbroken in the midst of their brokenness, and yours.

Love risks being strong. Dare to quiet with grace when all things brash and brazen are flung at you, dressed up as conversation. Steel yourself against the snide and the sulky and fling wide with strong arms the love that covers (1 Peter 4:8). Have the strong presence of mind to remember that someone's antagonism probably says more about them than it says about you. And then muster all your strength to fall to your knees, and forgive.

Love risks being sensitive. Pray for discernment and go with your gut. Love risks being supple. Bow low in the wisdom that breeds humility that leads to greater wisdom. Bend easy around other people's imperfections as far as you hope that they'll bend around yours.

Do you dare today to be soft, strong, sensitive and supple, and cut someone some slack?

Jesus, I want to take some radical love risks. Make me brave. Amen.

My kid's smarter than yours

Let someone else praise you, not your
own mouth – a stranger, not your own lips.

Proverbs 27:2 NLT

Pride poses a formidable threat to personal relationships. Legitimate parental pride – or pride in a friend's or colleague's stature or achievements – can flip over into a form of boasting or arrogance. (Like, we share happy news – the milestone or the promotion – because it reflects favorably on us.) Sometimes, taking pride in our kids' achievements or behavior says more about us and our priorities than it says about their success.

The opposite is true too. When we're disappointed in our kids or other loved ones – when we're embarrassed by their conduct or performance – it splashes our pride for all to see.

Of course we need to cheer for our little and other loved ones – affirm and encourage them. But maybe when healthy encouragement morphs into unhealthy pressure to achieve, then the key to tackling this area of pride is to take Solomon's advice: Let others praise you (and your kids too), not your own lips. Let your biggest concern be that your kids, your spouse or your friends know that they are well loved.

Is there a competitive edge among the women you hang out with, when it comes to kids or colleagues or social connections? What could you do today to break the trend?

God, help me to love, encourage, affirm and support my loved ones. But help me to leave the loud trumpet blowing to You. Amen.

Fun to live with

Everyone will share the story of Your wonderful goodness;
they will sing with joy about Your righteousness.

Psalm 145:7 NLT

D. Edmond Hiebert said, "Love is the highest blessing in an earthly home, and of this the wife is the natural center." Which means, if Mama ain't happy, ain't nobody happy. This is probably true for women of all ages, in all stages of life, because we have an innate ability to make or break the mood in offices, car parks, inboxes and church pews.

Maybe all it takes for us to grow in our relationships – and change the world – is to be intentional about finding ways to express our joy in God, and celebrate His character as we do life alongside all the other people He has created. We could pray for ways to make the best memories on the mundane plains of quotidian life. We could bless those around us by sometimes letting fun win out against common sense, hygiene or bedtime. We could live excellently before a watching world something of the abundant life that Jesus gives.

Are you fun to live with?

*Lord, create in me an infectious joy
that draws people into the wonder of You.* Amen.

Brave loving

Love is patient and kind. Love is not jealous or boastful or proud or rude. It does not demand its own way. It is not irritable, and it keeps no record of being wronged.

1 Corinthians 13:4-5 NLT

Paul's descriptions of love all start with a decision. One of the powerful, daily miracles of being a follower of Jesus is that whether we feel like loving someone or not, it *is* possible to love them.

You can choose to love someone by tearing up the evidence of what they did to you so that you can't use it against them in court, or in conversation, or in the sleepless hours of the night. Of course, you're not stupid. You have a mind that stores memories and you won't necessarily ever forget how you were sinned against. But you can choose not to replay the memory like a movie you love.

You can also choose to love someone by not living on the back foot – always defending and protecting yourself. Choose rather to play an *offense* position, not a *defense* position. Make a brave move towards someone. Get in there before they know what's hit them. Blind-side them – surprise them – love them first.

What love decisions do you need to make today?

Jesus, keep reminding me that I'm always only one decision away from loving someone. Amen.

AUGUST

Four-part harmony

Choose my rhythm and
My rock: I'll sing loud and bright –
The fragrance of You.

Heart, soul, mind and strength

"You must love the Lord your God with all your heart, all your soul, all your strength, and all your mind."

Luke 10:27 NLT

Doing life alongside other people is like singing our notes close up against each other to make a common, complex, beautiful resonance. So if we're off pitch – too flat, too sharp – we'll throw others off their notes. Things could get noisy, and nasty.

But before we can harmonize with others we need to practice our pieces alone with the Maestro. We need to find harmony with God. Moses sang one clear note: "Hear, O Israel! The Lord is our God, the Lord is one!" (Deuteronomy 6:4). Then he split the chord: "And you must love the Lord your God with all your heart, all your soul, and all your strength" (Deuteronomy 6:5).

The theme echoes and swells right through the gospels: love God with your heart, soul, strength and mind.

Whatever today holds, stretch your fingers across the keys of these twenty-four hours to play those four notes in sync with the Father. Playing your piece in the right key is the key to peace on the inside and the outside of life.

If you get nothing else done today, how could you play the four love notes – heart, soul, strength and mind – and let the rest of frenetic life happen around them?

God, I want to practice these holy harmonies until they get gloriously stuck in my head. Amen.

All your soul

"Study this Book of Instruction continually. Meditate on it day and night so you will be sure to obey everything written in it. Only then will you prosper and succeed in all you do."

Joshua 1:8 NLT

Meditation isn't mindlessness. It's mindful chewing on God's Word, to feed the soul. So, to love God with all your soul, you may want to start each day chewing on a little more Scripture than I offer here. Read. Think about how you might explain what you read to someone else. Reflect and re-read.

If you're already in the habit of Bible reading, you'll know that some days it's easy. A couple of psalms or a chapter of the gospels has you filled up and ready to tackle life. Other days it's thick-sludge trudging. Thoughts roam. Eyelids close ... It helps to tell yourself the truth, every day, that all Scripture is God-breathed (2 Timothy 3:16), and He wouldn't have put something in His book without good reason.

Make loving God in the Word your urgent to-do. Find ways to keep it fresh: use markers and margin-scrawling. Light a candle or read a passage out loud. Meet the King on the pages of His Word, so that it may be well with your soul.

Are you brave enough to love God with all your soul, by feeding it well?

God, flood my soul with a love of truth. Amen.

All your strength

Don't you realize that in a race everyone runs, but only one person gets the prize? So run to win! All athletes are disciplined in their training. They do it to win a prize that will fade away, but we do it for an eternal prize.

1 Corinthians 9:24–25 NLT

Loving God with all your strength is crucial because your flesh and blood and the skin that holds it in is what you've been given to work with, in your allotted earth time. It's where all your potential is stored. You get this one body to use for loving God and loving others. You need to do what you can to make it strong.

So, without obsessing, exercise. Even just for five minutes, twice a week. Something's better than nothing. Drink water. Shop healthy. Live a daily balance, not allowing the pendulum to swing idolatrous either way. That is, don't make food or fitness, fat or fat-free, a god. Before every meal, treat or temptation, pray, "God, choose my weight, choose my plate."

Loving God with your strength takes daily courage, and makes for an excellent, beautiful, useful you.

In terms of your eating, exercising and health in general, where do you need to build your strength?

Jesus, I give You my body. I want to use it to love and glorify You. Amen.

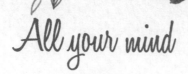

All your mind

I am doing a great work and I cannot come down.
Why should the work stop while I leave it and come down to you?

Nehemiah 6:3 NASB

Loving God with all your mind means staying on the wall, like Nehemiah did.

He had a thing to do. His secular vocation and connections gave him the skill set to unite and mobilize his people, spiritually and politically, against Persian opposition. The mission: rebuild Jerusalem's walls. He was humble. He was building a wall, not a résumé. He traded palatial influence for hard labor. He trusted that God was his promoter and he was excited about doing God's will, for God's glory.

There were distractions. Some guys who didn't like what Nehemiah was doing invited him for drinks in the nearby village. He knew they were out to get him, so he sent messengers to tell them that he wasn't coming down from the wall.

Your wall is the thing that calls and compels you. The thing you know is God's thing for you in this season. The thing that's most often and easily threatened by distractions. Stay on the wall and do your great work, even if people think your great work is inconsequential. Whatever your calling is, wherever you are – corporate ladder climbing or cookie baking – let your hands do the work of the moment. Do it bravely and beautifully.

What's your wall?

God, I am doing this great work for You.
I will not come down. Amen.

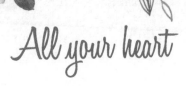

All your heart

Love each other with genuine affection,
and take delight in honoring each other.

Romans 12:10 NLT

Loving God with all your heart could mean forgetting about you and being fully present to others: giving all of you for all of those whom God scripts into your day. It might mean shutting down the distractions and devoting yourself to other human hearts.

Today, try to slow into the very tick of a second. This is where it's at: right here, now, where God has you breathing. You'll arrive at the future in good time. And if you mess up by missing out on the now, it won't *be* the future you're so feverishly imagining.

You could love God today by doing what today demands. Live each moment so it bulges into the next, making the minutes fat and full. Even the difficult minutes.

Weigh your words. Don't stress out about trying to save time, then lose that time forever because you've marred the minutes with hurry. There's enough time each day to do God's will, and giving people your undivided attention is never time wasted. It may even change the world.

Who could you really listen to, today?

*God, teach me to reach out with genuine affection
to those whom You've called me to love.* Amen.

Knee time

Devote yourselves to prayer with an alert mind and a thankful heart.

Colossians 4:2 NLT

We can all put on all sorts of performances and pretend to be all sorts of things. But when we're alone before the living God we can only ever be our very real selves. That's what Robert Murray M'Cheyne meant when he said, "A man is what he is on his knees before God, and nothing more."

If you want to be the truest, bravest, most excellent and most beautiful you, then prayer needs to be central to how you do life. You may need to figure out for yourself what "devote yourself to prayer" looks like in your world. Early mornings on your knees? Out loud in the traffic? Nighttime stargazing and conversation with the Creator?

Paul wrote to the Colossians that they should pray with an alert mind and a thankful heart. So, however and whenever you pray, make it intentional. Engage your heart and your mind. And give thanks. Praise God for His mercy and magnificence. Be, on your knees, the kind of woman you want to be in all the rest of life.

Have you prayed about it as much as you've talked about it?

Lord, keep me wide awake and excited to connect with You in prayer. Help me to take note when You bring someone to mind. I want to be obedient to Your nudging, and pray. Amen.

Oxygen

Pray in the Spirit at all times and on every occasion. Stay alert and be persistent in your prayers for all believers everywhere.

Ephesians 6:18 NLT

It takes courage and humility to make prayer the life-breath of your existence. Because no one sees or knows about your daily, breathe-in-breathe-out, quiet prayers. But imagine every believer on every patch of the planet walking through their days murmuring, thinking, sighing out one-liners to the King as they sign deals and homework diaries; as they drop kids at school and seeds into earth. Those kinds of prayers whispered out of our ordinary are never as small as they seem. They're world-changing.

So, set up prayer reminders throughout your day to keep you focused on breathing prayer. Like, when you're straightening your hair, pray, "God, make my paths straight." When you open the blinds in the morning, pray, "Lord, please open our home to those needing refuge or comfort." When you switch on a light, pray, "God, help us not to try to shine our own light but only to reflect Yours." Driving to an appointment, or setting the table, pray, "God, wisdom, wisdom, wisdom. Please, wisdom." You get the idea.

These habits develop rhythm, consistency and simplicity around prayer. They keep us breathing deeply the air that makes us fully alive.

Which boring chore or practical to-do could you use as a prayer trigger?

Jesus, keep me in conversation with You. Amen.

Found in translation

And we are confident that He hears us
whenever we ask for anything that pleases Him.

1 John 5:14 NLT

Jesus-followers with different traditions and temperaments pray differently, and it's pretty wonderful. It's sobering, humbling and encouraging to remember that God sees the heart of every person who prays. Anyone in any context can use prayer to show off. And anyone in any context can pour themselves out unaffected in the deep, otherworldly dialect of prayer.

How the words are rehearsed or stumbled out, honest and raw, is not for us to judge. It's also a relief to know that, "… the Holy Spirit helps us in our weakness. For example, we don't know what God wants us to pray for. But the Holy Spirit prays for us with groanings that cannot be expressed in words" (Romans 8:26).

When it comes to the language of prayer, all that we're responsible for is having the courage to *speak up*. Intercede. Actually *pray*, because if we pray for nothing then for sure we'll get no answer. None of us is totally fluent in prayer, but the way to learn any language is just to speak it. You're speaking prayer to God, and He won't laugh.

Could you practice speaking a bit of prayer today?

God, thank You that You understand me better than I understand myself. Make me brave to keep talking to You even when I don't have the right words. Amen.

I surrender my will;
I declare my dependence

"May Your Kingdom come soon. May Your will be done on earth, as it is in heaven. Give us today the food we need ..."

Matthew 6:10-11 NLT

You may have grown up reciting, at church or school, what's known as the Lord's Prayer. When it comes to the spiritual discipline of prayer, it's not necessary to rehearse and deliver a specific set of words in order to be heard by God. But for sure, the Lord's Prayer is a beautiful piece of gospel truth – the Messiah's careful instruction to His friends on how to pray.

I've heard it explained that the essence of what Jesus taught was this: I surrender my will (*Your Kingdom come, Your will be done ...*) because it's never about me and always about His glory; and, I declare my dependence (*give us this day our daily bread ...*) because I desperately need His help and provision.

For life's ordinary dreariness or shocking disasters, it can bring energy and resolve, or it can quiet the crazy and bring peace and perspective, to pray simply, *I surrender my will; I declare my dependence.*

Would you be brave enough today to submit to God your preferences, desires, and desperate necessities?

Jesus, have Your way. I trust You for all that I need. Amen.

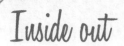

Inside out

How wonderful to be wise, to analyze and interpret things.
Wisdom lights up a person's face, softening its harshness.

Ecclesiastes 8:1 NLT

Spiritual discipline – placing yourself in the pathway of God's grace so that He can work in you – is never neutral.

Sure, you'll do it in secret, in the stillness of your own heart. There may not be any immediate or obvious tangible change in what your life looks like, and it may not feel as if intentionally seeking God has had, or will have, any influence on those around you.

Yet you couldn't be more wrong. Finding ways to love God – honestly, in your areas of greatest vulnerability, and with all your heart, mind, soul and strength – *will* have an effect on the outside of your life, and that *will* have an effect on others.

As you search the Scriptures for truth, and as you stay close to God in prayer, you'll increase in wisdom – which always leads to humility. And humility is displayed in soft features turned to God to reflect His light. It's so very becoming.

What can you do today to seek out – on purpose – the loveliness of wisdom?

God, I long for more of Your wisdom. Increase my understanding and discernment. Let wisdom light up my face, and my life. Amen.

Writing a good read

"In the same way, let your good deeds shine out for all
to see, so that everyone will praise your heavenly Father."

Matthew 5:16 NLT

Aristotle was born 384 years before the greatest story ever told – the one about a King who was nailed to a tree He seeded, bleeding so we could be free. But Aristotle knew a thing or three about storytelling. He reckoned that every good story needed:

Ethos – because a good story is credible and it has credentials. It's tried and trustworthy. It's true.

Logos – because a good story is compelling and clear and hinged upon logical connectors. There's structure and evidence and theme. It's excellent.

And pathos – because a good story moves and inspires and opens the heart. It's beautiful.

You and I, friend, are living our stories. People are reading the pages we're scrawling across days and months and decades. And our stories aren't supposed to be just entertainment or escape. They're to broadcast the majesty of our great God. They demand of us the courage and the craftsmanship to weave words of ethos, pathos and logos: truth, excellence and beauty.

Could you make today a real page-turner?

Jesus, give me the courage to write a true, excellent, beautiful story with all my days, to Your glory. Amen.

First things first

"But when you are praying, first forgive anyone you are holding a grudge against, so that your Father in heaven will forgive your sins, too."

Mark 11:25 NLT

For believers in Christ, this is not an option. It's a serious command. Jesus is explaining that there isn't much point discussing anything else with Him until you've forgiven those you are beating up in your heart.

Maybe, then, a good way to start your day in prayer is to ask God to hold up some mental flashcards – to remind you of the names of those you need to release to our just, righteous God. You could even do something practical, like write down the names (again?) on a piece of paper. Pray through the process of forgiving the people attached to those names. Then put that paper in the recycling bin – as a sign that you're done with the grudge, and you're trusting God to recycle the relationship.

When you talk to God, what do you typically start the conversation with?

God, before we go any further – would You help me let go of this person? You know the whole story, and how I feel about it. Will You carry the burden for me, so we can get down to other business? Amen.

Alphabet of peace

May the words of my mouth and the meditation of my heart be pleasing to You, O LORD, my rock and my redeemer.

Psalm 19:14 NLT

We waste words, every day. We say things we don't mean. We say things we *do* mean though they're things best left unsaid. We refer to ourselves in conversation, to swing the spotlight our way.

Jesus said that "whatever is in your heart determines what you say" (Matthew 12:34). Your words – in offices or department stores or on the phone with your friend or your mom-in-law – are as much a spiritual discipline as prayer or Word study.

Your words need to be brave, true, excellent and beautiful, to reflect your brave, true, excellent and beautiful heart.

Would you pray some poetry with me today? Here goes –

Jesus, help my words. Let my words land like soft thuds of truth in supple minds. Let smug words be shushed by the gulp of pride swallowed. Let love words be loud. Let laugh words dance light like candle flames. God, make me an alphabet of Your peace. Amen.

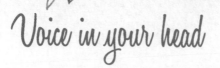

Voice in your head

My child, never forget the things I have
taught you. Store my commands in your heart.

Proverbs 3:1 NLT

Solomon was all about the wisdom. Wisdom was a matter of crucial spiritual mastery. You can almost hear him saying, "Kid, if you forget everything else I tell you, remember this …" He desperately wanted to be the voice in his son's head.

Who's the voice in yours?

Mocking, lying or unwise voices can come at you from obscure sources that you'll scarcely recognize as being destructive. It may be someone's silence that communicates volumes, and shrinks your confidence to nothing. It may be the social media perfection of strangers or friends, shouting that your life is boring or belittled. Maybe your mom, your Grade 2 teacher, your brother or your boss is the voice in your head, and maybe they're not all about the wisdom but all about making you feel worthless.

The only way to shut out the wrong voices is to turn up the right ones. Go out of your way to store God's commands in your heart and head. Discipline yourself to get wisdom.

Is there a negative voice in your head you're so used to hearing that you subconsciously make decisions to please it?

God of wisdom, I want to hear Your voice above all others.
I want to live according to what You say is true of me.
Help me to be disciplined about hunting for wisdom. Amen.

Salt submersion

"Salt is good for seasoning. But if it loses its flavor, how do you make it salty again? You must have the qualities of salt among yourselves and live in peace with each other."

Mark 9:50 NLT

What I love about swimming in the sea is not just surfing right up to the beach and laughing into wet sand with waves thumping me low. It's wading far out and diving under the swell where it's quiet and you can somersault through salt far below sun and bubble and froth and holiday shrieks.

Maybe that's what spiritual discipline is all about. Maybe it's less about riding the crest of the wave and more about diving deep. Against the current. Into the salt of truth that heals and preserves and flavors and sometimes stings. Maybe it's about the courage to swim lower and deeper against rising tides of compromise or controversy. Maybe it's about the more-ish flavor of humility – the delicious seasoning of peace.

Could you make time and space today to immerse yourself quietly in the truth?

God, I want to be drenched and salted with truth so that I can't help but change the flavor of everything around me. Amen.

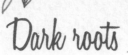

Dark roots

Work at living in peace with everyone, and work at living a holy life, for those who are not holy will not see the Lord. Look after each other so that none of you fails to receive the grace of God. Watch out that no poisonous root of bitterness grows up to trouble you, corrupting many.

Hebrews 12:14-15 NLT

We tend to think that because no one can *see* bitterness, we can hide it. And because we can hide it, it won't affect anyone else. This is *so* not true. Just like it's hard to hide ecstasy and it rubs off on those around us, it's hard to hide bitterness because it creeps out of us cloyingly and sticks to those around us too.

If you're a world changer, you'll want the right stuff to get all over those around you, because in turn they will grow good things wherever they go, and bit by bit the planet will become a better place and the fragrance of Jesus will fill the air (2 Corinthians 2:15).

If bitterness has taken root in you somewhere, you've got to rip it out. It grows fast and sends out sticky tendrils. Friend, be brave enough to tell yourself the truth about the destructive power of bitterness, and get gardening.

Is your irritability, apathy, anger or nastiness an offshoot of the bitterness that's rambling wild in your soul?

Lord, chop this bitterness off at the roots!
Dig it out! Free me! Amen.

It all adds up

"If you are faithful in little things, you will be faithful in large ones."

Luke 16:10 NLT

There is cumulative value to investing small amounts of time in certain things over a long period. Carving out little chunks of time each day for the important things has massive payoffs in this life, and the next.

There's no immediate benefit from a single time installment (like, one gym session doesn't transform your body) and there's no obvious cost if a time installment is missed (as in, you'll still have a pretty good day, even though you hit snooze instead of getting up to go running). But, over time, the returns on the time invested in achieving positive change are worth infinitely more than whatever else you would have spent that time on. The sacrifice of immediate pleasure is always worth the inevitable – eventual – advantage gained.

Being faithful in the small things – for a long time, over time – may not feel like living a brave, significant life. And yet as Mary Anne Radmacher says, "Courage doesn't always roar. Sometimes it's a quiet voice at the end of the day saying, 'I will try again tomorrow.'" Keep on keeping on. It all adds up to something spectacular.

How many small, good decisions might it take to change the terrain of today?

Jesus, keep me faithful in the small things. Amen.

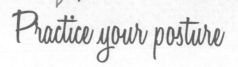

Practice your posture

Like newborn babies, you must crave pure spiritual milk so that you will grow into a full experience of salvation.

1 Peter 2:2 NLT

There's a Bible verse that makes our youngest son feel brave. It's stuck up by his bed, but you have to *lie down to read it.*

It makes me think how approaching God's Word is about posture and position. Too often I soapbox-stand over Scripture to fling it where it's convenient – to contrive, convince or cover up. Or I sigh and slouch over the pages. I make the Bible a pick-and-choose buffet, not daily bread: a feel-good Pinterest printable, not permanent truth and promise. I cut-and-paste it to prove or condone instead of breathing in what God breathed, then breathing it out – not as hot breath to wither, but life breath for a dying world.

Friend, what if we sat up straight – alert – and also bowed low – honest – and let the words of the Word find their way into crevices of hurt or confusion, hate or condescension? When we kneel quiet or lie still and let the Word read our inside stories – things change. The Word amends and adjusts our course, drawing hard lines of truth and painting brushstrokes of grace. It never bends to tendencies of culture but always bends tender around broken hearts. It reaches in, if you'll let it, to bring hope.

Have you read the Bible, or has the Bible read you?

God, I yield to Your ways, revealed in Your Word. Amen.

Be there

We prove ourselves by our purity, our understanding, our patience, our kindness, by the Holy Spirit within us, and by our sincere love.

2 Corinthians 6:6 NLT

Being present for others – in-the-moment attentive – can feel like time wasted. Hearing again your friend's perpetual struggle with her in-laws or listening to your kid unpack her day doesn't always feel constructive, or necessary, when there's a world of pressing problems to solve.

Yet we need to practice being present. Patient. Devoted and responsive, the way Jesus was to kids, crowds and lonely women. All our shared conversations, all the eye contact and the quiet spaces we leave so others can talk – all these add up to childhoods, friendships and solid-rock relationships. Don't wait to look at someone across a room and realize you're looking back over time, wondering how years could have been scoffed and wishing you'd taken the time to smear them thick with butter, to savor them slowly, by being there.

We can train ourselves to be there for the people in our lives, so that they hear the smile in our voices, not the sigh. It's the many moments of being there for each other that fill us all up, and make us brave and beloved.

Even if you have more urgent things to do today, could you pause for someone, and listen?

Jesus, help me to practice and get better at being there for others the way I need them to be there for me. Amen.

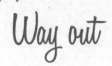

Way out

The temptations in your life are no different from what
others experience. And God is faithful. He will not allow
the temptation to be more than you can stand. When you are
tempted, He will show you a way out so that you can endure.

1 Corinthians 10:13 NLT

Some days unravel. The day's fibers whizz loose from my got-it-all-together ensemble. I'm stripped of kind composure, leaving loved ones to trip over tangled heaps of angry words at my feet and loose threads lying ugly to end the day threadbare.

Ever had a day unravel? How do we live that sort of day differently? How do we live a day *first* time round as if it was *second* time round and we knew *this* time round how to do it better? How do we pick up dropped stitches and tie tight the slack strings with truth and love?

Paul reminds us that God will show us a way out. Not a loophole, an easy exit or an *opt* out. A *way* out.

And we know the Way. Jesus said, "I am the way, the truth, and the life. No one can come to the Father except through Me" (John 14:6). We're not alone. The Way into the truth about how to live life is in the Father – He's right here with us in the mess, making it beautiful.

Will you look out for a way out today?

*God, thank You that You always
give me a way out of temptation. Amen.*

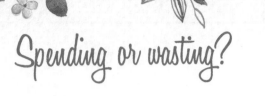

Spending or wasting?

Make the most of every opportunity …

Ephesians 5:16 NLT

Our car broke down once, in the middle of nowhere, on our way home from a long road trip. We waited for hours with two kids and a dog and tons of stuff on a pavement in a small town for a rental car coming from a slightly bigger town fairly far away. It was not fun. Our eldest son was five at the time. A couple hours in he asked me, "Mom, are we *wasting* our time or *spending* our time?" I realized the answer depended entirely on what I decided to do with my attitude.

No matter what unplanned or inconvenient circumstances overtake our schedules, we can always make the most of the time we find ourselves in. Waiting in line, we can pray. Waiting with friends or family, we can talk. It's never time wasted and always time well spent if we're asking ourselves the right questions, like: What's true about this situation? What courage does it demand of me? How can I spend this time excellently, and turn it into something beautiful?

What waste-of-time part of your day or your week could you reframe as time well spent?

Jesus, help me to see the opportunities in every slice of time, scheduled or unscheduled. Amen.

Holy comparison

But now you must be holy in everything you do,
just as God who chose you is holy. For the
Scriptures say, "You must be holy because I am holy."

1 Peter 1:15-16 NLT

At all costs, we need to discipline ourselves to avoid the comparison that leads to envy. But not every kind of comparison is bad. Like, it's good to compare prices in the supermarket and get the best deal. It's also good to compare yourself to others if your goal is to emulate their godly behavior.

Better still, if you're prone to comparing yourself to others? Compare yourself to Jesus. Because living brave for Him, *like* Him, will bring such deep peace and pleasure – such immense fulfillment – that it won't even occur to you to compare yourself to friends, colleagues or anyone else. You'll enjoy these people like never before, because the taught tension of constant comparison would have been cut slack by the kindness that Christ is forging in your character.

In all your actions and attitudes, dare to make it your spiritual discipline today to copy Christ.

Could you pick one aspect of your character, and compare it to Jesus? It's a cliché because it's true, so go ahead and ask yourself, "What would Jesus do?"

Jesus, I want to keep on looking to You as my example. Thank You that I needn't compare myself to anyone or use any other standard, because You have set the perfect paradigm. Amen.

Hidden

The Lord our God has secrets known to no one. We are
not accountable for them, but we and our children are
accountable forever for all that He has revealed to us,
so that we may obey all the terms of these instructions.

Deuteronomy 29:29 NLT

I love to see God *revealed*. Because God made manifest, obvious,
discernible and unmistakable – that's glory. Like Red-Sea-parted,
stick-turned-snake, call-down-fire, dead-man-raised kind of glory.

And yet there's glory in God *hidden* too. Glory in Elijah unharm-
ed, unfound by a brook. Glory in Jesus slipping unseen through
a crowd. Glory in galaxies measureless to man and glory in small
swirling electrons unobserved. Glory in our obedience – our highest
worship – which happens in the hidden heart where pretension is
laid low and only God sees.

Maybe we shouldn't always glory hunt under bright lights for big
things because maybe the most splendid beauty, and maybe the
greatest rewards, are in the secret, holy, hidden things.

Are you ok with what God has chosen to keep on the down low? Are
you ok to be one of His best-kept secrets?

God, I praise You for all that You keep hidden for Your glory. Amen.

First words

The LORD is close to all who call on Him, yes,
to all who call on Him in truth.

Psalm 145:18 NLT

As children, we learn to speak because someone speaks to us first. We learn the vocabulary that is spoken to us, near us, over us. God spoke to us first – through His Word – so that we'd learn the divine vocabulary of our heavenly Father.

Kids don't stress out wondering how they should talk to their parents. And parents are great at interpreting when their kids don't have quite the right words, because parents can decode the intentions of their kids.

Speaking to God is not that different. We can speak the truth of His Word – the words He spoke to us first – back to Him in prayer, knowing that He knows every thought and intention of our hearts.

Do you have a favorite part of Scripture that you could read back to God in praise, gratitude, love or longing?

God, I don't always know what to say to You or how to say it. Thank You for going first – for reaching out to me and starting the dialogue. Amen.

Whatever it takes

> My child, don't reject the LORD's discipline, and don't be
> upset when He corrects you. For the LORD corrects those
> He loves, just as a father corrects a child in whom he delights.
>
> *Proverbs 3:11-12* NLT

We've forgotten how to be ok with difficult truth. When stuff starts getting a little off-culture we stare at the floor or do the nervous laughter, let's-rephrase-that thing. Like, we're fine with the wounds of the Savior as long as we don't get scratched.

But what if the Savior is so deeply, wholly motivated by love that He will do whatever it takes to make you holy – even make you severely uncomfortable?

The challenge is this: if you're following Jesus, be afraid and don't be afraid. Be afraid because He's the living God of blinding splendor and He will not be mocked. Don't be afraid because you are His wholly beloved, forever redeemed child and heir, and He delights in you.

Is the Holy Spirit making you uncomfortable? Is He prompting you to wrestle with the truth, the whole truth and nothing but the truth? Which parts of the truth do you find most difficult to get your head or heart around?

God, I'm amazed that You love me enough to want me to be the best, most beautiful version of me. Thank You for delighting in me enough to discipline me. Amen.

Big rocks

The one thing I ask of the LORD – the thing I seek most –
is to live in the house of the LORD all the days of my life, delighting
in the LORD's perfections and meditating in His Temple.

Psalm 27:4 NLT

At this time of year, Christmas might still seem far away. It's closer than you think. So here's a question I've been challenged to live with: *When I get to sing my Silent Night at the end of the year, what do I want this year to have been about? What will have made it a success?*

You know the universal principle: that into the metaphorical container of your life you need to put in the big rocks *first* so that the small stones and the gravel and the fine sand all fit.

In your mind's eye, jump to Christmas – and be brave enough to look back. What do you hope to see? What needs to be there? The big rocks aren't necessarily the big *measurable* things. They're likely the things no one else will ever know about – time invested daily in important relationships, for example. Yet they're the things that will make all the difference, and they're the things that will last.

If priority determines capacity, what do you need to put first so that you've got space for excellence?

*God, show me the non-negotiables
and help me to put them first. Amen.*

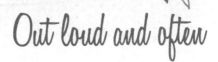

Out loud and often

When they heard the report, all the believers
lifted their voices together in prayer to God …

Acts 4:24 NLT

The "report" that's mentioned in this verse is of Peter and John's bold encounter with the Temple authorities, who were none too pleased with the message and the miracles that Peter and John were preaching and performing. When the other believers heard how things had gone down, their immediate response was to pray, courageously and out loud and all together.

Regular prayer with others – aloud and often – needs to become the habit of your life and mine. We need to constantly hold each other accountable to confident, faithful prayer being our first port of call, not our last resort. We need to be praying for each other – for the world – the way we would want to be prayed for, bringing our longings before God.

Are you comfortable praying out loud with others? Is it part of how you do life?

God, I want to include others in my conversations with You, to encourage them and me. Help me to step over any awkwardness that may get in the way. Amen.

Complaint rations

Do everything without complaining and arguing …

Philippians 2:14 NLT

Some time ago we tried something radical as a family. We limited ourselves to one complaint a day, each. One complaint per person per day. It didn't last long. Complaints slithered in. But here and there we could say, "Whoa! Save it for your one complaint tomorrow morning!"

The spiritual discipline of not complaining demands courage, because the truth is that it may affect some of your relationships. Griping and gossiping are the heart and soul of some friendships. We fuel each other's discontent.

Arguing and fault-finding are the standard operating procedure for some family relationships. We don't know how to relate to one another without nit-picking in some way. World-changers don't need to fill the silence with another objection. They uplift and encourage; listen and give thanks.

Who are the people you tend to complain to, or with? Who brings out the moan in you? Could you avoid those people, or rewrite the narrative of your conversations with them?

Jesus, help me not to whine. I want my words to be edifying, not destructive. Please change my heart, and keep me accountable by Your Spirit to speak as someone, not disgruntled or entitled, but satisfied with grace. Amen.

Sold out to freedom

*So Christ has truly set us free. Now make sure that you
stay free, and don't get tied up again in slavery to the law.*

Galatians 5:1 NLT

When my husband and I spent some time in Zanzibar's Stone Town, I was acutely aware that the people walking and working in those narrow streets were descended from people who were once labeled "thing", and sold. We wandered past the towers where slaves were stuffed to suffocate, and the old slave market – the last of its kind to be shut down forever so that freedom could be handed down from people, to people, to free people who could sing about amazing grace.

Except, *really*? Are we free and handing down freedom? Do our children look up to see us living free under grace? Does free spill from our lives to splash over theirs, to run full and free into their futures, and on to their children's children's free children?

The truth is that we *are* free. We just need to be brave enough to kick off our shackles of sin, cynicism or legalism – and *be* free.

What makes you feel trapped?

*Jesus, thank You so much for setting me free!
Thank You that I don't need to be a slave to
anything other than my desire to love You.* Amen.

Let it rain

… I have trusted in the Lord without wavering.

Psalm 26:1 NLT

One night at the coast, it rained all night. A soft steady pattering just audible above the wave roar. It wasn't a rain to take notice of, or to get people talking. But it went on *all night*.

Next morning, chunks of tar had washed clean out the road, into the sea. The river was a wide boiling torrent. Fish flopped in roadside puddles. Crowds turned out like so much driftwood on the beach to gaze awestruck at the flood wonder. There was no ignoring what the all-night right-here boring ordinary drizzle had done.

Maybe the way to flood the world with wonder is to let the rain keep falling, all night. The unremarkable routine rain of making beds, food and love. The everyday pitter-patter of wiping sinks and heart-slates clean. The humdrum rain-on-the-roof of paying tax and staying faithful, even when – *especially* when – no one is looking.

All that unremarkable goodness will collect in the furrows, ditches and widening waterways of a desperate world because God can turn tides and do something remarkable with straightforward faithfulness and simple faith. If we unremarkable people leading unremarkable lives would *be* the all-night rain, maybe people would turn out on the beaches to see the remarkable, irrefutable marvel that Jesus is our hope, and the hope of the world.

Would you be willing to believe that your seemingly unremarkable life can make a remarkable difference?

God, Your grace rains, and reigns. *Amen.*

Resolved

> Taste and see that the LORD is good.
> Oh, the joys of those who take refuge in Him!
>
> *Psalm 34:8 NLT*

At the beginning of this month, we took hold of the idea that spiritual discipline is the beautiful harmony of loving God with all your heart, soul, mind and strength. What we call "spiritual discipline" – Bible reading, prayer, fasting and the like – takes rigor and commitment and can somehow be misconstrued as being punitive when really, spiritual disciplines are just another way of describing ways of enjoying God. They're a gift, not a slog.

We could pray that, at the end of this month and at the end of every ordinary day lived well, there would be no dissonance in the music we're making. We could pray that every chord would resolve to truth. We could pray for the courage to say no to stress and no to mediocrity. We could pray for the courage to say yes to an uncomplicated life – yes to the simplicity of loving with heart, soul, mind and strength – so that even when life's load gets heavier, the harmony of the music we're making would lend rhythm. And, maybe, change the world.

Between now and the end of the year, what spiritual disciplines are you resolved to take with you?

Father, I want to position myself so that I get to know and experience You more deeply in every area of my life. Amen.

SEPTEMBER

Break bread, build bridges

"We all mold one another's dreams. We all hold each other's fragile hopes in our hands."

– *Anonymous*

Next door and beyond

"Love your neighbor as yourself."

Matthew 22:39 NLT

Christians have always been accused of forming holy huddles – shutting out those who are "other" and embracing the comfort and self-perpetuating credibility that comes from hanging out with those who are the same as us.

Except that, when Jesus told the Pharisees that loving your neighbor as yourself was the second greatest commandment – right alongside loving God – He didn't mean just the folks next door, or in the next pew. He meant every other fellow human.

Loving your neighbor doesn't mean unconditional approval of everything that's going down in someone's life. But it does mean deciding to be unconditionally committed to being actively compassionate to a wider community. It means being brave enough to make disciples and to live tenderly alongside them with the discernment to meet them where they're at – at home, at church, at work, online and in the world at large. It means understanding that to *have* community, you need to *be* community. Invite people into your home, not because the dishes are always done and the dog never walks mud across the kitchen, but because it's a place of peace where Christ is King. Love your neighbor by being a refuge – practically and emotionally – for world-weary travelers.

In this next month, what first step could you take to walk, not just next door, but a little farther down the street?

Jesus, You opened Your heart to comfort people with Your love. I want to be like You. Amen.

Essentials and non-essentials

Finally, all of you should be of one mind. Sympathize
with each other. Love each other as brothers and sisters.
Be tenderhearted, and keep a humble attitude.

1 Peter 3:8 NLT

We've been hosting a Thursday night cell group in our home for close on a decade. We laugh a lot, eat a lot, argue Apple versus Android, election versus free will, pray, laugh some more.

Our group is a mix. On the spectrum of Calvinist to Catholic to occasional charismatic, we've pretty much got everyone covered. We represent three local churches, which is unusual for a Bible study group but works just fine for us. We're a fusion of different passions, personalities, callings and careers. We have strong temperaments that don't water down opinion for the sake of another's ego. And yet there's deep love, acceptance and genuine care. We do life together – kids, work, stress and joy. We celebrate promotions and sympathize over setbacks. We mark births, deaths and adoptions.

And someone usually falls asleep on a couch. So we build rest into our community – meet for six weeks, rest for the seventh – and we rest on what Augustine said: "In essentials unity. In non-essentials liberty. In all things love."

Are you sure that you're so sure of the essentials of your faith, that you'll be comfortable with someone's different viewpoint on a non-essential?

God, keep me standing on rock-solid gospel.
Make me gentle and flexible to invite people in,
with their difficulties and differences. Amen.

The courage of soft

Above all, clothe yourselves with love,
which binds us all together in perfect harmony.

Colossians 3:14 NLT

Most communities – churches, families, schools, organizations and nations – go through sweet spots and sticky hard-going spots. But the truth is that communities keep going – keep growing – if you have the courage to keep building them with soft steel.

Being soft takes courage. Hard hearts are easy to keep. And they keep others out. Hard hearts scoff that soft hearts are pathetic. Weak. Soft in the head.

The hard hearts, however, have it wrong. Because it takes the marvelous strength of the brave to be soft. It takes courage to live the truth that *not* loving people is not an option for Jesus-followers. His love for us compels us to keep a soft heart and open doors to people in our lives and communities.

Whenever God calls us to do so, we need to be in the soft heart space of being ready to receive people, whether they arrive with sharp edges or whether they arrive with no edges and need to be held together.

Is God prompting you to be a little softer towards others? Could you write down some names?

*Jesus, even with infinite might, You are perfectly tender.
Please make me brave, and teach me to be soft.* Amen.

The courage of steel

As iron sharpens iron, so a friend sharpens a friend.

Just as it takes courage to be soft, it takes courage to be steel.

In our insular, individualistic culture, flaking out is the easy default. We make vast, shallow social media connections and it costs us nothing to hit "like" on someone's Facebook post because we don't really have to commit. We don't have to leverage time or resources – who we are – for the sake of someone else and their best interests.

It takes courage to be steel because people are heavy and you may need to carry them for weeks – years – a lifetime. You may need to be the steel that reinforces the faith of those God has given you to love. And sometimes you need to steel yourself against judgments or nasty remarks because of the people in your community. They're not perfect, and neither are you.

Being soft steel to others – being brave enough to say *yes* to community – means learning how to navigate people with wisdom, discernment and sensitivity, translating your good intentions into their reality. You'll need to be brave, but the beautiful outcome will be worth it.

Do you tend to make excuses for someone's questionable choice or irresponsibility, or are you willing to hold them accountable?

God, strengthen me to strengthen others. *Amen.*

No words

Then they sat on the ground with him for seven days and nights. No one said a word to Job, for they saw that his suffering was too great for words.

Job 2:13 NLT

When our baby boy was diagnosed as blind, we were broken. My husband didn't want people to offer him cheer-up-God's-in-control Bible verses. He didn't want to hear what a privilege it was to be chosen for this trial.

Some people avoided him because they didn't know how to penetrate his anger and grief. And he'll never forget what it meant to him when a friend arrived at his office in the middle of a work day and said, "I don't know what to say. I don't have words. But I'm praying so much for you." And when another friend took him for breakfast and said, "Me too. I know about being angry at God. I don't have answers but I'm with you and I'm praying."

Like Job's friends (before they totally messed up with stupid advice), they just sat silent with my husband in the dust, right there with him in his affliction. The power of that kind of soft-steel community? No words.

Have you ever been offended by someone's good intentions? Is there someone who needs you just to be there for them, rather than to be the solution to what they're facing?

God, give me the wisdom and sensitivity to know how to sit quietly with someone in the midst of their sorrow. Amen.

Say your best yes

Crowds of sick people – blind, lame, or paralyzed – lay on the porches. One of the men lying there had been sick for thirty-eight years. When Jesus saw him and knew he had been ill for a long time, He asked him, "Would you like to get well?"

John 5:3-6 NLT

There'll be times when you'll need courage enough to say *no* to community. Because a community can gather velocity and momentum and you can be swept up by the vision and compulsion to do *everything*.

Except that Jesus didn't do everything. He didn't heal everyone at the pool of Bethesda. For reasons we'll never know (and He doesn't owe us an explanation), He healed just that one man. He also didn't preach everywhere. He did the work of each day and He did it well.

We'd do well not to fill all the gaps that need filling in a community. We'd do well to do the work that we're uniquely called to do because less really is more. A few things done well are always better than a dozen things slapped hit-or-miss together. We're not supposed to be able to do everything or be involved everywhere. We're created with gaps, too, and there's something beautiful about giving those around us the space and freedom to use their gifts to fill us.

Why do you really find it hard to say no?

Lord, in my community, help me say the best yes, so that the right no takes care of itself. Amen.

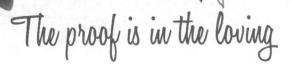

The proof is in the loving

"So now I am giving you a new commandment: Love each other. Just as I have loved you, you should love each other."

John 13:34 NLT

Jesus teaches His friends about community over their last meal together. Judas has left the room to split on Him. Jesus knows. Death is near. He's about to enter His glory – about to leave them. He looks with love around the table and gives His parting instruction: "Love each other. It's the thing that will convince the world that I'm for real" (John 13:35).

He doesn't say, "Memorize Scripture and build houses for Habitat for Humanity to prove to the world that you're My disciples." Though both are excellent ideas, He says, "Just as I have loved you, you should love each other."

Prioritizing love doesn't mean compromising beliefs. Even when it was offensive, Jesus never sidestepped the truth to placate or fit in. He was *steel*. Yet He had boundless mercy for sinners. He was *soft*. Community love means keeping on going back to Scripture – together – to wrestle with raw truth – thrashing out theology and leaning into grace and holiness in this culture of anything goes because, "By this everyone will know that you are My disciples, if you love one another" (John 13:35).

If aliens landed in your city today, would they figure out who you follow, by your love for His followers?

Jesus, let me be the yes for someone wondering if You are who You say You are. Amen.

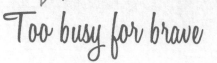

Too busy for brave

And let us not neglect our meeting together, as some people do, but encourage one another, especially now that the day of His return is drawing near.

Hebrews 10:25 NLT

There's no escaping creation's design. We're made for relationships. It's obvious, because God keeps making more and more people and putting them all on this one small planet. It's like He's saying, "This isn't crowded. This is community."

To which we say, "Sorry, but I don't have *time* for community."

And yes, the bad news is that people are busy. But the good news is that people have choices. We can decide to link into a community and spend energy forging relationships that are close, deep and strong.

It takes courage to trust God to order our private worlds and to bring across the tidy lines and blank margins of each day whomever He chooses. Because if we're honest we know that good days aren't about measurable achievements or what got ticked off a list. They're about our attitudes and actions, and how they affected the warm bodies around us. Maybe we need to bring this kind of community to dinner parties, school car parks, prayer groups and WhatsApp chats because by *this* everyone will know that we are His disciples. And by this, we might just change the world.

Is it possible that you're giving someone the impression that you don't have time for them?

God, transform me so that the busier I am, the better my choices. Amen.

Common ground

All the believers were united in heart and mind.

Acts 4:32 NLT

Cultures change. Churches and communities change with them. Worship bands playing off click tracks might be your current Sunday reality, and yet hymnals may be in your living memory. You can trace changes throughout Scripture in the way people got together to worship God. Attending a service in the tent of meeting in the Sinai Desert would have looked way different to meeting in the homes of New Testament early church believers.

And that's ok. Changing cultural expressions of our worship are great – so long as the culture never compromises the truth of God. Progress has been God's plan for humanity from the start. And yet shifts within the church can be hard to swallow, because things that have made you feel comfortable might change. There's grace for you. And really, your only response and responsibility is to make sure that your heart and mind are united with those of other believers, under the banner of unchanging, irrefutable truth.

Are you in quiet – or not so quiet – rebellion against how your church or community is changing? If you're the one longing for change, how can you begin to live the positive changes you hope for?

God, give us the grace, wisdom and discernment to never water down the truth in favor of the flavor of culture. Help us to be flexible in expression; steadfast in truth; united in heart and mind. Amen.

Accept and release

He did not retaliate when He was insulted,
nor threaten revenge when He suffered. He left His
case in the hands of God, who always judges fairly.

1 Peter 2:23 NLT

The power of Jesus is so evident in this verse. He withstood the blinding urge to retaliate. He wasn't in denial; He just rested in the power and justice of His Father.

If there's someone in your community intent on judging or annoying you, no matter how hard you try to make things right: *It is what it is.* This is your reality, in this relationship. Accept that you can't change the other person. As far as it depends on you, be at peace with all people (Romans 12:18). Entrust yourself to the God who judges righteously. He's got your back (Psalm 139:5). Honor the other person as much as you can for the strengths you see in them. Let go of the rest. Decide to be kind. Choose to let love blanket the bristly bits of your opponent (1 Peter 4:8).

Don't forget that you need others to spread that blanket over you too, and kiss you on the forehead as you snore on the couch of oblivious imperfection.

Could you accept someone today, release them to God, and stop trying so hard?

Father, help me to recognize that people don't fit into tidy boxes;
me least of all. Help me to be at peace with that. Amen.

Community critic

"And why worry about a speck in your friend's
eye when you have a log in your own?"

Matthew 7:3 NLT

When we're in the thick of community, it can be easy to take offense because inevitably we'll bump up against someone who will splash their coffee on our clean clothes. And when that happens, it can be hard to see how we're also spilling our disapproval and casting our caustic judgments on those around us.

Carry your words carefully. Sift them, and only choose to share those that make souls stronger. Because what you're saying to someone – your kid, your pastor, your colleague or the store manager – it might be *true*, but it may not be necessary, or helpful, or conducive to progress emotionally, spiritually, socially or practically.

It's embarrassing to admit, but I'm always either living for my glory, or God's. To check which one it is, I check my criticism levels. In real life or in my imagination, am I ranting against anyone who doesn't think, live, drive, parent or work like I do? My fault-finding shows that I'm all about me. I know then that I should consider not saying another word until I've remembered that God is on the throne, not me.

How are your criticism levels? What are they reflecting about your walk with God?

O Lord, my digging for dirt and flinging it freely just shows my own ugliness. Help me to extend grace. Amen.

Irrational

A person with a changed heart
seeks praise from God, not from people.

Romans 2:29 NLT

You can probably think of a time when your pride was injured and your lashing out went a little overboard. And afterwards – when you had calmed down and your vision, blurred by injured ego, had cleared – you cringed and regretted it. I sure can.

Pride can make us irrational. Like, if you ask God to use you, then you shouldn't be indignant when you feel used. And if you say you don't do things for the thanks, then you shouldn't be piqued when thanks doesn't come. And if you're totally honest? Sometimes you don't even necessarily take pleasure in the attention you're craving or manipulating your way into getting. You just take pleasure in the fact that you have more of it than someone else.

We're smart enough to know that thinking like this is not a good use of our brains, right? If we seek our recognition from God alone it will keep our pride in check, and that will make us far more reasonable, realistic, beautiful women of God.

What are the triggers that make you react irrationally to injured pride?

God, humble me. Help me to think straight. I want to seek affirmation from You, first and foremost. Amen.

Glass

We now have this light shining in our hearts, but we ourselves
are like fragile clay jars containing this great treasure. This makes
it clear that our great power is from God, not from ourselves.

2 Corinthians 4:7 NLT

Glass comes in kaleidoscopes of beauty and brutality. It's stained cathedral windows, stories high and brilliant. It's beer bottles jagged and bloody. It can be an old vase loving kitchen roses or a cracked tumbler swilling something strong or dusty panes made soapy-clean on a bright day.

People are like glass: we may look different and have different stories, but we're all fragile. Glass, however, isn't always broken. People are. And because we're broken we cut, and others bleed. Sadly, and too often, we don't even realize that we have sharp edges.

The good news is that Jesus sweeps up our shattered lives. He shapes them, and shines them to dazzle. So perhaps the brave thing to do is to kneel in the shards that slice and scratch, and pray for His molten touch to blow and cleanse – reform – renew – reflect – and blaze His glory.

Are you the glass that cuts, or shines? Do your words wound others, or hold water to refresh?

Jesus, help me to live transparently.
Make me a clear reflection of You. Amen.

Above and beyond

"So he returned home to his father. And while he was still a long way off, his father saw him coming. Filled with love and compassion, he ran to his son, embraced him, and kissed him. His son said to him, 'Father, I have sinned against both heaven and you, and I am no longer worthy of being called your son.' But his father said to the servants, 'Quick! Bring the finest robe in the house and put it on him. Get a ring for his finger and sandals for his feet.'"

Luke 15:20-22 NLT

Imagine you work in a store. You're caught with your fingers in the till. You get fired. Then your boss finds you, forgives you, and not only gives you back your job but makes you manager. Promotes you, just because he's so thrilled to have you back on the team.

That's how God forgives us. He doesn't just call it quits. He clothes us in righteousness (Isaiah 61:10), adopts us and calls us daughters of the King. He *more than* restores us to a right relationship with Him.

We need to imitate God in the way we forgive others, in whatever community we find ourselves. Our forgiveness should be more than just begrudging consent that a debt has been cancelled. It should illustrate something lavish – something entirely undeserved – and breathtaking in beauty.

How can you go above and beyond today?

God, help me not to sulk. Be my strength and joy to love. Amen.

Things that go bump

So encourage each other and build each other up,
just as you are already doing.

1 Thessalonians 5:11 NLT

I've learned that whenever I commit to any community – church, family, friends, marriage – God sends people my way to reveal things about me. Communities make me bump into all sorts of folks but mostly I just bump into myself. I don't know the dark depths of my character or my intuitive reactions until I'm backed into a corner or challenged or annoyed or envious.

And the key to being transformed, as I live and move through the big and small Venn-diagram communities that make up the patterns of my life, is humility, and hunting for ways to encourage and add value to those around me. This means that the posture of my heart should be so kind, so honoring, that every handshake or hug or casual "Hi" should say, *"You're more important than me."*

The privilege of living in community is that all sorts of people show up to give us what we don't necessarily want. Almost always it shows us how much we need Jesus. Almost always it's a sparkling opportunity to choose a response that will show the world some of His grace.

Who have you bumped into this week?

Jesus, thank You for giving me up close and personal opportunities to humble myself and encourage others. Amen.

Understood

Each heart knows its own bitterness,
and no one else can fully share its joy.

Proverbs 14:10 NLT

You probably have a handful of inner circlers who understand you almost perfectly. But the truth is that none of us will ever be fully – wholly, ultimately – understood by anyone but God. None of us can climb completely inside another's skin and really – *really* – know what life feels like for them.

You will be misunderstood. Guaranteed. The King of kings – the One with whom you've had the courage to align your destiny – was misunderstood. So it shouldn't surprise you or stress you out when people misunderstand your goals, dreams or priorities. It shouldn't surprise you or stress you out when they think you're pathetic or paranoid, weird or wasting time, myopic and missing the big thing. Trust Him who sees the big picture to *choose for you*: your appointments, your direction, your friends, your schedule, your level of involvement in work, ministry or social events. Take responsibility for your slice of the relational pie in each of your connections – try your best to understand your people – and then rest in the truth that the King of the universe understands you, perfectly.

Are you satisfied with being understood by the One who made you, loves you, and shapes your destiny?

Jesus, with You, I never have to explain. Thank You! $\mathcal{A}$*men.*

Reaffirm your love

I am not overstating it when I say that the man who caused all the trouble hurt all of you more than he hurt me. Most of you opposed him, and that was punishment enough. Now, however, it is time to forgive and comfort him. Otherwise he may be overcome by discouragement. So I urge you now to reaffirm your love for him.

2 Corinthians 2:5-8 NLT

What I love about Paul is that he's real about the devastation caused by the person who sinned against him and, it would seem, the whole community. He doesn't sweep it all under the church carpet. He is compassionate towards those who have been hurt – he commiserates – and yet he is brave enough not to allow himself and the community involved to wallow or to keep on kicking up the mud of what the perpetrator has done. He calls the community to reach out and comfort the guy, because love always goes first. He calls them to reaffirm their love for him by re-establishing a relationship.

It's one thing to put behind you what someone has done and move on. It's quite another to face them – engage with them – and be tender.

What would it look like, practically, for you to reaffirm your love for someone today?

Lord, thank You that You are fully aware of the effects of sin in our community. Show me how to have a soft heart towards others in the middle of the mess. Amen.

Christian karma?

"Do not judge others, and you will not be judged.
Do not condemn others, or it will all come back against you.
Forgive others, and you will be forgiven."

Luke 6:37 NLT

We live in a cause-and-effect world. Study hard, and you get good grades. Sneak out at night, and you get grounded. Whole religions have been developed around this universal principle.

Yet, this is just the thing that sets Christianity apart. There's no cause-and-effect at play in the salvation miracle. God broke the natural order and did something radical by sending His Son to pay the price we should have paid for our own sin. He removed the cause-and-effect punishment we had coming.

But we still live in a cause-and-effect world. How you treat others has an influence on how you will be treated. For sure, you should never be frightened by the empty threat or lulled by the false promise that what you do will come back to bite you, or bless you. But your actions and reactions influence others because they are the bricks with which you're building relationships. Build wisely.

Yesterday, who did you treat as well as you'd hope for them to have treated you?

God, I want to honor You by the way that I show grace and goodness to others. Not so that I can get some sort of reward, but because it brings joy. Amen.

Ego trip

… Don't think you are better than you really are.
Be honest in your evaluation of yourselves, measuring
yourselves by the faith God has given us.

Romans 12:3 NLT

You're probably aware that pride damages relationships in a community. It can drive and dominate our actions and attitudes. Maybe, like me, you refuse help because you want to prove that you can manage just fine on your own. Maybe you push your opinions and push others right over in the process. Maybe you enjoy feeling superior to someone else because you're convinced that *you* have made far better life choices.

We know that we can repent of pride, be forgiven and have the assurance of eternal salvation. We can rest in the relief of grace and God's goodness in justifying us for ultimate glorification in eternity. But between justification and glorification comes sanctification: walking with Jesus in the now so that He rubs off on us. And we only need to walk a few steps with the Savior before His fierce gentleness has us dealing with pride. Like, every day. After day. After courage-mustering day. Daily cleaning out our hearts. Daily asking Him to sharpen our conscience, quicken our senses, prod us, humble us, and love us, to love others.

Where does pride trip you up?

*God, help me change the narrative in my head
and in my relationships, so that I don't promote
myself in my thoughts or conversations.* Amen.

Make music with much

How good and pleasant it is when
God's people live together in unity!

Psalm 133:1 NIV

My son had a favorite bath toy when he was little: a plastic trumpet with tubes that he could fill up to different levels with water, so that each plastic knob that he pressed produced a different cute plastic pitch when he blew into the thing.

So, you can fill a plastic trumpet tube with just a little bath water, and *it makes a sweet sound*. Or you can fill a plastic trumpet tube with a lot more of the same water, and *it makes a sweet sound*. The sounds are different – higher, lower – but both are sweet. It's the same with relationships.

Some relationships are deep: meaningful, close, harmonious. Thank God, and pray against complacency. Those relationships still involve human beings, who have a long track record of doing stupid things to hurt each other. Be deeply at peace with the people you're deep with, and make a sweet sound.

Of course, cancerous malice and misunderstanding can lurk even in deep relationships, which is unspeakably painful. Decide to love. Decide to honor. Play the notes of that person's strengths. Listen for a sweet sound and keep playing those notes. Don't necessarily expect a symphony to echo back. Not immediately, anyway. Love is patient.

Could you let someone you love know today how much you enjoy doing life with them?

*Lord, You've surrounded me with the sweet
sounds of amazing people. Thank You! Amen.*

Make music with little

Do all that you can to live in peace with everyone.

Romans 12:18 NLT

Back to the plastic trumpet we played yesterday. Some relationships are shallow – superficial and possibly fraught with glaring incompatibilities. But fortunately, it's not about you. It's actually quite freeing to think that it's ok to feel injured, judged or disregarded. You don't have to have deep, harmonious, I-totally-get-you relationships with everyone. You just need to *make a sweet sound*. You just need to put a little bathwater in those tubes and play the notes you know.

So with those people? Choose your attitude. Be kind. Be interested. Surrender your pride. Keep praying that God would best position you to reflect His glory and the grace of Jesus. And relish the moments of connection that do magically happen now and then in those I'm-not-sure-I-trust-you relationships – a shared laugh, or the fact that you both love licking the icing off your Oreos, or whatever. Know in those congruous moments that something is resonating with God's image stamped in you.

How can you avoid playing bars of discordant conversation with casual acquaintances?

God, with people whom I don't know well, and who don't know me, help me to play the sweet sounds I do know. Amen.

Do not react

> Most important of all, continue to show deep love
> for each other, for love covers a multitude of sins.
>
> *1 Peter 4:8 NLT*

It's hard to keep calm when you're slighted, and it's usually even harder when someone wrongs your kid or your husband or your sister. Claws come out, right? This makes you a normal human.

We'd be wise to ask God to help us snuff out smoldering situations with love. Buy yourself time to calm down, and process. Do. Not. React.

Victims react. They lash out livid and all it screams is *desperate* and *afraid*. And you're not a victim. You're an overcomer (Romans 8:37). Do not react, because maybe *you chose* part of the difficult reality you're facing? How much of the wrong are you possibly responsible for? Do not react, because it may not be as bad as you think. And do not react, because you know it's stupid to make the call or send the mail before you're calm and kind again. Process. Bide your time. Clutch wisdom. But –

Do. Not. React.

Is there an inflammatory situation or a volatile relationship over which you could throw a blanket of love? Could you put your anger to bed under that same blanket?

God, help me not to react furiously and thoughtlessly.
Help me to forgive my offenders or the offenders
of those I love by covering their sins with love. Amen.

Then, react

Dear brothers and sisters, if another believer is overcome by some sin, you who are godly should gently and humbly help that person back onto the right path. And be careful not to fall into the same temptation yourself.

Galatians 6:1 NLT

When you or someone you love has been sinned against, and you've calmed down enough to analyze and decide, *then* you can react.

React in prayer and practical wisdom. React by telling yourself or your loved one that we can't do much to make others more patient or perceptive, more considerate or observant, but we can work on the insides of us. We can become the kind of people the world needs more. React by reminding yourself to reach out to others in a way that inspires reciprocation. React with discernment. Judge others on their good intentions. Be kind. Judge yourself on your actions. Be courageous. React on the run. You can't predict life. You can take all the right advice – make all the right rules and routines – but still only God knows what's coming. Try to be ready for, well, anything. You're going to have to make sense of the pain right here and now in the rhythm and the real of life.

Are you ready to react?

God, I want to honor You in all my actions and reactions. Give me wisdom with my ways and words. Make me brave to reach out and react rightly. Amen.

Every breathing soul

The generous will prosper; those who refresh
others will themselves be refreshed.

Proverbs 11:25 NLT

I heard a preacher say once, "D'you know how to tell if someone needs encouragement? If they're breathing." Because every one of us – every breathing soul – needs encouragement.

I sometimes hold back from encouraging someone because my encouragement feels so small – so insignificant. And yet encouragement is *never* small when you're on the receiving end of it. It's never a small thing when you realize someone has stopped to notice – seen what stirs your heart – and offered words to give you strength to keep going.

En-*courage*-ment means just that: to be engendered with courage. And the thing about encouragement? It's the people you think need it least who need it most. The bravest are also the most vulnerable. Our visually impaired son throws himself fervently at most of life. He's pretty unaffected by the doings of others, because he can't see them. I want to be that kind of brave: oblivious to my own insecurities. So, instead of feeling like the uncool mom on the edge of the cool conversations of cool moms who always have great hair and don't need my encouragement, I should risk encouraging someone who looks cool but probably isn't. Maybe you should too.

Need refreshing? Whom can you refresh?

God, show me today the people I can encourage. Amen.

Who do you say I am?

Then He asked them, "But who do you say I am?"
Peter replied, "You are the Messiah."

Mark 8:29 NLT

There are going to be people who disagree with how we live out our faith. Somebody probably rolls their eyes at you because you call yourself a Jesus-follower instead of a Christian, or because you're doing Lent and they're speaking in tongues, or because you raise your hands and they have tattoos, or because you're into Word study and they're into world saving. Or whatever.

The issue isn't how we who's-who others. It's who we say Jesus is. He asked His disciples, "Who do people say I am?" (Mark 8:27). And people were saying all sorts of things which didn't bother Him because He knew who He was and His heart was only after what His disciples believed.

The brave, beautiful thing to do, then, is to let the truth of *just that* slice through our debates and dislikes. Because for those of us who name the name of Christ – who declare that He's the Son of the living God, Savior of the world – it's ok to argue Christian culture, but it's never ok to be anything other than a kind, gracious answer to, "Who is Jesus?"

What would change in your community if you and others let Christ's character in you overcome the differences you have with one another?

Jesus, You are the Messiah. Help us to remember that, in every heated discussion and icy silence. Amen.

Blind spot

"… To open their eyes, so they may turn from
darkness to light and from the power of Satan to God."

Acts 26:18 NLT

Everyone has an actual blind spot: the optic nerve's point of entry on the retina. It's insensitive to light.

We all have personality blind spots too: areas where the truth about ourselves is obstructed. The fantastic thing about being created for community is that God gives us close friends and prayer warriors who see things we don't, and help us. There isn't one of us who doesn't need the help and insight of others.

Personality blind spots can also obstruct our view of the church. Too many churchgoers are all about being satisfied. They want church done on their terms, according to their needs, desires and personality preferences. And when we lose perspective, we get demanding.

When we stop seeing what church is actually all about – meeting with others to build our faith and theirs – we start wanting church to be about what suits us. As soon as our focus is back on Jesus and being the fragrance of hope in a desperate world, then we can see again how spacious our community is – how much room there is for a diversity of personalities.

Have you ever asked someone who knows you well to tell you what your blind spots are?

God, help me to let others help me to see myself. *Amen.*

Know your type

Don't be selfish; don't try to impress others.
Be humble, thinking of others as better than yourselves.

Philippians 2:3 NLT

Your personality – more than shared interests or experiences – is possibly the most significant determining factor in how well you get on with others. Within community, it's good to understand whether you're outgoing or reserved, self-expressive or self-controlled, cooperative or competitive. Each of these traits can set you up for relational disaster if misunderstood or mismanaged. If you *know* who and how you are, you can temper your relational course more realistically and successfully. You will also better understand others.

Knowing your personality type makes you more aware that, if someone irritates you, you can be pretty positive that you irritate them. Keep close that bit of reality – and keep checking it. It keeps us gracious, tolerant, and forgiving. Often, it keeps us quiet.

But be encouraged: you are not responsible for anyone else's happiness. And no one but you is responsible for yours. If you feel hemmed in – discouraged from serving – because your personality type doesn't quite fit the context you're leaning into, then check your heart. Check your motives. Check for sin. If your tests come back clear, then go ahead and serve, with a strong spirit and a soft heart.

How does being an introvert or extrovert influence how you relate to colleagues, family members, friends, or others in your church community?

God, You created my personality.
Help me to use it for Your glory. Amen.

Energized

For you have been called to live in freedom, my brothers and sisters. But don't use your freedom to satisfy your sinful nature. Instead, use your freedom to serve one another in love.

Galatians 5:13 NLT

If we've yielded our lives to Jesus, then we're called to serve as He did: to leverage all of ourselves for the sake of others, in all the ways we know how.

And yet the church is full of tired, disgruntled, disillusioned people who feel used – unappreciated – unthanked. People who have signed up to commit, commit and overcommit to every possible committee. People whose self-induced martyrdom doesn't attract anyone to the gospel. People who have believed the lie that burnout and busyness equals godliness or success.

And yet when we stay close to God – reading, repenting, praying and positioning ourselves to listen – and when we lean into the thrill we feel at an opportunity to serve – then we are *energized* by serving, not burned-out.

If you're not sure what kind of ministry would suit your personality? Determine whether you favor high-risk or low-risk, people or projects, following or leading, teamwork or going solo, routine or variety. Steve Jobs would have asked you, "What makes your heart sing?" Knowing this will help you wash the right feet, as you discover or create opportunities to serve excellently.

What ministry opportunities make you go, "Now that I could do"?

Father, show me where my passion and my aptitude can collide for Your glory. Amen.

Cyber-community

History merely repeats itself. It has all been
done before. Nothing under the sun is truly new.

Ecclesiastes 1:9 NLT

Doing community in the no-man's-land of social media can be tough. We risk being hit by the shrapnel of those who run wild and stupid through virtual minefields.

To be brave, beautiful women of God, we need to navigate the technosphere: harness its power; detect its dangers. Devices have changed the way we plan, process and form relationships. Links to vast audiences ultimately isolate us. I once taught a boy who, busy on his tablet and annoyed at the guy looking over his shoulder, said, "Dude, it's an iPad. Not an usPad."

Yet, there's grace for our generation and the generations coming after us. Thanks to social media, never in history has it been faster or easier to spread hope.

But we need to be brave enough, online, to model honesty and accountability. We need to be brave enough to be credible Christians: willing to engage and *listen* in a screen world to show that we care, because the purpose of social media is relationships and it's a beautiful means of being all things to all people (1 Corinthians 9:22).

The Greek word that gives us *icon* meant more than image or picture. It meant window. When someone clicks on the icon of your life, does a window open with a view to Jesus?

Jesus, let my values online and offline
be consistent with Your truth. Amen.

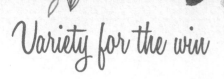

Variety for the win

O Lord, what a variety of things You have made! In wisdom
You have made them all. The earth is full of Your creatures.

Psalm 104:24 NLT

The Bible's *first verse* reads, "In the beginning God created the heavens and the earth". The Hebrew subject, "God" (*Elohîm*), is plural, yet the action it does – "created" (*bara*) – is singular. So, the Creator is a plural-yet-one Being. Variety is part of His very essence.

When it comes to people, God shows off His creative multiplicity by making inspirers, caregivers, performers, executives, visionaries and hundreds of other personality types within a miscellany of nations, cultures and socioeconomic spheres. He makes all these people in the dazzling multicolors of His image because His image mirrored in His handiwork glorifies Him.

All those personalities can mean it's difficult to understand – never mind get along with – people who interpret life differently from us. Yet the psalmist says, "In *wisdom* You have made them all." A *wise* God made the people you think are weird. And to display God's glory, we need to be a plural-yet-one community, embracing our personal differences instead of taking our differences personally. The differences are necessary to reflect God's complex magnificence. He takes pleasure in all He has made. That goes for your, and every other, personality too.

Do you see evidence of God's creativity in the temperament of someone you don't necessarily get along with?

*Creator of atoms, galaxies, introverts and extroverts,
thank You for displaying Your glory through rich diversity.* Amen.

OCTOBER

Night-lights and lullabies

"There are no 'ifs' in God's world. And no places that are safer than other places. The center of His will is our only safety … let us pray that we may always know it!"

– *Corrie ten Boom*

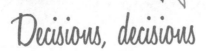

Decisions, decisions

Then Elijah stood in front of them and said, "How much longer will you waver, hobbling between two opinions? If the LORD is God, follow Him! But if Baal is God, then follow him!" But the people were completely silent.

1 Kings 18:21 NLT

Elijah was about to call down fire from heaven to prove that God was God and Baal was not. He was committed. Courageous. Dedicated and decisive. And his demeanor was in sharp contrast to the people he addressed, who vacillated – dithered – between conflicting beliefs.

Life is a series of decisions. We have to decide what to do about what has happened to us, and what hasn't. We have to decide to make certain things happen and decide to prevent other things from happening. Yet we never know what will happen in the future, not even with all the world's scenario planners airing their predictions on talk radio and Twitter.

Decisions involve the heart as much as the head. And if the heart is shadowed by doubt, confusion or regret, then making good decisions – or any decisions – isn't easy. We waste time. We miss opportunities. Like Elijah, who knew the truth about God and threw his weight behind it, we need to weigh things up wisely and commit courageously.

Are you struggling to make a decision? Do you have all the facts? If not, do you believe that God does?

God, when the time is right, help me to be decisive and dependent on You for wisdom. Amen.

Eliminate

If you need wisdom, ask our generous God, and He will give it to you. He will not rebuke you for asking. But when you ask Him, be sure that your faith is in God alone. Do not waver, for a person with divided loyalty is as unsettled as a wave of the sea …

James 1:5-6 NLT

Sometimes decisions are obvious. Other times, they're complicated and emotional. There can be a raft of compelling, well-researched reasons that support each side of a should-we-or-shouldn't-we argument. Sometimes, neither decision is wrong in and of itself. We can talk ourselves into or out of almost anything.

So we worry. What's right? What's God's will?

When we had tiny babies who cried at night, I'd bring them into the light. In the glow of the lit passage, I'd go through a process of elimination. Hungry? Wet? Hot? Cold? Coughing? Puking? I would feed, change, wrap, unwrap or drive to the emergency rooms depending on the evidence. If it seemed nothing was the matter, I did what seemed good and wise in the moment. I would rock, shush, or hold them close. Until the fear passed, theirs and mine.

With decisions, switch on the light of God's Word. Go through the elimination process. Clear commands? Obvious principles? The truth sets us free from fear, and that freedom lends us the courage to choose.

Does God's Word say anything specific about the decision you're making?

Lord, give me wisdom to know which options I should eliminate. Amen.

Loud and clear

Wisdom shouts in the streets. She cries out in the public square.

Proverbs 1:20 NLT

God's Word doesn't have a *thou shalt* or *thou shalt not* for every situation. Thankfully, wisdom is shouting in the streets. Wisdom is available. Unconcealed. Loud, if we'll just listen. And wisdom – common sense – looks at how the world predictably works and traces cause-and-effect patterns, using these to make decisions. A great question one preacher asks is, "In light of my past experiences, my current circumstances, and my future hopes and dreams, what's the wise thing to do?"

From common sense, move back to the Word. Let Paul's wisdom quiet you. He reminds us that we needn't obsess about finding God's will because it's not lost. He wrote, "Don't copy the behavior and customs of this world, but let God transform you into a new person by changing the way you think. Then you will learn to know God's will for you, which is good and pleasing and perfect" (Romans 12:2). He went on to say, "For the Kingdom of God is not a matter of what we eat or drink, but of living a life of goodness and peace and joy in the Holy Spirit" (Romans 14:17). Which gives you this checklist:

☐ Is the decision you're making good, pleasing and perfect?
☐ Will it result in goodness, peace and joy?

Thank You, God, for common sense and concrete truth. Give me clarity, insight, discernment and understanding. Help me listen for wisdom. Amen.

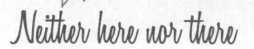

Neither here nor there

The LORD is my light and my salvation – so why
should I be afraid? The LORD is my fortress,
protecting me from danger, so why should I tremble?

Psalm 27:1 NLT

When you're faced with a decision where you could go left or right with no glaring curse or abundant blessing either way, you may need to settle your decision-making fear with God. Where there are convincing reasons both for and against a decision, wrestle and pray and read and think and talk and listen until the resulting peace or turbulence makes it clear what God is nudging or plunging you into.

And if you really – *really* – feel neither peace nor turbulence – if there has been no clear directive – do what seems good, right and wise. Pray for the courage to do the Next Right Thing and rely on God to adjust your course if you're heading in the wrong direction. He loves you. If you're seeking Him and if your heart's desire is to want what He wants for you, then you absolutely have to believe that He will not let you be led astray.

Will you be brave enough today to take a decision that needs to be taken, one way or the other, and trust that God is guiding your steps?

*God, I'm leaning heavily on You for peace and safety
as I face this uncertainty. Give me the confidence
I need to take the next step.* Amen.

Threatened

Have mercy on me, O God, have mercy!
I look to You for protection. I will hide beneath
the shadow of Your wings until the danger passes by.

Psalm 57:1 NLT

Sometimes fear asks, "What if I'm not good enough?" This kind of fear roadblocks you from journeying into your full potential, and making good time. It's built on the self-doubt that sneers, *Loser.*

Strangely, it's also the fear that can lash out as prejudice, which is so often the result of insecurity. (Think Nazism, and apartheid, and most of human history.) If we don't know enough about a person or a group of people, or we feel threatened by them, we oppress or prejudge unfairly.

The way through this fear is to know who we are in Christ. There wasn't much in it for God when He gave His Son to buy our freedom. And yet He did it: redeemed us, welcomed us into kingly courts as heirs having no righteousness of our own but made new, made clean. And He made plans for us. He gifted us. His strength is perfected in our weakness. His commands empower us.

This kind of soul-stirring truth eradicates self-doubt and insecurity. It gives us sit-up-straight courage.

Are you stalling a decision because you're worried you don't have what it takes?

Father, thank You for mercy and protection. I will not fear. Amen.

Guidance and gut feel

"When the Spirit of truth comes, He will guide you into all truth. He will not speak on His own but will tell you what He has heard."

John 16:13 NLT

The Holy Spirit brings clarity to decision-making, through the wisdom of friends, family and mentors who know your blind spots. But choose your counselors carefully. Don't only ask those whom you know will tell you what you want to hear. Seek out honest, mature visionaries who walk closely to God and who love you enough to be truthful and rational.

And allow God's Spirit to blaze bright on your motives. Is the decision all about you? Is it about your comfort or lack of trust? Is there God-honoring motivation for a decision, either way? Ask God to floodlight your heart. Where is the dirt? What nuances of sin or selfishness are you hiding? Ask Him to lay His desires on your heart even if you know that you might not like them. Ask Him to help you to want to want what He wants for you. And pay close – and honest – attention to your gut.

Do you recognize the prompting of the Holy Spirit? Are you willing to act on it?

Holy Spirit, thank You for Your constant presence and power, and for guiding me into perfect truth. I trust You to make me sensitive to Your leading, so that I'll steer clear of danger, and be brave to take action for good. Amen.

Working shifts

*Don't worry about anything; instead, pray about everything.
Tell God what you need, and thank Him for all He has done.
Then you will experience God's peace, which exceeds
anything we can understand. His peace will guard your
hearts and minds as you live in Christ Jesus.*

Philippians 4:6-7 NLT

Changes in your working life can be seriously disconcerting. Expectations that others have of you may change. Expectations that you have of yourself may change too. Whether you've been promoted, demoted, sidelined or sacked, a change at work means finding new rhythm – and often it means digging deep to find new skills and new direction, and getting your head around a new way forward.

Paul's instructions to the Philippians are clear: Do. Not. Worry. Jesus said the same thing (Matthew 6:25-34). Peace is always the by-product of prayer, and bringing your needs before God – trusting that He knows your needs, and thanking Him for how He has always met them in the past – will result in a supernatural peace that you won't find around the staff water cooler or in your inbox.

Have changes at work unsettled you? Have you called a meeting with God, or only with your boss?

*Jesus, You know all that I need, and You
know my heart's desires. Be my peace.* Amen.

Don't fight

The LORD Himself will fight for you. Just stay calm.

Exodus 14:14 NLT

Moses said these words to the Israelites just before raising his staff to part the Red Sea. That is some kind of divine intervention. And the same God who fought for the Israelites while they stayed calm, is fighting for you.

Making big scary decisions can feel like slaying so many big scary dragons. Some of those dragons have scales of jagged ice. They suck in warmth and leave the landscape of your life frosted and airless. They stalk the temperate climes of happy moments, slavering for enthusiasm and optimism. They feast gluttonous on your hope and passion.

The dragons that stalk your mind when you're trying to make good choices are fixed on having you believe that you don't have the scope to live significantly or to make the world a better place. Often, their tactic is to wear you down with whispered lies and trivial disappointments, sometimes for years. And a girl can get kind of panicky.

Friend, the beautiful truth is that there is One who fights for you. Just stay calm.

Will you let God be your warrior in the fight you face?

Father, thank You that I don't have to figure out a battle strategy all on my own. Keep me calm. Amen.

Not just a pretty face

A prudent person foresees danger and takes precautions.
The simpleton goes blindly on and suffers the consequences.

Proverbs 22:3 NLT

Solomon points out that a fool is someone who knows that what he's doing is wrong or unwise, yet he goes ahead and does it anyway.

As believers, we have the Spirit of God to guide us. We have God's Word to instruct, warn, direct and deliver us from our own idiocy. We have community – God's people – to hold us accountable and to encourage and inspire us to walk wisely. What we don't have, really, is an excuse to be foolish.

If you know what's tripping you up – what's causing you to stumble and sin – and yet you keep heading down those same cluttered, disastrous streets to do the same things with the same people, Solomon would probably call you a fool. Ouch. The great news is that you can take the next exit. If you're a woman saved and surrendered to Jesus, then you don't have to keep riding foolish roads. There's a more excellent way.

Are you willing to trust God for the wisdom to know what to do, and the courage to do it?

God of grace, I don't want to be a fool.
Show me where I'm being stubborn or naïve. Amen.

Preapproved

Obviously, I'm not trying to win the approval of people, but of God.
If pleasing people were my goal, I would not be Christ's servant.

Galatians 1:10 NLT

It's hard to make decisions confidently when you've been disregarded. In fact, not being taken seriously can lead to paralyzing fear.

The dread of being ignored may have less to do with pride (though your pride probably comes into it) and more to do with deep insecurities that you've somehow gathered and guarded. And so, perhaps, much of what you fling yourself into is to prove the world wrong. If you know you have it in you to be the best at something, you don't stop until you've done it – so that people will see and affirm. You study and slave so that you always have something to add to the career conversation or the *savoir faire* of the school car park. You work impossibly hard at being as impossibly thin, brilliant, funny or beautiful as you possibly can be, because impossibly amazing people are always respected.

Friend, stop. Your efforts will never buy all the approval you're hoping for. You'll never meet the imaginary standard of perfection you believe that others are holding up for you. You'll never be taken seriously by others until you realize how seriously God takes you.

What's really making you try so hard to win people's approval?

*Thank You, Jesus, that Your redemption
declares me preapproved. Amen.*

Rejoice

*For the LORD your God is living among you. He is a mighty savior.
He will take delight in you with gladness. With His love, He will
calm all your fears. He will rejoice over you with joyful songs.*

Zephaniah 3:17 NLT

This Scripture is a splendid, life-altering truth to celebrate. God gives you victory over the defeating, deflating fear of being trapped in a changeless frame of identity. His love has the power to calm your fears, so that your fears need no longer affect your relationships and decisions.

Rejoicing in how much God rejoices over you brings profound relief, release from strongholds, and change. Nothing much on the outside of your life will change, mind you.

The change comes in the subtle, growing realization that it doesn't matter so much anymore who does or doesn't *get* you or appreciate you because you'll be able to climb out from underneath the weight of others' opinions. You'll be able to stand free and see clearly the truth of who you are to God, and who you can be for others.

Could you take five minutes today just to be still and enjoy the truth that God rejoices over you?

*Mighty Savior, Your love has revolutionized
my life and my identity. Thank You!* Amen.

She's with me

For if we live, we live to the Lord, and if we die, we die to the Lord.
So then, whether we live or whether we die, we are the Lord's.

Romans 14:8 ESV

If you're worried about your self-absorption levels, relax. You won't need to take yourself too seriously – and you'll be a lot less hung up on others taking you seriously – when you begin to understand how God sees you.

Imagine you're a nobody walking into a room full of somebodies. The King is there too. And He greets you. Calls you by name. Hugs you and asks you how you're doing. Do you care if all the somebodies still think you're a nobody? Abso-frikkin'-lutely not. It's enough that God took you so very seriously that He wrote a cosmic love story and sent His Son to carry out the ultimate rescue operation on your life, paying the highest price in history to buy you back by taking on Himself all the punishment that was rightfully yours. Not because He got anything out of the deal or because you were worth it. But because it was His good pleasure to impute worth, for His glory. He mapped your life from eternity past and Rubik's-cubed your DNA just so. You're beautiful.

Which room might you walk into more confidently, knowing that you walk in on the arm of the King?

God, it's such a relief that I don't have to live for something as small as me. Amen.

Good company

"If the world hates you, remember that it hated Me first."

John 15:18 NLT

For better or worse, we get a sense of security from other people. Like, if a particular couple thinks that the school is good enough for *their* kids, you feel ok sending *your* kids there too. If certain people in your life were to emigrate or change churches or gynaecologists or supermarkets, you might feel kind of unsettled, and want to change too. It's nice to be doing what the *in* crowd does.

Spelling it out like that is kind of crazy, and kind of embarrassing, right? We know in theory that we shouldn't be so easily swayed by others. Being and doing instead like Jesus – *that* makes sense. Following His lead, and allowing Him to live His life through us – *that's* wise. We need to have more faith in the ability of the Shepherd to lead us, than in our ability to follow.

Of course, being led by Jesus does also mean that you'll suffer, because He suffered. If you want all of Jesus, that's part of the package. And He assures you: everything's going to be ok.

Are you content to move as Jesus moves, even if it means you'll take flak from others?

Jesus, thank You that if I suffer for loving God,
then I'm in the good company of my King. Amen.

Medicated

When Jesus heard this, He told them, "Healthy people don't need a doctor – sick people do. I have come to call not those who think they are righteous, but those who know they are sinners."

Mark 2:17 NLT

Competitiveness leads to poor choices because we pick winning over wisdom. But to cure competitiveness earth-side, we can probably only hope for long-term semi-permanent remission with daily anti-retrovirals. Still, a course of treatment for ambition sufferers might look something like this:

Take two capsules of Reality Check. It's not about you. Whatever your strain of ambition, channel it into Kingdom purposes. You are nothing more than dust-to-dust transience. Any enduring impact you hope to have is in reflecting God's glory. Inject yourself daily with Now. Enjoy the present. Don't only crave future possible (or impossible) successes. Love the work (today) not the result (hopefully tomorrow). Celebrate the process. With the Now, take a double dose of Trust. God knows what He wants to do with the talents He gave you. Leave it to Him. Cut out all forms of Worry. Don't let it get to you when people are dismissive. Don't stress out about proving or defending yourself. God will fight for you (Exodus 14:14). If and when the time is right He will display you, for His glory.

Which of these treatments do you need most?

God, help me to choose daily to put the right things into my heart and mind, so that I will be spiritually healthy. Amen.

Excuses, excuses

But as for me, I almost lost my footing. My feet were slipping …
For I envied the proud when I saw them prosper despite
their wickedness … These fat cats have everything their hearts
could ever wish for! … Did I keep my heart pure for nothing?
Did I keep myself innocent for no reason?

Psalm 73:2-3, 7, 13 NLT

Comparison cons you into making excuses. "How am I supposed to get ahead by doing the right thing? Look at her. She totally disregards God. She does whatever she wants. Not only does she get away with it, she thrives."

If you compare yourself to others, you can always make excuses – which stall you or depress you. If you compare yourself to *yourself* by asking yourself how you're doing in the race set before you, then you make progress.

Do the wicked really prosper? Sometimes yes, for a while. Sometimes for all their lives. Sometimes not at all. They're on their own journeys. You can trust that God sees all their doings and misdoings, and He judges righteously. Trying desperately or cynically to understand their apparent or real opulence or affluence will only blind you to your own startling, dazzling riches.

Do you know any fat cats that seem to be winning at everything? Does it puzzle you, or make your angry?

*God, I want to make progress, not excuses. Help me
not to whine about what's happening in other lives,
but to thank You for what's happening in mine.* Amen.

Appetite

But it was the LORD's good plan to crush Him and cause Him grief. Yet when His life is made an offering for sin, He will have many descendants. He will enjoy a long life, and the LORD's good plan will prosper in His hands.

Isaiah 53:10 NLT

Jesus experienced the ultimate rejection. His own Heavenly Father forsook Him in His dying moments on the cross (Matthew 27:46), never mind His closest friends (Luke 22:57). Surely that kind of betrayal strikes fear – clouds judgment – *nauseates*?

Incredibly, when His betrayal was imminent and He knew fully the hours of agony He would suffer – physically and emotionally – He ate with His disciples. He was actually *able* to eat with His disciples.

When I'm aware of approaching pain, I can't eat. And yet Jesus was so convinced that God had a plan, He trusted so fully that God was in control, that He even had an appetite. He had settled God's sovereignty over His suffering and rejection, and apparently that settled His stomach. He still prayed and asked God to take the pain, rejection and humiliation from Him (Luke 22:42), yet knowing that He was God's beloved enabled Him to face it.

What truth might settle your nerves today, even if you're dealing with sickening hurt or fear?

Father, give me a strong stomach for trials. Still the waves of angst with the sure knowledge of Your wisdom, love and power. Amen.

Peeling the onion

But I will keep on hoping for Your help;
I will praise You more and more.

Psalm 71:14 NLT

Most regular humans have long-term suffering in their lives. Stuff that isn't going away anytime soon. Like a difficult (and inescapable) family relationship, a physical disability, or the very obvious consequence of a bad decision. Hopefully, you've learned to be content despite whatever thorn pokes your side (2 Corinthians 12:7), but probably, the suffering will flare up from time to time. You'll want to kick yourself because really, by now shouldn't you have dealt with it? How can you be struggling *again* to process the pain?

Long-term suffering is a bit like peeling an onion. Not just because it makes you cry, but because you will keep being confronted by the suffering as the reality of it crops up in different sets of circumstances. The bad news is that, yes, you'll have to get your head and heart around it all over again. But the good news is that as you keep on peeling that onion, God hones your character. Layer by layer, He softens your heart as you again surrender to Him. Layer by layer, there is grace enough.

What good decisions did you make to get through the last layer of suffering that you peeled?

Lord, I want to be a quick learner of the lessons You are teaching me over and over. Amen.

Steady

As for the rest of you, dear brothers and sisters, never get tired of doing good.

2 Thessalonians 3:13 NLT

Maybe to conquer the fear that can numb you and stop you from making good choices, you need a vision to hold you steady. Ask God to give you a Scripture – like this one today? – to be your filter for decisions, and your encouragement when doubt and fear creep in.

A vision keeps you keeping on in the right direction. It keeps you remembering that everything's going to be ok, and it helps you to look ahead, intentionally and hopefully. You might try picking a point in the future – one, five or ten years from now – and choosing a theme that will help you to stay the course or stretch your wings or dig deeper right where you are. Maybe you'll be parenting – or grandparenting – from toddlers to teenagers in ten quick years and what happens in this next decade – it's the big thing. You need to decide to be heart-soul-mind-strength present, on purpose.

Is there something you could memorize or stick up on the fridge – a verse, a prayer, two words? – that will keep you focused, and free of fear?

Father, please lay on my heart a clear vision or an idea from Your Word that will conquer my fear and inform my decisions, in this next season. Amen.

Don't be afraid of the enemy

But the Holy Spirit produces this kind of fruit in our lives: love, joy, peace, patience, kindness, goodness, faithfulness, gentleness, and self-control. There is no law against these things!

Galatians 5:22-23 NLT

When all hell breaks loose in your life – maybe literally? – don't be afraid. No kidding, Satan is powerful and we should be on our guard against his schemes (1 Peter 5:8). But a friend reminded me once that the fruit of the Spirit is *patience*. We have the Holy Spirit, and so we have patience. Satan doesn't have the Holy Spirit, and so he doesn't have patience. Stand firm (Ephesians 6:11). Eventually, his patience will run dry and he'll give up trying to make you quit because he knows as well as you do that greater is He who is in you, than he who is in the world (1 John 4:4).

There's also no goodness in the enemy, but by God's transforming grace, there's plenty in you. Paul wrote to the Romans, "Don't let evil conquer you, but conquer evil by doing good" (Romans 12:21). You have no reason to be afraid, because you have everything it takes to be a brave and valuable warrior.

Are you willing to go to battle by praying for patience?

God, thank You that I am branded as Yours and that no one can steal me away from You. Give me courage to stand firm, patience to endure, and the peace of knowing that You are my protector. Amen.

Don't be afraid to feel

Jesus wept.

John 11:35 NIV

This is a pretty famous verse because it's the shortest one in the Bible. But really what should astound us about it is that it shows us the heart of our Savior. Jesus felt all the feely feelings we do, and He wasn't afraid to feel them.

One night my four-year old yelled out to me from the bath, "Mom, how's it going in your heart with Jesus?" It was the highlight of my day. I want him to keep on asking me, and keep on asking himself. I want him to understand that sin breaks relationships. That we need to own our feelings and keep on finding each other in the soft strong circles of mercy. That no matter how violent and sweaty the tantrums that he and I and others throw – we need to keep asking the hard questions. Keep asking forgiveness. Keep forgiving. Keep feeling.

When last did you surrender all your emotions to the God who created them?

Lord, help me to accept humbly the emotional invasions You allow, but shield me from needless hurt. Give me margin for grace and gentleness so that I might bless others by being uncomplicated: weeping with those who weep, and rejoicing with those who rejoice. Amen.

Don't be afraid to try

For I can do everything through Christ, who gives me strength.

Philippians 4:13 NLT

"I'll try anything once," you hear people say. I tend to agree (barring the obvious no-no's, like heroin). As believers, we should indeed be known for being gung-ho. As in, if you see a need, step in and serve. You may not like it. You may not be the best person for the job. But maybe the fumbled efforts of someone trying to help are better than nothing?

You don't have to love everything in life. You don't have to love crowds and noise and new things. Or books and concertos and Thai food. But sometimes you have to try anyway. When the waterslide is too high and you really don't want to go down it, sometimes you have to slide anyway. Try. At least once. Because your sliding might lead to an astonishing personal discovery. You might be surprised at who is cheering from the sidelines, hoping to be splashed by some of your courage.

What comes to mind as you read today? Is there something you've been putting off? Are you willing to give it a try? What's the worst that could happen?

Jesus, make me brave to try, at least once. Amen.

Don't be afraid to lead

This is my command – be strong and courageous! Do not be afraid or discouraged. For the LORD your God is with you wherever you go.

Joshua 1:9 NLT

It's the leaders – the people you think should be super confident – who are regularly filled with fear. Because it can be terrifying out front where you're the one pushing back boundaries. It takes courage to love others consistently and to say the hard things that people don't want to hear but that sometimes need to be said. It takes courage to make the hard decisions that no one wants to make but that sometimes need to be made.

Friend – beautiful woman with subtle or obvious influence on the people around you – face your fears. Don't shrink so easily from challenge or discomfort. Because those who make the greatest advances face the greatest fears. Those who are afraid are likely living on the edge – which is the most fertile place to cultivate faith.

In what kind of life spaces do you find it particularly scary to lead others, or set an example?

God, I give You my fear of being a front-runner. I want to make myself available for You to use in whatever ways You choose. Amen.

Don't be afraid to hope

He called out, "Fellows, have you caught any fish?" "No," they replied. Then He said, "Throw out your net on the right-hand side of the boat, and you'll get some!" So they did, and they couldn't haul in the net because there were so many fish in it.

John 21:5-6 NLT

Jesus had a thing for fish. He drew His inner circle rough with the grit of men who caught fish for a living. Taught them how to fish for souls (Matthew 4:19). Multiplied fish on a hillside (Matthew 14:19). Paid tax from a fish's mouth (Matthew 17:27). Cooked fish on the beach for His friends (John 21:9).

And Jesus was into flinging the fishing nets wide, hauling them in heavy and unbroken.

Those first disciples didn't know if the nets would come back full. They threw them out in faith, trusting God for the catch. Like them, we could offer what we have – fling the stitched up, patched up sagging strings we have – and *trust God for the catch*. He works all things for our good (Romans 8:28), even the disappointments we wrestle back into the boat. And what spills from our lives if we trust and obey is all good, all glory.

Will you tug back to the beach the nets teeming with the glistening minutes of today, to marvel at the mercies of today's catch?

God, thank You that tomorrow, there will be time enough and grace enough again to fling wide the nets, and hope. Amen.

Whatever

Take delight in the Lord, and He will give you your heart's desires.

Psalm 37:4 NLT

The psalmist isn't saying that God will give you whatever you want, whenever you want it. He isn't saying that we can do what we want, when we want, with whom we want. He's saying that if we're taking delight in our King, Friend and Redeemer – if we're reveling in our relationship with Him – then His best ideas will rub off on us, and we'll want what He wants. His desires will become our desires, in which case, *do whatever you want.*

You and I could be more deliberate about habitually placing ourselves in the pathway of God's grace so that He can work in us. The intricate, traceable patterns of our lives could reflect a desire to walk closely to Him. That kind of beautiful, brave living will mean that *whatever* in our vocabulary won't be accompanied by attitude and resigned eye-rolling. We'll be able to say *whatever* with the ecstatic, no-fear freedom of living for Christ.

Are you willing to allow God to put His desires on your heart?

God, thank You that You've saved me, filled me with Your Spirit, and committed to sanctifying me. I submit to You, and I'm even willing to suffer for You. Thank You that I can be, do or decide whatever You're laying on my heart to be, do and decide. Amen.

It could all go up in smoke

You are my rock and my fortress. For the honor
of Your name, lead me out of this danger.

Psalm 31:3 NLT

One hot spring afternoon when our eldest son was three years old, he switched on a heater just for fun. It was leaning hazardously against a bed, and the bed subsequently, quietly, caught fire. Our son hurtled merrily downstairs, oblivious to his pyromania. Something made my husband go upstairs – for no apparent reason – just to check. Just to prevent, as it turned out, our house from burning down.

That same day, we heard from a friend whose parents, after forty years of building lives and loving their kids and others into bright futures, were separating. We felt punched in the gut. We were speechless and ineffably sad.

The burning bed incident gave us that *life*-is-so-fragile wake-up call. Everything could, in fact, go up in smoke. Any day. Any time. Choose to treasure the things that matter.

The broken marriage news gave us that *we*-are-so-fragile wake-up call. A marriage can also go up in smoke. Even the strongest, godliest people are only one bad decision away from messing up. We need to make the brave choice every day to stay close to Jesus, and each other.

Do you smell smoke? Where do you need to depend more on God for daily decisions to keep tangible and intangible responsibilities safe?

God, thank You for Your sustaining grace. Keep me from ever being complacent about life, or love. *Amen.*

No-fear zone

My people will live in safety, quietly at home. They will be at rest.

Isaiah 32:18 NLT

The context of this Scripture is Israel's ultimate deliverance, but it gives us a picture of the kind of home you and I could be building. The preceding verse reads, "And this righteousness will bring peace. Yes, it will bring quietness and confidence forever" (Isaiah 32:17).

Take a moment to think about how the world would change if we as believers built homes like that?

Our homes could be and should be, safe and simple. Warm and welcoming. Clean (sort of) and neat (mostly). Beautiful, and always open to any that God chooses to bring. A refuge where we and others are free to rest and wrestle as God calls out from us the people He made us to be. A place where the fog of fear can clear and decisions are made easier. A place of peace where Christ is King.

Do you feel completely at ease in your own home? How could you eradicate fear and build a space that is safe for all the backing and forthing you may need to do, to make your big decisions?

Father, I fervently and expectantly pray that You would transform my home with a tangible sense of Your presence, Your peace and Your great love. Amen.

Halt

The wise are mightier than the strong, and those
with knowledge grow stronger and stronger.

Proverbs 24:5 NLT

You've heard the old advice, that before you make any decision, big or small, you should H.A.L.T because you shouldn't make a decision if you're Hungry, Angry, Lonely or Tired. (You also shouldn't be in the chocolate aisle of the supermarket if you're Hungry, Angry, Lonely or Tired.)

You can probably look back on a decision you made once when you were in one of those four physical or emotional states. It's probably a decision you regret entirely, or at least, had you waited and made the decision in a better frame of mind and body, the repercussions of the decision would have been different.

To make the best possible decision, you need to look after your heart and mind, your body and your brain, so that you're in a fit state to be as wise as possible. That might mean *not* sending that text or *not* swiping that credit card until you've slept, eaten, cleared your thoughts and calmed down completely. It might mean saying no to attractive distractions for the greater good of what God has called you to be or do.

Are you eating enough? Sleeping enough? Spending time with people who are kind and courageous?

Jesus, please hold me back from making stupid decisions because I'm not in a good place. Protect me from myself, and help me to be intentional about my health. Amen.

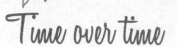

Time over time

Do not despise these small beginnings,
for the LORD rejoices to see the work begin …

Zechariah 4:10 NLT

We've meditated already this year on how it's small deposits of time – all the time – over time – that add up to what's critical. As in, one decision doesn't get you to where you want to go. On the road to our desired destination, our mode of transport needs to be decision, after decision, after decision. Even when each of those decisions feels so very small and insignificant – like just another slow ordinary moment that doesn't rock the world.

You're right. Those moments and decisions don't rock the world. Not today. Probably not even tomorrow. But maybe – just maybe – they'll rock the future.

We need to learn the immeasurable worth of doing on purpose the mundane and the miniscule every day, all our days. Because, lived as worship, the mundane and the miniscule are the grains in life's hourglass. Maybe a lifetime from now when our kids are all grown up they'll see how these small days began in them the great days of knowing who they are – because they'll know how they were loved.

Could you decide today to keep making the small, crucial decisions that will keep your life headed in the right direction?

God, open my eyes to how, even when nothing feels extraordinary, the extra is there in the ordinary all the time. By Your grace, it's there in the day in, day out done well; and in faith. Amen.

You've got what it takes

Don't be dejected and sad, for the joy of the LORD is your strength!

Nehemiah 8:10 NLT

Whether you *feel* it or not, you have to start believing that you've got what it takes to make a wise decision. You are strong enough.

The moment you committed your life to Jesus Christ, His Spirit filled you (Romans 8:9). And as you've continued to walk with Him, that Spirit has grown the evidence in you: fruit, like love, joy, peace, patience, kindness, goodness, gentleness, faithfulness and self-control (Galatians 5:22-23). Nehemiah reminded his people that it's the joy we get from the Lord that gives us our strength. Our joy *equals* our strength. The more you delight in Him – the more you rest content in His peace and presence, grateful for the gifts He gives in the chaos and the calm of life on this planet – the stronger you'll become. Strong enough, certainly, to make the decisions you're so afraid to make.

Do you know someone who is "dejected and sad" at the moment? How could you encourage her to allow the joy of the Lord to be her strength?

Heavenly Father, thank You for the simple, sustaining strength You give me as I rejoice in You. Amen.

You've been heard

> Then he said, "Don't be afraid, Daniel. Since the first day you began to pray for understanding and to humble yourself before your God, your request has been heard in heaven. I have come in answer to your prayer."
>
> *Daniel 10:12* NLT

Too often we get disillusioned because, from where we're standing, it seems God is ignoring us. We bring before Him our aches, needs or debilitating insecurities, and we're greeted with silent indifference. Daniel must have felt the same. Three weeks of fasting and praying with no result. Others – throughout Scripture, all of history, and in our world today – wait *years* for answers or resolutions from God. Many – maybe you? – are still waiting.

But the angel who appears to Daniel brings such cosmic perspective and peace. "Since the first day you began to pray … your request has been heard in heaven."

Regardless of how you're experiencing God's answering, or not, hold on to the truth that no prayer on your lips or in the quiet of your mind has ever escaped God's notice. He longs to hear from you, and though He may not always answer you in the way or at the time that you think He should, He is at work for your good and His glory. All. The. Time.

What has life thrown at you, to throw you? Will you commit to humbling yourself and praying for understanding, trusting that every one of your prayers is heard?

God, thank You for hearing me. Amen.

Decisions in the dark

> The light shines in the darkness,
> and the darkness can never extinguish it.
>
> *John 1:5 NLT*

When my son asked over breakfast "how the sperm gets to the egg", I told him. He was pretty unfazed. Kept spooning in the cereal. He couldn't fully fathom the intricacies that play out miraculous between two people and escalate into life even before those two people know it.

And really, God gives birth to all of life that way. We're the last to see what He has been watchfully secreting into days and decades and since eternity past. He maneuvres puzzles and people long before we're aware of it. Sometimes we're never aware of it. There's life born around us all the time and we hardly notice it unless it intersects our reality in an obvious, ironic or serendipitous way. God works in the darkness all the time, and when it's too dark to see what He's doing we'd be wise to *listen* to what He's saying, because His voice is all we have to go on.

You may even find that you hear *better* in the dark, because the din of bright life can drown out what's really being said. And in the dark – of depression, tough decisions or a painful relationship – you can't see anything but the next, obedient, courageous thing. The thing that – if you're watchful – swells with hope.

Are you listening?

*God, help me hear Your voice in the dark,
and to trust that it's enough to go on. Amen.*

NOVEMBER

Feet first

"What lies behind us and what lies before us are small matters compared to what lies within us."

– *Ralph Waldo Emerson*

You'll be remembered for November

I have fought the good fight, I have
finished the race, and I have remained faithful.

2 Timothy 4:7 NLT

"You'll be remembered for November." It's what a friend said to me one November, years ago, and I've said it to myself and anyone who will listen every November since. Because as much as we're heading into what's arguably the best, most joyfully celebrated time of year, November can be the most frenetic, most stressful, most crucial time of year. Performance appraisals. End-year functions. Family Christmas logistics looming. Strategic planning. Frazzled nerves. Short fuses. Tightropes of stretched patience. Fatigue.

It's too late to finish strong in December. The year's over by then. People are eating, tanning or skiing. Every year when November approaches – and the silly season that it heralds – we need to take cover in prayer, because our own strength isn't enough to finish strong. It doesn't matter how well you've done from January to October. A crass remark to some colleagues at the coffee machine? Arriving late and missing the small tinsel-haloed angel's performance? One stupid decision because you felt tired or angry or lonely? These are the things people will remember.

There's a better, more beautiful way to finish strong.

How will you finish this never-to-be-echoed calendar year bravely and well by fighting the good fight, finishing the race, and remaining faithful?

God, I want to finish strong! *Amen.*

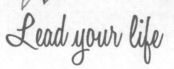

Lead your life

And you yourself must be an example to them by doing good works of every kind. Let everything you do reflect the integrity and seriousness of your teaching.

Titus 2:7 NLT

Anyone who wants to change the world is a leader so that's what makes you and me leaders, friend. Leadership is simply *influencing others*. It's always about others, and never about you.

If you have a desire to change something – to influence anyone at all, in any way at all – then you're a leader. Moms and dads are leaders. Small people look to us. Teachers and architects and entrepreneurs and physiotherapists and gardeners and accountants and friends are leaders. Anyone who is passionate about maximizing time and potential and leveraging influence for the Kingdom is a leader.

And if you're convinced that you're so *not* a leader? You're leading a life. That makes you a leader. All your days you'll be putting one foot in front of the other. And if you do that well – if your life is a lavish expenditure of your time and your potential within the context that God has set you – you may look back and find a bunch of people following you.

If it's true that you're leading a life, and that others are watching, where do they see you going with it?

God, You've given me this one life to lead. Give me the wisdom, discernment, strength and integrity to lead it well, and to Your glory. *Amen.*

Barefoot bravery

The Sovereign LORD is my strength! He makes me as surefooted as a deer, able to tread upon the heights.

Habakkuk 3:19 NLT

Every truth about leadership demands that you be brave because the soul of leadership is courage – remembering, of course, that courage isn't the absence of fear; it's simply acting *despite* of your fear.

It takes courage to lead because leaders are initiators and early adopters. Leading requires walking out front, stubbing toes on obstacles misjudged or unexpected because we're the first to get to them. Really, being a successful leader is being brave enough to put one foot in front of the other. Left. Right. Left. Right. Love. Righteousness. Love. Righteousness.

No matter what new or daunting or routine leadership challenge you face, you may feel as if there are critical eyes on you. People watching and wondering and waiting for you to fail. Know that God will protect, establish and promote you. Let those three words be your mainstay on tough days. Let the truth that God's got your back energize you to lead boldly and without fear of recrimination. God is encircling you: you are protected. Your feet are on the rock: you are established. And He has the power and wisdom to hide you or display you as it seems good to Him.

Will you take off your shoes – worship God on holy ground – and trust Him to lead you down the right path?

Jesus, choose the strike of my every step. Amen.

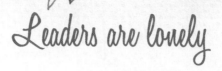

Leaders are lonely

> But the LORD was with Joseph in the prison and showed him His faithful love. And the LORD made Joseph a favorite with the prison warden.
>
> *Genesis 39:21* NLT

Joseph was lonely. As a slave, in the top strata of Egyptian aristocracy, and in prison: he didn't fit in. The psalmist writes, "Until the time came to fulfill his dreams, the Lord tested Joseph's character" (Psalm 105:19). So, when the time eventually did come, Joseph was promoted. God chose his position even though he didn't have the right qualifications by any stretch of his CV. And Joseph was used mightily, in his own generation and beyond.

We serve the same God that Joseph served. The God of eternity and every day. The God who split the Red Sea and can write your résumé and protect your reputation. The God who is with you in your organization, community or family when you're out front – plotting a course – launching – deciding – sticking with it. There's confidence in knowing that God is your promoter in career and community, friendships and family. Corporate steps and closed circles are nothing to Him. He will put you where He wants you, for your good and His glory. You needn't shoulder-rub or name-drop to find out or fit in. Just be faithful to give your very best self to the circumstances in which you find yourself.

When do you feel particularly lonely?

Lord, when I'm on the edge making a stand,
remind me that I am never alone. Amen.

Feet of clay

… Do not be arrogant, but tremble.

Romans 11:20 NIV

My feet just aren't pretty. I had a boyfriend once who thought it would be funny to quote Psalm 139 at me: "You're fearfully and wonderfully made," he said. "But your feet – they're just fearfully made."

Yet I've come to accept my feet. They're the feet God chose to make for me; they've taken me to beautiful streets and beaches and mountaintops; and they keep me humble. A big head gives me a better view of my feet so when I get proud it just takes a glimpse of them for my head to shrink back to an appropriate size.

My not-so-pretty feet also remind me that my feet, your feet, and everyone's feet are made of clay. Like the feet of the statue in Nebuchadnezzar's dream (Daniel 2), they spell destruction if we think we can do leadership alone. The moment we get proud and stop depending daily on Jesus for insight and guidance – the moment we stop cleaning out the sin that builds up in our hearts – our leadership becomes inefficient, ineffective and detrimental to those who are following.

Do you ever feel invincible in an area of your life? Would it be worth doing a reality check to refocus your belief in God's strength and goodness, rather than your own?

God, You know better than anyone that I stand on clay feet. Any excellence or beauty in me comes straight from You. Don't let me forget! Amen.

Stand on your own two feet

So, my dear brothers and sisters, be strong and immovable.
Always work enthusiastically for the Lord, for you know
that nothing you do for the Lord is ever useless.

1 Corinthians 15:58 NLT

When I was heading up a high school English department, my mom used to remind me that if everyone liked me, I probably wasn't doing my job.

The truth is that a leader needs feet that stand firm. She needs to know exactly where she's standing, and why. She needs to believe in the value of her cause, her message or her mission – enough to be brave enough to promote it in a world that might ignore her, or drown her out. She needs to be comfortable with the idea of taking a stand, and standing there for as long as it takes.

And when it comes to stepping on toes – because, um, you will – a leader should take advice from Dr Seuss who said it best: "You have brains in your head. You have feet in your shoes. You can steer yourself any direction you choose … So be sure when you step. Step with care and great tact and remember that Life's A Great Balancing Act."

Are you brave enough to stand up for a cause or a course of action, brave enough to stand up to those who may disagree, and brave enough to keep standing?

Jesus, I want to be the kind of brave You modeled, leading tenaciously with resolute passion and infinite compassion. Amen.

Wash feet

… Then He began to wash the disciples' feet,
drying them with the towel He had around Him.

John 13:5 NLT

More important than standing on our own feet is washing another's.

That's how Jesus led. He simultaneously held together the atoms of all creation while stooping low to wash filth from feet. Mighty hero. Humble servant.

In the Upper Room with His disciples – death drawing near – Jesus gave us an astounding lesson on leadership. He knew that the Father had given Him authority over everything and that He had come from God and would return to God. So He got up from the table, took off His robe, wrapped a towel around His waist, and poured water into a basin. Then He washed and dried His friends' feet.

So, Jesus dwelt on the truth that *all power was His*. And the very next thing He did was to get up and wash feet. He said that same night – God with skin on: "For I am among you as one who serves" (Luke 22:27).

God's Kingdom is always the crazy beautiful upside-down opposite to what the world yells about power and pre-eminence. And as leaders, in whatever capacity, the more power we have, the more we should be serving. That kind of leadership? It might just change the world.

What could you do for someone today, knowing that there's nothing in it for you?

*Jesus, humble me so that I can
influence people the way You did.* Amen.

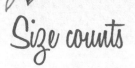

Size counts

These are just the beginning of all that He does, merely a whisper of His power. Who, then, can comprehend the thunder of His power?

Job 26:14 NLT

As leaders, our battle with pride will likely rage on, present continuous. We've got to keep fighting because, as Solomon said, "pride leads to conflict" (Proverbs 13:10) and we should be all about soft hearts and harmony. So, since bad habits are defeated by good ones, there are some things we can do to kick pride in the teeth.

Start each day by telling yourself, *size counts*. When we dwell on how incomprehensibly big our God is, we automatically remember how infinitesimally little we are. The bigness of the world helps us feel our smallness, and yet even this planet of staggering heights and depths is only a speck of dust in a vast and boundless universe. When we slow our thoughts on this, we no longer kid ourselves that God *needs* us. That He's so lucky to have us and that He couldn't possibly spread His kingdom without us. Um … no.

But you and I both know that we're fickle and quick to forget. Realizations that move and humble us wear off and we downsize God again – relegate Him to bite-sized convenience – and supersize our agendas.

The smallest people with the most beautiful influence stay mindful of the truth that they serve an enormous God.

How big is your God?

God, I can't begin to fathom Your magnitude. I worship You. Amen.

Reverence and rejoicing

Serve the LORD with reverent fear, and rejoice with trembling.

Psalm 2:11 NLT

Scriptures like this put into beautiful perspective the pride that so often makes us stumble.

I love how King David, whose heroism as a leader is carved deeply into his nation's history, understood the posture of a godly life.

He understood that our humility before God isn't a groveling terror, but rather a joyful, unpretentious surrender to His greatness. Because as soon as we're focused on the splendor of the Savior, our pride melts away, ludicrous and irrelevant.

The psalmist also understood that a life bent on serving God is a paradox. You should walk upright in the confidence that you are a child of the King, clothed in the royal robes of righteousness. And you should bow low. Bow *very* low. Because your great worth and your great beauty in His eyes are His gifts bestowed, for His glory.

Are you ever confused or put off by the concept of fearing God – trembling before His greatness – or do you see it as a source of great joy – something that empowers you as a leader?

Father, thank You for imparting worth to me, when You alone are worthy. Amen.

Forget

God has given each of you a gift from His great variety of spiritual gifts. Use them well to serve one another.

1 Peter 4:10 NLT

When I'm battling with pride, I try to forget about humility. Because *trying* to be humble can feel a bit like looking for love. As in, you'll seldom find the man of your dreams when you're out looking for him. Mostly love hits you from behind – in like, a loving way – when you least expect it and definitely on the day you should have washed your hair.

If I'm *trying* to be humble, then I keep checking on how I'm doing – as I would if I were trying to achieve anything – and if I'm checking my humility barometer, then the mercury invariably shoots up to arrogant.

So I try to forget. Which is actually not as impossible as it sounds, especially when we remember that leadership is always about others and never about us. My thoughts run quickly and easily away from me-me-me when I set them busily on you-you-you and God-God-God. It's hard to self-obsess or gloat when I'm getting my hands dirty for a cause bigger than me.

How can you distract yourself today by serving God and others, so that you forget a little about how fantastic you are and focus rather on the magnificence of God?

God, give me some good ideas of things I can throw myself into, to maximize You and my influence for the Kingdom. Amen.

Get wise

For wisdom is far more valuable than rubies. Nothing you desire can compare with it. "I, Wisdom, live together with good judgment. I know where to discover knowledge and discernment."

Proverbs 8:11-12 NLT

Another way we can be excellent leaders and combat pride is to grow desperate for wisdom. Firstly, because no one who knows what's good for them wants to follow a fool. Secondly, because wisdom breeds humility, and no one wants to follow an arrogant fool.

We need to pray for wisdom daily, because God promises to give it if we ask (James 1:5). We need to look for it. Listen for it shouting in the streets (Proverbs 1:20). Make notes on our phones. Memorize. Cup our hands around wisdom and swallow it hot.

Because the more we know, the more we know how little we know, and that right-sizes us. We feel small again, in the hands of a great and omniscient God.

Wisdom also counsels us that the world doesn't revolve around even the most influential of leaders. We're all just flecks in the wave of history that rolls on deep and wide and all for God's glory.

Do you go out of your way to get more wisdom? Do you find a way to hang out with wise people? Read wise books? Listen to wise words? How does gaining wisdom change your view of God?

Jesus, I long for the wisdom that downsizes me and blows my mind with Your magnitude. Amen.

Less is more

He must become greater and greater,
and I must become less and less.

John 3:30 NLT

Less can be more. In fact, less is almost always more.

Sometimes *backwards* (in the logical career, relationship or financial progression expected of a grown-up on planet earth) means *forwards* (in the eternal kingdom of God).

What looks to the world like a step down into a smaller life is most likely your debut into God using you bigger. In most scenarios, you probably won't see your eternal impact, until eternity. And your earthly impact may feel inferior. This is hard to swallow, because of pride. Yet you're in the world, not of the world (John 17:16), so don't measure your life according to of-the-world standards.

As a leader, your choices to step away from common or cultural expectations may be seen by the masses as *less*, and yet there are some in the realm of your influence who are watching and wondering – starstruck by how you choose significance over success, and by how beautiful that makes you.

Do you need to remind yourself or someone close to you of the truth that less may actually mean more?

God, I want more of You and less of me. Help me to see that that is actually the greatest thing imaginable for my life. Amen.

Do it anyway

"… I say, love your enemies! Do good to those who hate you …
Pray for those who hurt you … If someone demands your coat,
offer your shirt also. Give to anyone who asks; and when things
are taken away from you, don't try to get them back. Do to
others as you would like them to do to you."

Luke 6:27–31 NLT

If you want to be a difference maker, it's only a matter of time before you'll hear the reverberation of your dreams shot down. And yet, a leader fights pessimism with enthusiasm. *Do your thing anyway.*

If anyone understood cold shoulders and hot accusations when their God-heart was only ever mind-bending love, it was Jesus. Yet He never said it was ok to be pathetic – to hide behind a victim mentality. He said get up, get over yourself and get busy loving the critics.

So, some people think your ideas are wild or stupid. Think of ideas anyway. Some moms pretend not to see you in the school car park. Smile and wave anyway. Some friends don't text you back. Text anyway. Sometimes you do all the inviting. Invite people anyway. Sometimes you make delicious food and your kids say, "Yuk!" Make delicious food anyway. Leaders are brave enough to keep leading, and to keep loving.

What will you do today, anyway?

*Jesus, thank You for Your example of relentless,
selfless love in the face of naysayers.* Amen.

Self-esteem doesn't solve stuff

When I look at the night sky and see the work of Your
fingers – the moon and the stars You set in place – what
are mere mortals that You should think about them,
human beings that You should care for them?

Psalm 8:3-4 NLT

Self-esteem is all the rage. School teachers, life coaches, magazines
and mentors will all likely tell you that it's crucial to happiness and
success. It seems logical too that a high self-image is necessary to
fortify ourselves against criticism, and to lead well.

There's an element of truth to that. But the whole truth is that
self-esteem – how highly or lowly we think of ourselves – comes
from comparing ourselves to others, or to a standard that the world
has established. If you've ever compared yourself to anyone else
(and who hasn't?), you'll know that comparison makes you either
vain or depressed. Neither response makes you a better leader.

The secret is to stop worrying so much about esteeming you, and
rather *esteem God*. Live in the joy, thanks, confidence and security
that because He has imputed righteousness to you, He esteems
you as child and heir. That truth lets the pressure of being someone
great slide right off, freeing you to live and lead excellently.

How's your God-esteem?

*God, help me to forget myself and how all the combined
elements of life make me feel. Help me to lift You high
with my life and rest, poised and protected, in You.* Amen.

Hollywood hero

As they stoned him, Stephen prayed, "Lord Jesus,
receive my spirit." He fell to his knees, shouting,
"Lord, don't charge them with this sin!" And with that, he died.

Acts 7:59-60 NLT

This is a seriously dramatic scene from Scripture. It fits a big screen Hollywood hero-martyr – directed by Ridley Scott and accompanied by a swelling Hans Zimmer soundtrack. In his dying moments – when he has every right to lash out bitter for being killed for his innocence – Stephen turns to God. He surrenders to his Savior and then he prays for his attackers. He asks God to forgive them.

People long to follow this kind of leader, with this kind of Hollywood heroism. And this kind of heroism is how you and I are supposed to lead. It's how you and I are supposed to forgive, every time. Surrender to God – your thoughts, emotions, attitudes and actions – and pray for your accuser or attacker or ignorer or snide remark maker. Your fearless daring and intrepid strength will point to an Almighty God, and your life will begin to influence others in beautiful ways.

Will you trust God to protect you, and pray for someone today, that God will forgive and restore them?

*Jesus, make me more like You. You didn't self-flagellate.
You didn't self-congratulate. You just didn't think of Yourself at
all. You thought of others. Turn me into that kind of hero.* Amen.

Threshold

As for me, I look to the LORD for help. I wait confidently for God to save me, and my God will certainly hear me. Do not gloat over me, my enemies! For though I fall, I will rise again. Though I sit in darkness, the LORD will be my light!

Micah 7:7-8 NLT

Micah – prophet and poet – writes a God-honoring account of misery turned to hope. His confident conviction despite dire conditions demonstrates how even pain that shoots beyond our threshold can empower us to lead.

His experience is believable, because a threshold is a limit – a ceiling – a this-far-and-no-farther. And a threshold is also a verge – a brink – a beginning. It's the groom carrying his bride into new life and love. It's the lamb's blood smeared on thresholds of ancient slave slums promising that the Lamb would endure the ultimate pain threshold and say, "It is finished." Then stand on the threshold of the grave, and rise again.

You are your bravest and most resourceful, your most creative and committed, when you absolutely have to be. You're also your most beautiful. Whatever the threshold upon which you're teetering, pray for courage to trust the Creator of your capacity. He knows just how you may need to break so that pain can flood through as the inception of beauty.

What's your threshold?

God, turn my pain into passionate confidence so that You will hear me, and You will save me. Amen.

Tongue-tied

But Moses pleaded with the LORD, "O Lord, I'm not very good with words. I never have been, and I'm not now, even though You have spoken to me. I get tongue-tied, and my words get tangled."

Exodus 4:10 NLT

God quickly puts Moses in his place by saying that *He* will give Moses the necessary words (Exodus 4:11-12). It's a brilliant leadership hack: remembering that your strength doesn't come from you at all but from God, and that deflecting the glory back to Him turns the attention away from you, allowing you to operate more confidently.

To lead our own lives beautifully – and so lead others – we don't need big faith. We just need simple faith in a big God. Living and leading with simple faith means letting all of life fall onto a mirror to reflect the tender mercies of the Giver.

It's not trivial or trite to bow low in gratitude for every sunrise, every gap in the traffic, every smile at the school gate. We needn't be afraid of speaking out often and assuredly of the goodness of God because it reminds us and others that we're not the center of the story.

Could you quit worrying about saying too much or too little, and just speak freely and courageously of the goodness of God?

God, when my words get tangled and I feel like I don't have what it takes, loosen my tongue to take the lead in giving thanks to You. Amen.

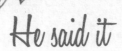

He said it

But Balaam replied, "I will speak only the
message that the LORD puts in my mouth."

Numbers 23:12 NLT

King Balak is rooting for the prophet Balaam to be the bearer of feel-good news. So when Balaam delivers the message that God *really* has for Balak, the king yells, "What have you done to me? I brought you to curse my enemies. Instead, you have blessed them!" (Numbers 23:11).

Balaam's courage under fire is a stunning example of how leadership is nothing more than stalwart obedience to whatever God is telling you to do or say. It's not stubbornness or pride; just quiet, immovable deference to the will of God.

And if you're not sure what message God is putting in your mouth, do the Next Right Thing. Do it bravely and excellently, where you are, just today. Be a brave, excellent student or parent or maker of French toast or manager of millions. Bring up your kids to be brave, excellent citizens of the world and the Kingdom. Deal excellently with every person who intersects your life, today. In your sphere of influence, control what you can – bravely and excellently – and throw yourself on the mercy of God for the rest.

What breaks your heart? Could you lean into that area today, and bring truth, courage, excellence and beauty?

*Heavenly Father, I'm willing to say whatever
You want me to say, and do whatever You want me to do.
The buck stops with You. Amen.*

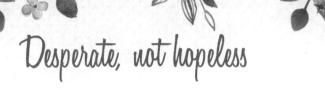

Desperate, not hopeless

"Who has done such mighty deeds, summoning
each new generation from the beginning of time?
It is I, the LORD, the First and the Last. I alone am He."

Isaiah 41:4 NLT

To lead well, and to pass the baton of leadership to the next generation, we need to know that we, and they have been beckoned to the stage of this century for such a time as this.

No matter how the darkness darkens, there is hope for this generation, and the next, because God has summoned us from the beginning of time.

We need to remind each other that God is still in control. He keeps building His church, and all the powers of hell can't conquer it (Matthew 16:18). Like He did for His people long ago, He will make a way when a way seems impossible.

The psalmist writes, "Your road led through the sea, Your pathway through the mighty waters – a pathway no one knew was there!" (Psalm 77:19). He will give us the compassion and courage to make a difference. And though we may feel desperate, we are never, never hopeless.

Do you feel cornered into making an impossible decision? Do you feel as if the odds are stacked unfairly and immovably against you? Could you preach truth to yourself, reminding yourself that there is always hope?

*Father, thank You that, even at this time in history,
I can walk in confidence because You reign in glory. Amen.*

Courage to commit

Commit everything you do to the LORD.
Trust Him, and He will help you.

Psalm 37:5 NLT

We admire those with the courage to commit to arduous physical challenges – marathons and mountain bike stage races and cliff scaling. Because the kind of brave that does those things says one thing: *Commit*. Commit to the strain of the hills and the rhythm of the flats and the thrill of the downs. Commit to knowing you can't fall farther than the ground. Commit to pedaling or walking or climbing or swimming, and then some. Just. Commit.

But the courage that ricochets through generations is the courage to commit to things that don't win medals. It's easy – it may even be selfish – to be a hero committed to physical courage; whereas committing to moral and relational courage day after day is the real freedom fight.

We need to be the kind of heroes who lead by example, habitually bending our agendas to the needs of others and the cause of Christ. We need to model the quiet courage that washes dishes and feet. Because heroes have the courage to commit.

How's your staying power when it comes to living heroically in relationships?

*Jesus, give me the stamina to commit,
whether or not anyone applauds.* Amen.

Leaning on those you lead

> As long as Moses held up the staff in his hand, the Israelites had the advantage. But whenever he dropped his hand, the Amalekites gained the advantage. Moses' arms soon became so tired he could no longer hold them up. So Aaron and Hur found a stone for him to sit on. Then they stood on each side of Moses, holding up his hands. So his hands held steady until sunset.
>
> *Exodus 17:11-12* NLT

Moses was an incredible leader. He was also ordinary flesh and blood, like you and me, and he needed the help of those around him.

As a leader, never believe the lie that you're self-sufficient. Stay humble. Be willing to learn from, and lean on, even those who are younger and less experienced than you. Don't be jealous of their growth or the opportunities they get. And seek out those who are older and wiser too. Learn from and lean on them. Harvest the strengths of every generation in a family or community. Let the energy of the young enthuse you. Honor the old. They've walked this planet a long time. Also, one day you'll hope for the same respect.

An excellent, courageous, beautiful leader knows it's ok to risk being called weak to garner the strength of those surrounding her.

Who is God asking you to lead, learn from or lean on?

God, keep me unpretentious and respectful as I call on those You've called me to love and lead. Amen.

Community, contentment, consistency

> When the storms of life come, the wicked are
> whirled away, but the godly have a lasting foundation.
>
> *Proverbs 10:25* NLT

We could braid those three words into a leadership philosophy: three words all starting with *with*. Community – with people. Contentment – with peace. Consistency – with sameness. Because consistently being at peace with the people around us will make us secure leaders and secure followers.

Perhaps the way to peace (contentment) in our habits (consistency) and relationships (community) is a person – another *with* – *Emmanuel* – God *with* us. Trusting that God's presence is with us all the time as we lead and as we follow will make us braver to move with His promptings, instead of hanging back insecure until the feeling passes and we don't do or say what we know we should have.

Maybe it's in active obedience to Him – not passive complacency in us – that we'll find significance in the season we're in, and real fellowship. Maybe, for the glory of God and by His power, we'll even change the world.

Would it help you to be at peace with one of your leaders, to be content and to love them more sincerely, if you found a way to consistently show respect?

God, thank You for the community You have placed me in.
As far as it depends on me, help me to be at peace
with all people, and to be consistently content. Amen.

A voice for the voiceless

Learn to do good. Seek justice. Help the oppressed.
Defend the cause of orphans. Fight for the rights of widows.

Isaiah 1:17 NLT

Women of every generation would be wise to be extraordinary leaders, because there's a huge gap in the market. There's plenty of mediocrity around. *That* market is flooded. What the world needs is extraordinary, and we could be those extraordinary women. We've got everything going for us to make an extraordinary difference to the oppressed, the orphan and the widow, and to leave an extraordinary legacy. Don't aim for average. Keep asking yourself, "In a hurting world, what would an extraordinary woman do?"

A leader uses her voice, not to ask questions that skim shallow and safe, but that slice to the crux. Not to hurt or condemn but to do the open-heart surgery of changing grace. A leader is ok to risk discomfort to bring hope. And a leader doesn't ask, "God, what am I supposed to do with my life?"

A leader knows that Christ *is* her life (Colossians 3:4), so she asks, "God, what do You want me to do with *Your* life, in me?" She echoes the Persian poet who said, "Raise your words, not your voice. It is rain that grows flowers, not thunder." She's more than a patron for the patronized. She's a voice for the voiceless.

What's stopping you from speaking up for those who can't speak up for themselves?

Jesus, break my heart for what breaks Yours. Amen.

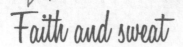

Faith and sweat

The eyes of the LORD search the whole earth in order
to strengthen those whose hearts are fully committed to Him.

2 Chronicles 16:9 NLT

Intrepid explorer and evangelist David Livingstone is reputed to have once asked Charles Spurgeon, "How do you manage to do two men's work in a single day?" Spurgeon responded, "You have forgotten that there are two of us." Spurgeon understood something of what the angel of the Lord said to Gideon: "Mighty hero, the Lord is with you! ... Go with the strength you have ..." (Judges 6:12, 14)

Leaders work as if it's all up to them: they sweat. And they wait as if it's all up to God: they have faith. They rest in the truth that His yoke is easy and His burden is light (Matthew 11:30) and that it's not by force nor by strength but by His Spirit that they live the lives He's called them to live (Zechariah 4:6).

They know that, since God is totally committed to His glory, His kingdom and His people, it's in His best interests to position them best, for His best use. And then they keep on showing up to take the opportunities He gives them to change the world.

If you keep going back to WHY you do what you do, you'll keep at it, even when times are tough. So, what's your WHY?

*God, I'll do anything You ask. Give me the faith
and perseverance to do Your will. Amen.*

Kudos

> LORD, You will grant us peace;
> all we have accomplished is really from You.
>
> *Isaiah 26:12 NLT*

If you have a positive influence over someone, you're likely to be thanked, praised or complimented. Maybe, like me, you can float on a good compliment for weeks, and then the only thing keeping your feet close to the ground is the fact that a big head is also heavy.

So what do we do with compliments?

Don't look for them. A wise man said that it's better to be brilliant in the dark than to switch on the light prematurely to show up your own mediocrity. Let others find you. And let God take His glory.

Don't get all self-deprecating if someone tells you that you're awesome. Jesus didn't walk around grinning sheepishly and saying, "No, no, I'm not that great. I'm probably not even the Son of God ..." He was never arrogant, but He knew who He was and He lived it confidently.

Remind yourself, "What do you have that God hasn't given you? And if everything you have is from God, why boast as though it were not a gift?" (1 Corinthians 4:7). Then with the sincerity that makes you truly beautiful, just say, *thank You.*

Do compliments generally make you feel awkward, or arrogant?

Jesus, thank You for sending people now and again to encourage me by affirming me. Help me to accept and appreciate their words, but never to expect them. Keep me humble. Amen.

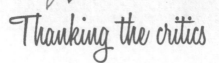

Thanking the critics

And I want you to know, my dear brothers and sisters, that everything that has happened to me here has helped to spread the Good News.

Philippians 1:12 NLT

Paul wrote that from prison. He had the high-minded generosity of spirit to view his grim circumstances from God's perspective, and be thankful.

You may not be in prison for your faith, but you do know that sometimes people can be plain mean. Other times people love you enormously and want to help. Either way, you can't predict all the criticism, opposition and rejection that you'll face. But if you have the courage to lead, you can be sure there will be haters. If you're resolved to live out your potential and be used by God as He chooses for His glory in a wrecked world, then be prepared to meet resistance.

The grace-laden irony is that criticism, opposition and rejection give you occasion to display the strength and the loveliness of Jesus. I pray that you will have the courage to look your antagonists straight in the eye. Walk past them gentle and fearless. And find the clarity of vision to turn around and thank them.

Regardless of someone's motives for criticizing you, can you make peace with the truth that they will be held accountable? Can you find the good fruit that has come from the difficulty?

Loving God, thank You for what opposition has wrought in my life, to Your glory. Amen.

Welcome

Therefore, accept each other just as Christ
has accepted you so that God will be given glory.

Romans 15:7 NLT

I'm reminded of a comedian who said he wasn't into *getting laughs* from his audience. He was all about *giving laughter*. He wanted to add value to the people he cared about, so he risked making his influence about others, not himself.

Maybe the best way to love and lead people is to stop inviting them and start *welcoming* them so that they really believe that there's room at the table. I met a man once who said that he didn't want to be popular; he wanted to be helpful.

Allow people – yourself included – to make mistakes, because no one is good at anything the first time they try it. But the way to *get* good is to start. Make that first attempt. Don't let perfection get in the way, and be willing to laugh at yourself. Make sure people know that you value what they have to offer more than the perfection of their delivery.

Welcoming others makes for the kind of counter-culture leadership that has people sitting up and taking note. It's the kind of leadership that has you showing up, over and over, to offer something to others that you don't necessarily yet have yourself.

How do the people that you look up to make you feel welcome?

Jesus, help me to welcome those on the fringes of belonging. *Amen.*

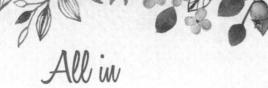

All in

Has the LORD redeemed you? Then speak out!
Tell others He has redeemed you from your enemies.

Psalm 107:2 NLT

God's call on Isaiah's life starts with a mind-blowing vision of the holiness of God, which brings him to a shattering understanding of his own unworthiness. God meets him in his sorrow and repentance, and cleanses him. And Isaiah's immediate response is, "Pick me!" (Isaiah 6:8).

It's exactly when you feel least worthy to be used by God – least worthy of His attention or affirmation, least sure of His plans for your life – that you need to cling to His kindness and surrender to Him, to will and work in beautiful ways.

You can start today. Practice being brave to speak out about what God has done for you, and in you.

John Maxwell says that consistency gives you a compounding that no other trait will. So, you needn't wait for the perfect opportunity, saying, "I'll speak out *then*. I'll work hard *then*. I'll be all in for God *then*." Speak out and work hard and be all in, today. And then tomorrow, and the next day, and the next.

Are you a pocket of excellence, in your family, your friendship circle, your career network or any other circles of influence? Are you all in?

Jesus, use all that I am, for Your kingdom and Your glory. Amen.

The hope of glory

… And this is the secret: Christ lives in you.
This gives you assurance of sharing His glory.

Colossians 1:27 NLT

Uncertainty can be paralyzing, yet it's exactly in uncertain times that we need leaders. Fear of an unknown future and the unsettling of a restless culture may be your greatest obstacle and your greatest opportunity, to lead excellently.

Another Bible version renders the end of Colossians 1:27, "Christ in you, the hope of glory." When we shift our perspective from the future and the culture, to a *person* – the unchanging Savior – then uncertainty dissipates.

Recognize that you'll need to be brave to make wise moral and relational choices that fly in the face of our society's permissiveness and indiscretion. You'll need to make wise financial choices that are counter-culture in a consumerism age. You serve a Creator, not a killjoy, and the universe has been designed around the paradox that surprising, overwhelming freedom floods in when we play by the rules. The terms and conditions set upon our lives by the Architect of galaxies and molecules are only ever to shield us and to liberate us to live fully, with the hope of glory.

Regardless of the variables, unknowns and pressures, could you relax and lead comfortably today, because Christ is in you?

Jesus, thank You for the absolute security and confidence
I can enjoy because of Your indwelling Spirit. Amen.

Shoes off

Then the Lord said to him, "Take off your sandals,
for you are standing on holy ground."

Acts 7:33 NLT

I once dressed for the day and left my slippers on. I was vaguely aware that my feet were unusually comfortable, but only realized my error when I arrived at my son's preschool. It was too late to turn back. I asked him if he would prefer me to go in with slippers on, or barefoot. He yelled, "Barefoot!"

The whole experience made me think that, as a leader in any small or massive capacity, it's good to go barefoot sometimes. Going barefoot ensures that you don't get ahead of yourself. The sharp gravelly bits slow you down. Barefoot gives you time to think about Who is really in charge, and Who it's really all about. It's a simple holy-ground reminder of your smallness and God's bigness.

Barefoot also means you feel the tremors of others' pain, which is less melodramatic than it sounds. All it means is that arrogance has you walking on air. It numbs you to people's trauma, and that renders you ineffective to those God has given you to love. A brave, beautiful leader is ok to show her feet.

Is there a way you can walk barefoot – actually or metaphorically – for the people over whom God has given you a certain influence? How might you make yourself vulnerable in order to understand and lead them better?

God, keep me standing awestruck on holy ground. Amen.

DECEMBER

Rock hard

"There are far, far better things ahead than any we leave behind."

– C. S. Lewis

Platform

… I plead with you to give your bodies to God because of all He has done for you. Let them be a living and holy sacrifice – the kind He will find acceptable. This is truly the way to worship Him.

Romans 12:1 NLT

These days, it's all about platform. Entrepreneurs, artists and CEOs punt the idea of building your army of followers, friends and fans, to make you feel famous.

A platform is nothing more than something you stand on, to establish or elevate yourself. As believers, our lives should be established on the altar of sacrificial love and thanksgiving. And the only thing we should ever stand on, to gain a bit of perspective, is the Rock (Psalm 61:2).

Our greatest success doesn't lie in how much our careers progress or how many creative ideas go viral. Our success lies in how much we serve, with truth and courage, the people God has given us to love.

We all get just one shot at this gig called life, and our highest calling is not to build a following, but simply to follow Jesus.

What are you standing on?

Rock of Ages, I want to build altars that honor You, not platforms that promote me. Amen.

The best possible memory

So be careful how you live. Don't live like fools,
but like those who are wise.

Ephesians 5:15 NLT

I love to travel. It's my idea of living fully. The glorious sensory assault of being thrust from the rhythms and routines of normal gives me big-picture freedom to live adventurously. I've slept on a beach in Spain, on an airport floor in Tel Aviv, on a train platform in Berlin and on a bus through Morocco with vomit sloshing side to rock-reeling side under the seats.

These are all great stories to tell (except maybe the one with the vomit) because I felt so alive when I was living them. I was pushed to look at the context and say, "It is what it is." And then use the time available and the potential of the situation to make the best possible memory.

But the fact is that travel isn't just about passports, plane tickets and foreign streets. We're travelling all the time. We're all travelling through time, all together. All the sunrises it takes us to get from birth to death. And we can make that same choice, in every context. *We can decide to make the best possible memory.* We can decide to live fully.

What memories are you planning to make today?

God, I want all the stories of my journey to be about how You were most glorified in me when I was most delighted in You. Amen.

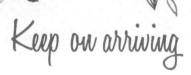

Keep on arriving

Fight the good fight for the true faith. Hold tightly
to the eternal life to which God has called you, which
you have confessed so well before many witnesses.

1 Timothy 6:12 NLT

This side of eternity, we've got to keep traveling. We've got to keep on arriving, over and over, only to find that there are a hundred other places to go.

We've got to keep on traveling and keep on arriving because a *full* life is an *alive* life and alive things keep growing and changing. The truth about living fully is that we need to keep on applying all the truth we've learned and keep on learning – when it's easy and obvious, when we fail and forget, when there's challenge and change. Battling the external pressures of life and ruthlessly eradicating the enemies of our own hearts has to be our habit, all our days.

It sounds exhausting. Yet God's grace is enough for each leg of the journey (2 Corinthians 12:9). And truth applied and re-applied, lived and relived, is startlingly refreshing. You are never too old to start living out your calling, and never too young to have already found beautiful expressions of it in your passions and pursuits. Keep on.

Are you willing to keep on living out the things God has taught you this year?

*Jesus, sustain me as I keep on arriving at new destinations
in the journey You have mapped out for me.* Amen.

Paint your life

Each time He said, "My grace is all you need. My power works best in weakness." So now I am glad to boast about my weaknesses, so that the power of Christ can work through me.

2 Corinthians 12:9 NLT

We'll never be perfect. Redeemed, yes. Even rehabilitated. But body-bound we're never completely free of the upshots of sin. That means we will never use our time faultlessly or live out all our potential.

Jesus knew this and it blows my mind that He still appointed us to be world changers (Acts 1:8). He gave us power through His Spirit to do the impossible, and that power is perfected in our weakness. I'm staggered to think that I might be used by God despite all the obvious gaps in me that need filling. And I'm amazed at how He fills those gaps with other people, and Himself, so that my life – and yours and everyone's – can look like art.

The truth is that the world around us would begin to change if we began to figure out the primary colors of our characters, which blend into the shades of relationship, which paint the landscapes of our lives, which would change the color of history.

Are you willing to let God paint on the canvas of your life?

God, I'm awed that, though You don't need me or anyone, You love me, use me and include me in the bright Kingdom colors You're painting. Amen.

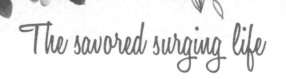

The savored surging life

Yet I still dare to hope when I remember this: The faithful love of the Lord never ends! His mercies never cease. Great is His faithfulness; His mercies begin afresh each morning.

Lamentations 3:21-23 NLT

To live a full life, we need to savor life, *and* let it surge.

Savor life. Because big dreams grow slowly, like big trees. They give shade for generations. Be patient. You can't hurry God. He's never late. Life is short, sure. But life is also long. There's time. And, *let it surge.* Because the surging life is the bristling, teeming, bursting, *abundant* life.

The courage life demand is that we hold that tension. Savor it. Let it surge. Don't try to escape time but rather keep pace with time and live it wild. Don't waste a moment. Fill up your days. Earn your years. Dig deep, live loud, and leave the planet better than you found it.

Don't lose your sense of wonder, not ever. Don't settle for safe or beige or bland (even if safe, beige and bland are also lucrative). Reach for the kaleidoscope and the tang that explodes from your gifts. Day by slow dawning day.

What threatens your sense of wonder?

Lord, thank You that every sunrise comes with enough mercies for the day it heralds. Amen.

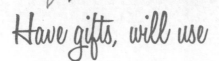

Have gifts, will use

A spiritual gift is given to each of us so we can help each other. To one person the Spirit gives the ability to give wise advice; to another the same Spirit gives a message of special knowledge … It is the one and only Spirit who distributes all these gifts. He alone decides which gift each person should have.

1 Corinthians 12:7-8, 11 NLT

To live fully, you've got to know your gifts, and embrace opportunities to use them. You've been created with passions and talents to be used for good and if you know what they are, if you know yourself, and if you have the courage to own your potential, then you hold the key to a full life.

I pray that you will see the truth about yourself and have the courage to live out what God has put inside you, in obedience to His calling.

To figure out your passion and potential, ask yourself what energizes you and flips your stomach. What do you do that makes people go, "Oh, look, she's in her element!" And being in your element is simply the space in which your abilities and your interests coincide: you're good at it, you love it, and the combination is beautiful.

What excites you before you do it, while you're doing it, and when you think about it afterwards?

Father, You've wired me just so. Use what You have instilled in me to Your glory. Amen.

Spill

And God will generously provide all you need. Then you will always have everything you need and plenty left over to share with others. As the Scriptures say, "They share freely and give generously to the poor. Their good deeds will be remembered forever."

2 Corinthians 9:8-10 NLT

More important than finding your sweet spot or being in your element is deciding what you want to give to this world. Not what you want out of life, but how you want to contribute.

The psalmist reminds you that God saw your unformed substance. He knew the number of your days before the first one dawned (Psalm 139). Despite your (and everyone's) congenital sin defect, He crammed your DNA with uniqueness and latent possibility – astonishing capacities to be freed by Jesus' blood – so that you could be all He created you to be.

We should be passionate about encouraging one another to be a generation authentically resolved to live out the God-dreams that He wove in us, in the darkness of the womb. There's a lot at stake. If we waste our gifts, others suffer. Using our time and potential to live excellent, brave, beautiful lives is not for us, but for others.

What do you love being good at? What gift do you want to give to the world?

God, lay the right dreams on my heart.
I want what You have blessed me with to spill
over into the right places, at the right time. Amen.

Singing in the dark

Yet You are holy, enthroned on the praises of Israel.

Psalm 22:3 NLT

Heading to the end of this year, and into a new one, it will take courage to live fully. It takes courage to celebrate in a dark world where there is most often more reason not to celebrate. But when you stop looking for answers in the mess – when you look up – when you boldly declare that there is hope in the grace and goodness of the living God in this life and the next, you will spread the light and the scent of Him wherever you go.

So, celebrate. Sing. Turn the truth up loud and rock it. God inhabits the praises of His people. The world will be different if your life declares His greatness.

A friend's son has a degenerative condition with a sinister prognosis. She feels as if they're traveling on a treacherous pass. She can't see what's coming round the next corner. But she says that she would rather be on that road, where the view is spectacular and she's learning to drive really well, than on the easy flats of the wide open. She says she has reason to celebrate – that she wouldn't swap their journey for anything – because there is breathtaking beauty that can only be glimpsed by those with the courage to ride dangerous, difficult roads.

When is it hardest for you to celebrate life?

God, put a new song in my mouth,
no matter how the sky darkens. Amen.

Bright star

"But those who exalt themselves will be humbled,
and those who humble themselves will be exalted."

Matthew 23:12 NLT

Like me, you probably want to live a full life – a sparkly, shiny life – but you don't want to get proud.

Look up at the stars.

I'd love to be a star. Not a rock star, but a twinkle-twinkle, diamond-in-the-sky star. I'd love to live a life *that* beautiful. I was moved by a wise woman's account of how she was looking up at the stars, so bright and so brilliant, and the thing that struck her was that *the stars are always small*. No one is attracted to the person who is always trying to make herself or her life bigger. In fact, people who try to make themselves bigger end up looking shriveled. Pitiable. Embarrassing.

So rather, I'm living desperately into the truth that it's in making myself small – going lower – passing on the glory because it's not mine to clutch and it's too holy to handle – that my life becomes beautiful, like the smell of cinnamon and the sound of waves crashing. And stars. I long to live not so that my presence will be missed but rather to make Christ's presence known.

Can you write out a list of the attributes of the most beautiful, most admirable person you know? Does the list include arrogance or self-promotion?

God, I long to make myself small: just a small star shining brilliantly for Your glory. Amen.

Doing something right

"God blesses you when people mock you and persecute you and lie about you and say all sorts of evil things against you because you are My followers."

Matthew 5:11 NLT

This verse sounds ludicrous but it's beautifully true – that the very best kind of criticism is the kind leveled at you for loving Jesus.

You may not be called to lose your life for the gospel. You may not be stoned or fired, spat at or slandered on Twitter for your faith. But if you are? You're probably doing something right.

Of course, that kind of opposition is still difficult and damaging. It's not something you should seek out to be some kind of hero.

But for sure, if you're walking in integrity, close enough to God to hear Him calling you, then you needn't fear it. And He promises that if persecution is a road you need to walk, He will bless you.

Do stories of martyrdom and persecution freak you out? Or fascinate you? You may not have faced a firing squad for your faith, but have you known the sting of rejection from colleagues, friends or family, because your life is associated with Jesus?

Jesus, I'll follow You no matter what the world says or does to stop me. Help me? Amen.

Depresshilaration

And the One sitting on the throne said,
"Look, I am making everything new!"

Revelation 21:5 NLT

Depresshilaration is just a word I made up to combine *depression* and *exhilaration*. Like, it's depresshilirating that right now somewhere – a baby is born to loving parents. A woman is raped. Paper is recycled. Toxic waste is dumped into the sea. Two people fall in love over lattés. A child dies of starvation.

God sees all these things, all the time. He sees the beauty, and takes His glory. He sees the tragedy, and does nothing. Why doesn't He press control-alt-delete on earth? We know that with God, all things are possible, even impossible things. If He can speak galaxies, surely He's big enough to fix our sorry mess?

He is. The fact that He doesn't – in the way we think He should – means He must have good reason. Sometimes we see the reason. Sometimes we don't. That's faith. And with faith, things get less depressing, and more exhilarating. God promises in His Word that He shelters the oppressed. Those who trust in Him won't be shaken. He's patient, inviting all people to turn to Him. He forgives, restores and judges righteously from the throne of grace, in this life or the next. He reigns forever, and He will make all things new.

Could you celebrate what's exhilarating, and ask God to help you hold what's depressing?

Lord, thank You that You see it all,
and all Your ways are just. Amen.

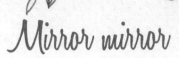

Mirror mirror

> Don't be concerned about the outward beauty of
> fancy hairstyles, expensive jewelery, or beautiful clothes.
> You should clothe yourselves instead with the beauty
> that comes from within, the unfading beauty of a
> gentle and quiet spirit, which is so precious to God.
>
> *1 Peter 3:3-4 NLT*

Beauty is part of our calling to live fully. But how much attention should we give to *external* beauty? How do we do our best with what we have, vanity-free, and honor God with our bodies?

When it comes to aging, everybody's doing it. We're all moving into the future at exactly the same rate. No pseudo-miracle surgery can eradicate Physics or the effects of the Fall, which have predetermined our inevitable decay. So if you think you're getting old, you are. But so are seven billion other people.

Perhaps the beautiful balance is brought when we're content to make an excellent effort. Your body is the temple of the Holy Spirit (1 Corinthians 6:19-20). If it's in good nick, so much the better for the Kingdom. So, within your budget and the realms of what's practical and possible, be your lovely self, inside and out. While you're here, you might as well make yourself as useful as possible – for God's glory, not yours.

Whether you're 22 or 50, what is it that really scares you about getting older?

God, keep me from worshiping myself. Help me to accept the passage of time, and to use the body I have, today, to worship You. Amen.

The wonder of younger

Look straight ahead, and fix your eyes on what lies before you.
Mark out a straight path for your feet; stay on the safe path.
Don't get side-tracked; keep your feet from following evil.

Proverbs 4:25-27 NLT

In case you missed yesterday's reading: don't worship yourself. When you look at yourself in the mirror and notice the changes, remember that *you* are a mirror designed to reflect God's beauty. We're all getting older, but we needn't blow what's left.

I have a theory that some people get freaked out on their birthdays because it reminds them that they haven't done all they wanted to do, or been all they wanted to be. There's no point going there. Repent, if you have regrets. Then focus. "Mark out a straight path for your feet," says Solomon. What will you do with the decades ahead?

The chronology of God's kingdom is diametrically opposed to the passing of time in the earthly dimension, because "Though our bodies are dying, our spirits are being renewed every day" (2 Corinthians 4:16).

Solomon also wrote, "The way of the righteous is like the first gleam of dawn, which shines ever brighter until the full light of day" (Proverbs 4:18). So the straight path I pray that we'd pick is the path to our younger, more wonder-filled selves. The best is yet to be.

What are you looking forward to?

*God, You know the days that are left to me.
I want to live them wondrously well! Amen.*

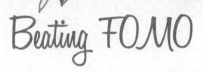

Beating FOMO

I have calmed and quieted myself, like a weaned
child who no longer cries for its mother's milk.
Yes, like a weaned child is my soul within me.

Psalm 131:2 NLT

FOMO – the Fear of Missing Out – can be a form of pride and jealousy. We're jealous of others' experiences or we think we deserve to be in on them. So, FOMO can be one of the fiercest enemies of living fully and contentedly.

You need to settle the fact that there's always stuff happening in other places that you're not a part of. Make peace with it. You're exactly where God wants you. He's doing things in and around you – things that you are integrally involved in – that indeed, others are missing out on. That's *not* a reason to get proud. It's just a reason to thank God that He sees you, knows you, and loves you – and He is at work.

If you are faithfully carrying out His assignment for you, then you are not missing out on His best.

Are there specific people or events that, when you're not with them or part of them, give you a serious case of FOMO?

*God, quiet me. Help me to rest and revel in the knowledge
that You are intimately aware of who I am, where I am
and what's going down in my life. I'm excited to be part
of what You're doing around me and through me. Amen.*

Get a grip

*So take a new grip with your tired hands and strengthen
your weak knees. Mark out a straight path for your feet so that
those who are weak and lame will not fall but become strong.*

Hebrews 12:12-13 NLT

Living a better, more beautiful life is being brave enough to beat comparison. But know that you don't have to be brave enough for the rest of your life. You just need to be brave enough for the next decision.

The next decision is to look straight ahead, or to pray, or to smile and celebrate. Because the better life is the wonder of simple, Next Right Thing obedience. The better life is leaving your case in the hands of God, who always judges righteously (1 Peter 2:23).

I want to challenge you, as you close out this calendar year and step into the next, to stop comparing – and see what happens. Because I know that when you move beyond the confines of comparison you'll enter the promised land of contentment. And o, the places you'll go!

Do you dare to stop comparing?

*Father, help me to get a grip on comparison. Make me
brave enough to travel the unique path You have for me,
without comparing myself to anyone. Make me brave
enough to keep on taking just the next step.* Amen.

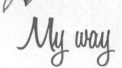

My way

Love each other with genuine affection,
and take delight in honoring each other.

Romans 12:10 NLT

At a wild time of year when family tensions surface around preparations for Christmas, be the bigger person – the more beautiful woman – and own the fact that the tension you feel is probably because, on some level, *you're not getting what you want.*

I was humiliatingly aware of this during an abysmal family photo shoot. I wanted us to look like the perfect framed family – so amazing that agencies would beg to use us for washing powder ads. Instead, our youngest son threw the mother of all tantrums.

The photographer couldn't get our son's face into any photos because it was burrowed angry in one of my armpits. I was embarrassed and furious, because I hadn't gotten what I'd wanted. I was pinning my happiness on my kids' behavior, which is unrealistic and unfair and sets them up for failure.

When other people don't follow the script we've written in our heads, it says more about us and our pride than it says about them. Let's live this Christmas season with the simple, excellent, brave beauty of being really ok with not always getting what we want.

Could you commit to loving with genuine, selfless affection, every day, for the rest of this year?

Jesus, when I don't get my way, help me to show the altruism that points to Your strength in me. Amen.

Who and whose

O Israel, the One who formed you says, "Do not be afraid, for
I have ransomed you. I have called you by name; you are Mine."

Isaiah 43:1 NLT

We live in a screen world that insidiously manipulates and defines us. Social media has us believing we need to be and belong like other people appear to, in their shiny, virtual worlds.

So, you and I need to keep on praying for wisdom and discernment so that we can answer ourselves truthfully when we question our own worth or identity. It's crucial to keep on walking by faith and in obedience so that we can live courageously and with integrity, online and offline.

Our integrity, after all, is directly linked to our faith in God, because if we really believe that God is who He says He is, then we'll trust Him to protect us and promote us, regardless of how others are defining themselves or foisting a definition onto us.

Before the Christmas lights flicker on and off again and the sun rises on a new year, settle *who* you are, and *whose* you are. The Internet has answers to almost all imaginable questions. But the living God knows your name.

Could you describe in 140 characters – just a tweet – who you are, and whose you are?

God, You called me by name and I belong to You forever.
Help me to never feel intimidated by how the world
tries to name me and own me. Amen.

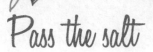

Pass the salt

"The people who sat in darkness have seen a great light.
And for those who lived in the land where death
casts its shadow, a light has shined."

Matthew 4:16 NLT

We can feel beaten by what seems irrevocably messed up in society. The world we're leaving to our kids seems to be drowning in the darkness of corruption, injustice, hurt, the fragility of life and the whip of so-little-time stress.

If we've embraced the truth of God, we need to embrace the *whole* truth of God, not just the feel-good parts but also the parts that make us uncomfortable and the parts that are hard to accept. And that can be seriously overwhelming.

We might try to treasure the truth that God gives us authority on our small patches of Kingdom ground. We might try to remember that when our lights shine out on our streets after sunset, the Light shines in the darkness, and the darkness has not overcome it (John 1:5).

We can live with an assurance that when friends and family grind salt at our tables, this Christmas and always, it's salt of the earth and won't be trampled underfoot but used to flavor, heal and preserve.

Today, could you create space to grind salt with someone, and offer the light and hope we celebrate at this time of year?

Jesus, make me brave enough to keep on passing the salt and shining Your light. Amen.

Space at the table

Jesus said, "Let the children come to Me ..."

Matthew 19:14 NLT

We're good at self-deprecation. We say, "Others are doing that, and doing it better. It's all been said, and said well." We feel we have no gifts for the King and there's not even space around the manger.

Before the year runs out and you run out of hope, here's the truth: God's wisdom never runs out. Cynics say the world is full up and fed up with great ideas. But God's wisdom is fathomless. You'll never know it all. Yet He offers it generously (James 1:5). You can keep going back to the One who made up *all* the great ideas.

God's power never runs out. He never relaxes His grip on you. He's the Father who never stops calling you, so your calling never runs out, not until He calls you home.

God's love never runs out. Jesus bled and said, "It is finished." He said it, did it and gave it all, leaving nothing for us to add to the gospel. Yet we are to spend all the saying, doing and giving of our lives telling that finished love story. Millions don't know it. We dare *never* say there's no space for us in the telling.

Until all your breaths run out, you're part of God's plan for the world. There's room at His table.

Ever feel like there isn't space for you?

Father, thank You for inviting me to Your table. *Amen.*

I'm dreaming of a simple Christmas

> She wrapped Him snugly in strips of cloth and laid Him
> in a manger, because there was no lodging available for them.
>
> *Luke 2:7 NLT*

I'd love to keep Christmas simple, like a mom wrapping her newborn in any snug thing available. But I find myself still baking, bottling, shopping and wrapping, according to tradition.

Yet, traditions (traditionally) show how *life* has passed from generation to generation. A simple Christmas, then, means not enforcing a tradition if the life has gone out of it because we've insisted upon standing on it – and suffocating it.

What if we simplified Christmas by using whatever we had available, and making it beautiful? What if this Christmas we decked the halls and set the tables with life-giving simplicity, instead of stress?

Just say no to the worry of matching up, the dread of patching up, the sweat of baking batch after batch and snatching at calories to cope. No to getting defensive – to putting *our* stamp on Christmas. No to nursing hurts and collecting offenses. No to stress.

Just say yes to *I am second* because if we don't get our way at the table or tree, that doesn't undermine us – like how it didn't undermine the majesty of the manger-born King who didn't "think of equality with God as something to cling to" (Philippians 2:6). Say yes to grace. Yes to simple.

Do you feel trapped by the trappings of tradition?

Jesus, I'm celebrating the sparkling simplicity of what You came to do. Amen.

Extravagant

For a child is born to us, a son is given to us. The government will rest on His shoulders. And He will be called: Wonderful Counselor, Mighty God, Everlasting Father, Prince of Peace.

Isaiah 9:6 NLT

Around Christmas, we hang lights in our street-facing windows and the world turns magical. It seems irresponsible, when we recycle all our paper-glass-tin-plastic, to burn lights all night for two months of the year. Ridiculous. Extravagant.

Maybe it is. There's too much about Christmas that doesn't make reasonable sense – in the same way that a woman pouring perfume on Jesus didn't make reasonable sense. Ridiculous. Extravagant.

It's also ridiculous and extravagant that the infinitely powerful and perfect stooped to be born in filthy straw on a broken planet among traitors. To love them despite their cruelty and criticism. To teach them despite their slowness and stubbornness. To save them despite their sin.

Lights remind us of all that – that as we give and get gifts in this season of joy, God unwraps the future. Lights remind us that although there are corrupt politicians, failing economies, frenetic schedules, imperfect relationships and relentless fatigue – Jesus brings rest, restoration, healing and hope. They remind us to live expectantly, to delight in new beginnings and to anticipate eternity.

Could you hang some lights as a shout-out to the world that you serve the God of extravagant devotion?

Father, all the Christmas lights in the world aren't enough to celebrate Your lavish love. Amen.

Something's gotta give

"Then if My people who are called by My name will
humble themselves and pray and seek My face and turn
from their wicked ways, I will hear from heaven and
will forgive their sins and restore their land."

2 Chronicles 7:14 NLT

This just-so-tilted planet-home is filled with God's masterpieces: soft snow, beach sand, red dust, hard rock, cafés, cathedrals, cobbled streets and every child's Christmas smile. He wraps the world in damp gray, bright white and true blue skies. He fixes time zones and buries bright stones beneath our feet. He sees it all, and takes His glory.

But despite how the world is shot through with beauty, *something's got to give* because sin's stain has seeped through centuries and blackened every page of history and, astonishingly, God hasn't ended it all. He has us here still carving out His kingdom in mud slums and fast-car cities. Because maybe, the *something* that's got to give is us.

We need to be so filled up with His spilling-over life that we can't help but keep on spilling changing grace. In a broken, beautiful world, we need to keep counting the gifts He gives, and being His gift to others.

What have you got to give?

*Savior born in a stable, wake us up like You did those shepherds.
Ignite in us a passion for Your purposes. Give us eyes to see
the gifts we hold, and courage to get busy giving them.* Amen.

Peace on earth and goodwill to all men

"Glory to God in highest heaven, and peace on earth to those with whom God is pleased."

Luke 2:14 NLT

Christmas is supposed to be a time of peace on earth and goodwill to all men. But for lots of people it's just feverish stress and strained familial obligations.

What if we prayed for each other, that we might live our Christmas stories differently this year? Pray for vulnerable, broken people who are dealing with frightening, tangible traumas: that this Christmas would be a watershed of healing and hope. Pray for polite, smiling, hurting people who are masking old damages: that this Christmas would mark their choice to stop lugging ugly unforgiveness, and to travel light into next year.

No matter who we are, where we're from, what we've done or what hangs over us: we are redeemed. Made new. Children of the Most High. Let's make this Christmas a celebration of that.

O come, let us adore Him.

What could you start doing, today, to spread peace and goodwill, even just to one other person?

Jesus, I stand in awe of You who broke into darkness to save the people who would later nail You to a cross. Thank You that because You came, I can know peace on earth and goodwill to all men.

Amen.

Gifts for the King

They entered the house and saw the Child with His mother, Mary, and they bowed down and worshiped Him. Then they opened their treasure chests and gave Him gifts of gold, frankincense, and myrrh.

Matthew 2:11 NLT

My prayer for you this Christmas is that you'd lay your gifts before the King – the gifts of your time, energy, resources and responsibilities – and see what He does with them in the coming year.

I pray that this Christmas you would remember that God promises to carry your burdens, and that if you're facing this next week, or this next year, thinking, "I can't!", that you'd know that you can do all things through Christ who strengthens you (Philippians 4:13).

I'm praying, despite the frenzies that inevitably broil around Christmas travel or Christmas cooking, that this Christmas would be a time of rest, and authentic, knee-bent worship.

I'm praying God would grow you and strengthen you to walk confidently into His coming plans for you. He's been with you this year. He'll be with you next year. That's reason enough to give Him your all.

What is God prompting you to give over to Him this Christmas? Are you brave enough to leave it at His feet?

God, I bow before You this Christmas, and like You lit the way to Bethlehem, I trust You to light up the path before me, even if all I can see is the next step. Amen.

Merry Christmas

"For I am about to do something new. See, I have already begun! Do you not see it? I will make a pathway through the wilderness. I will create rivers in the dry wasteland."

Isaiah 43:19 NLT

This Scripture is the ancient promise that burst starry over Bethlehem that first Christmas. Christmas has always been about newness, and it's always been about newness in us – in our characters, not our comfort levels.

The ultimate story that plays out year after year dressed up like shepherds in dish cloths reminds us that we hardly have room to be embarrassed about anything much if God wasn't embarrassed to arrive on earth in frail skin and filth.

It's a reminder that we've got to get over ourselves – our uncertainty or entitlement or indignation or fear. We don't need to carry those things anymore, because He makes all things new (Revelation 21:5).

And every Christmas since that first one has been a chance for new things. Because every Christmas is the cure for disappointment and discomfort – the closure on defeat. Every Christmas is our chance to leave sadness and setback at the feet of the King in the beautiful wrappings of surrender.

How can you celebrate newness this Christmas day?

Jesus, thank You that Your coming offered me the chance to start over. Amen.

Life is like the movies

And this is the plan: At the right time He will bring everything together under the authority of Christ – everything in heaven and on earth.

Ephesians 1:10 NLT

People say life's nothing like the movies. Maybe it's every bit like the movies – and better. In the movies and in real life we're inspired by those who do the hard, heroic thing. It moves us to watch people living resolutely. Obediently. Unwaveringly committed to the moral compass. We love those characters because movies need heroes, and so does life.

There are moments in movies when it seems the villain will trump the hero, yet our confidence is in the directors and screenwriters. They know the end of the movie. They wrote it. Just like God knows the end of your story. He wrote it.

The year's credits start rolling after Christmas, and yet we can be expectant and optimistic because the best is yet to be. There's no anti-climax in eternity. Before we get there, there'll be real-life close calls and real-life tragedies. But the good guys always win in the movies and, ultimately, so do we who have been rescued and relocated to the Kingdom of light (Colossians 1:13). When the real-life credits roll, we can be truly glad. There's wonderful joy ahead (1 Peter 1:6).

Do you believe that no matter what happens to you in this life, there's a happy ending?

God, thank You that You know how it ends, and that the end is just the beginning. Amen.

Future faith

"… I am the Alpha and the Omega – the Beginning
and the End. To all who are thirsty I will give freely
from the springs of the water of life."

Revelation 21:6 NLT

If you're a regular person like me, you've feared the future at some point. Like, you've wondered what life will look like for your kids decades from now. You've wondered if you're saving enough for your retirement. You've wondered if there's a future someone out there for you.

Psalm 112:7 says, "They do not fear bad news; they confidently trust the Lord to care for them." God was there at your beginning. What a relief to know that He will be there at the end.

There's no escaping that we will always need to live by faith, no matter where we live, and in what kind of circumstances. *Staying* somewhere requires faith. Packing up and *going* somewhere requires faith.

No matter where or how you choose to do life on this planet, you're called to live by faith. And the One who calls you is faithful.

What are your specific fears for the future? How does knowing that God will be there, change them?

*God, I'm thirsty. Please fill me with living water,
and help me to keep the faith.* Amen.

Give

"Give as freely as you have received!"

Matthew 10:8 NLT

As you start wrapping your head around a new year, maybe you could carry three words – give, save and live – with you. They're good words to manage your money – give before you save before you live. They're good words to manage all of life.

First, give.

Give your heart. At some point it will break, whether you give it or not. So, you might as well give it. Give your time. Give up your sleep if someone needs you. Give hugs. Give chocolate. Give counsel based on timeless truth and discernment in the moment. Give money. Give away more than what you spend on your own groceries because there are people starving in this world. Give people your books, your clothes, your personal space. Give them likes on Facebook and your undivided attention.

Give yourself over to the plans of your God. Take every opportunity to practice giving your best self to the world. Give your talents, your insight, your creativity, your energy and your sense of humor, no matter how these are received.

When you least feel like it? Give.

What do you possess that you were freely given? What could you freely give today?

Father, make me generous, like You. Change my heart, so that I long to give to others the way You and others have so liberally given to me. Amen.

Save

This world is fading away, along with everything that people crave. But anyone who does what pleases God will live forever.

1 John 2:17 NLT

What a privilege to abide in the truth that our lives are saved by the living God. It's a beautiful thing when we let the reality of our salvation play out in our decisions and our relationships.

For example, you could save on pain by making wise choices. "Wisdom shouts in the streets" (Proverbs 1:20). Position yourself to listen. If you're unmarried, save yourself. Sex is totally worth waiting for. Save the reference number when phoning government departments. Save memories. *Savor* them. Hold moments just a little longer in the present before they're consigned to the past. Once a day stop to watch the world coming at you. What does it taste like?

Save money. Sometimes, save your opinion because wisdom is a byproduct of humility. If people are coming over and you haven't done the dishes? Save time by putting them in the oven. (The dishes, not the people.) Save electricity. Save your own energy by planning for congruency and simplicity.

Save some of your stories for those closest to you, who see and know all of you. Don't worry too much about saving face. Trust God. And always save space for pudding.

What could you save today – instead of splurging it?

Lord, I can't ever thank You enough for saving me. Amen.

Live

I will rejoice even if I lose my life, pouring it out like a
liquid offering to God, just like your faithful service is an
offering to God. And I want all of you to share that joy.

Philippians 2:17 NLT

This is the fun part. You can blow this part of the life budget. Empty the coffers. Spend!

Live knowing that you are the beloved of God. Live knowing that you don't have to be defensive, because you are defended. Live knowing that you don't have to carry burdens, because you are carried. Live in confidence, and in Christ, and content – because God is greatly magnified by your life when you are deeply gratified in Him.

Live as if you've practiced and you're determined to get it right. A gazillion well-lived, intentional moments make up a life that counts in history and eternity.

Did I mention that you can just *spend*? Spend yourself on the work God has called you to. It's so profoundly satisfying. Spend money to bless people in your home. God will provide. Spend time trying to understand people. Spend yourself for the sake of community. Spend time with kids, with old people, alone, and outside. Spend your life truthfully, excellently, bravely, and beautifully.

Planning to do a little spending today?

*God, would You show me who I could spend time
with today, or what I could spend time or money on,
or how I could spend my gifts to honor You?* Amen.

The best is yet to be

Teach us to realize the brevity of life, so that we may grow in wisdom.

Psalm 90:12 NLT

My kids often remind me that perspective is everything. If I climb down from the jaded heights of all-grownup – if I bend low and make myself little – I see things new, big and different. I can re-frame naïve and call it magic. Re-frame parameters and see the possibilities. Re-frame problems and dig for promise and potential. Re-frame tragedy and find gratitude: relief that some of life's pain is over and done – under the belt – ticked off for glory.

Because Jesus never said we could have our cake and eat it. Not exactly. He said, "Here on earth you will have many trials and sorrows. But take heart, because I have overcome the world" (John 16:33). And He said, "I came that they may have life and have it abundantly" (John 10:10).

So maybe living the Jesus life – the deep-peace, great-joy life – means accepting that, earth-side, there's suffering to come, but that suffering is never how the story ends.

For us? The end is re-framed into just the beginning. Be wise, friend, as you live this short, beautiful life. Be honest. Be brave. Go with God.

As you stand on the brink of the future, will you thank God that the end of this year is another new beginning?

Faithful Father, thank You for bringing me through another whole chapter of life. Take Your glory. Amen.

About the Author

Dalene Reyburn is a writer and speaker, sharing weekly at www.dalenereyburn.com. She has a Master's degree in Applied Language Studies and was a high school teacher before giving that up to become a full-time mom, writer and speaker. She and her husband, Murray, have two sons and a golden retriever. They live in Pretoria, South Africa.